PRAISE FOR
JUST ACTION

"Now what? It's asked by many when facing brutal truths of racial discrimination and segregation. *Just Action* answers, offering hope. It defies the darkness of segregation's legacy by provoking our imaginations and providing examples of efforts that confront its impacts. This book will change minds, inspire public will, and revive communities."
—Rev. Natosha Reid Rice, vice president of
Habitat for Humanity International and Minister for Public Life
at All Saints Episcopal Church in Atlanta

"*Just Action* offers policy ideas for reducing residential segregation, much of which is the legacy of subsidized mortgages . . . designed to exclude Black Americans. Today, write the authors, 'Placing "Black Lives Matter" signs is not enough.'"
—David Leonhardt, *The New York Times*

"*Just Action* is just the book we need right now. Wise in its insistence on residential segregation as the country's number-one racial problem, optimistic in its lighting of an achievable path forward, it will enhance and focus the country's quest for racial justice."
—Nicholas Lemann, staff writer at *The New Yorker*
and former dean of the Columbia School of Journalism

"Every strategy for social change is grounded in an analysis of what's wrong with the way things are. With *The Color of Law*, Richard Rothstein helped us re-imagine what's wrong with segregated housing and wealth inequality. In *Just Action*, he and Leah Rothstein use their deep knowledge of history and policy to present the many things people are doing to build more equitable communities. This is an essential resource for everyone committed to building an economy that works for all of us."   —Reverend Dr. William J. Barber II, author of
White Poverty and co-chair of the Poor People's Campaign:
A National Call for a Moral Revival

"*Just Action* not only continues the exposure of the unfair policies and racial discrimination that plagues our housing industry but also gives us a 'call to action' and lays the foundation for ways to rectify the injustices."   —RZA, actor, producer, and member of the Wu Tang Clan

"*Just Action* will be an important source from which clergy, civic, and community leaders can draw strategic wisdom."

—Rabbi Jonah Pesner,
director of the Religious Action Center of Reform Judaism

"All too often, our cities are segregated and our suburbs are exclusionary. The bad news is that this is the result of a century of malicious policy. The good news is that policy can change. *Just Action* provides an engaging, practical guide for effectuating that change."

—M. Nolan Gray, research director of California YIMBY
(Yes in My Backyard), and author of *Arbitrary Lines:*
How Zoning Broke the American City and How to Fix It

"*Just Action* is a brilliant blueprint for how to finally successfully address racial segregation. It rightly recognizes that solutions are not going to come from the Supreme Court or Congress. It persuasively explains that action must come at the local level and it outlines dozens of inventive strategies local groups can pursue to redress segregation in their own communities. This is an essential book for all supporters of racial justice."   —Erwin Chemerinsky, dean of the
University of California, Berkeley School of Law

"The Rothstein father-daughter duo reminds ordinary people of their capacity to make extraordinary changes when they work together to take 'just action' to redress structural inequities, like residential segregation. The detailed vignettes between the pages of *Just Action* illustrate what it looks like to build relationships that can—in time—lay the groundwork for a more equitable, multiracial democracy."

—Karla McKanders, director of the
Thurgood Marshall Institute of the NAACP Legal Defense Fund

"We wrote a popular high school lesson based on *The Color of Law*. Students are surprised to learn of systemic causes of racial housing segregation, having been led to believe that individual families are to blame. They invariably ask, 'What can we do to remedy this injustice?' *Just Action* helps them answer that question. It's ideal for high school social studies classrooms, service-learning programs, and libraries."
—Deborah Menkart, codirector of the Zinn Education Project

"NCRC members . . . should read this valuable book that provides a toolbox for them to create integrated and vibrant neighborhoods."
—Josh Silver, senior fellow and former vice president of Research and Policy at the National Community Reinvestment Coalition

"*Just Action* opens conversations about how to remedy the inequities in homeownership that persist because of historic abuses by local, state, and federal government actions."
—John Gamboa, executive director of the National Alliance to Close the Wealth Gap

"After reading *The Color of Law,* the number one question asked by our real estate agents and community members was, 'What can we do to counteract the harm that was done?' With *Just Action*, we now have numerous tangible ways in which every one of us—neighbors, lenders, government officials, real estate agents—can create more equitable communities and neighborhoods."   —Amanda Lankerd, CEO of Battle Creek Area Association of Realtors

"*Just Action* is the 'starters guide' to a new civil rights movement. With clarity and foresight, the Rothsteins offer the blueprint to combat housing discrimination that has robbed communities of generational wealth. *Just Action* should be required reading for current and future leaders who aim to restore balance and eliminate the wealth gap."
—Raymond Doswell, executive director of Greenwood Rising in Tulsa, Oklahoma

"Historian Richard Rothstein, whose book *The Color of Law* exposed how federal, state, and local laws have perpetuated segregation, teams

with his daughter, community organizer and housing-policy expert Leah Rothstein, to argue forcefully that residential segregation underlies the nation's social problems. . . . A thoughtful, pragmatic manual for reform."
—*Kirkus Reviews*

"[An] impassioned guide to ending residential segregation in America. . . . Throughout, inspiring stories of people uniting to preserve their communities and redress segregation are interwoven with nitty-gritty policy details. It's a comprehensive and inspiring guide to solving a pressing social problem."
—*Publishers Weekly*

JUST ACTION

JUST ACTION

*How to Challenge
Segregation Enacted under
the Color of Law*

RICHARD ROTHSTEIN
and
LEAH ROTHSTEIN

Liveright Publishing Corporation

*A Division of W. W. Norton & Company
Celebrating a Century of Independent Publishing*

Frontispiece: Tulsa, Oklahoma. Twenty million Americans joined racially diverse protests in 2020 after the murder of George Floyd in Minneapolis. Most participants went home and displayed Black Lives Matter window and lawn signs but failed to follow up with action to challenge the residential segregation that allows police misconduct to flourish.

For information about permission to reproduce selections from this book, write to Permissions, Liveright Publishing Corporation, a division of W. W. Norton & Company, Inc., 500 Fifth Avenue, New York, NY 10110

For information about special discounts for bulk purchases, please contact W. W. Norton Special Sales atspecialsales@wwnorton.com or 800-233-4830

Manufacturing by Lakeside Book Company
Production manager: Anna Oler

Library of Congress Control Number: 2024949235

ISBN 978-1-324-09617-7 pbk.

Liveright Publishing Corporation, 500 Fifth Avenue, New York, N.Y. 10110
www.wwnorton.com

W. W. Norton & Company Ltd., 15 Carlisle Street, London W1D 3BS

10 9 8 7 6 5 4 3 2 1

CONTENTS

Part Four

Opening Up White Communities

AUTHORS' NOTES

In 2017, I published *The Color of Law*. A work of history, it set out to demolish the myth of *de facto* segregation: the broadly shared notion that our neighborhoods' racial inequality results from private business discrimination, whites and blacks freely choosing to live with others of the same race, or perhaps African Americans not trying hard enough to succeed. The evidence I cited told a dramatically different story, that federal, state, and local governments enacted racially explicit policies in the twentieth century to ensure that blacks and whites could not reside near each other. The policies were so potent that they continue to influence today's patterns of segregation and inequality. Of course, white citizens' bigotry played a role, but without government imposition of segregation, private discrimination could not have flourished.

Many readers of that book, and many who attended my talks about this history asked, "What can we do about it now"? They understood that undoing residential segregation would be difficult and that political support currently does not exist for policies that need to be as forceful in the redress of segregation as those that created it.

I am not a housing or policy expert. To answer my readers' question, I recruited a collaborator with expertise that I lacked. I knew one who had the necessary skills and persuaded her to co-author *Just Action*. I am so grateful that my daughter agreed.

—Richard Rothstein

I've been a community and union organizer, land-use policy consultant, affordable-housing development advisor, and criminal justice reform analyst for local governments—working to advance racial equity and reverse harms in small corners of a society that too often seems to be moving in the wrong direction. At its best, my work contributed to improvements in some people's lives, but it never led to the transformations I knew were needed.

After I read *The Color of Law* in 2017, I was one of those who asked my dad, "What can we do about it now?" He answered, "I don't know. It's going to be up to your generation to figure this out, not mine."

I went back to my work making slow, incremental change, but my dad's challenge nagged at me, so a couple of years later, I agreed to help research and write a new book to address the question I and many others had asked. The pages that follow are the result of our collaboration. I hope that our attempts can help us all continue to figure it out together.

—Leah Rothstein

JUST ACTION

JUST ACTION

INTRODUCTION

In 2020, after George Floyd's murder by a Minneapolis police officer, twenty million Americans took part in Black Lives Matter demonstrations, usually led by African Americans. Whites' participation in the protests and their support for eliminating the legacies of slavery and Jim Crow were unprecedented. When the demonstrations ended, black activists in segregated neighborhoods continued agitating for police reform, affordable housing, and a halt to evictions during Covid. Elected officials promoted policies that would narrow racial inequality with child allowances and other support for lower-income families, but with few exceptions (mostly to mitigate the pandemic's greater harm to those families) there was insufficient national political support for big reforms. Meanwhile, white demonstrators put Black Lives Matter posters in their windows or lawns, but most retreated to confront their personal challenges in a difficult time.

That was normal; even if a crisis event mobilizes millions, only a tiny number will become ongoing activists. From these protests, some African Americans were propelled to lead campaigns for police reform, with dwindling support. Few, though, white or black, mobilized to energize local civil rights organizations to win community victories that might challenge segregation and cascade into a national movement.

We don't pretend to understand all the reasons. But perhaps one is that those who want to do more don't know what they might accomplish, how to initiate campaigns, and what local issues are ripe to pursue. Many find it easier to consider national but unachievable policies than to meet with neighbors to take the first steps. More than half a century has passed since the civil rights movement engaged in militant action to win victories that narrowed racial inequality. Most Americans have little memory of that period and no models from which to learn. This book hopes to provoke the imaginations of activists and of the many more who would like to support them.

In the twentieth century, civil rights lawyers began to transform our nation—although not entirely. They investigated lynchings and attacked segregation in law schools, universities, and the military, and then, in 1954 persuaded the Supreme Court to ban legal segregation of elementary and secondary schools.

That ruling, *Brown v. Board of Education,* inspired sit-ins, marches, and demonstrations, led not by lawyers and policy advocates but by students, ministers, priests, rabbis, and ordinary citizens, black and white. Some were severely injured—like activists of the Student Nonviolent Coordinating Committee and "freedom riders," members of the Congress of Racial Equality, who were beaten severely and repeatedly as they rode buses in integrated groups through the South. Others were assassinated, most prominently the Rev. Dr. Martin Luther King Jr., president of the Southern Christian Leadership Conference, who had become the movement's leader and figurehead, and Medgar Evers, NAACP's first field secretary in Mississippi. Victims also included Viola Liuzzo, a thirty-three-year-old white mother of five from Detroit, shot when she came to Alabama to help register black voters; James Chaney, Andrew Goodman, and Mickey Schwerner, young volunteers, one black and two white, killed by a sheriff and vigilantes, also for helping to register voters; and uncounted scores of African Americans, murdered for attempting to register and as a warning to intimidate others from doing so.

Despite the dangers, demonstrators overcame massive resistance in the decade and a half that followed *Brown*, and as their local protests and civil disobedience cascaded nationwide, they forced the desegregation of Southern universities, lunch counters, buses, interstate transportation, public accommodations, parks, and swimming pools. They successfully pressed for a law prohibiting exclusion of African Americans from equal employment opportunities. They won passage of a constitutional amendment abolishing racially discriminatory poll taxes and then a voting rights act that enfranchised black voters in Southern states for the first time since the brief period of Reconstruction after the Civil War. And, in the wake of Dr. King's assassination in 1968, Congress passed a fair housing act that prohibited racial discrimination in the sale and rental of housing.

During the civil rights movement of the 1950s and '60s, many Americans came to understand that racial segregation was wrong, immoral, harmful to both blacks and whites, and incompatible with our self-conception as a democratic society. Yet when that movement faded, it left untouched the most powerful segregation of all: that every metropolitan area—north, south, east, and west—is residentially segregated, with clearly defined neighborhoods that are all or mostly white, and others that are all or mostly black. The two of us have lived in many metropolises: New York, Boston, Chicago, Denver, Charlotte, Los Angeles, Oakland. Each is characterized by racial segregation. This is no separation of equals; black neighborhoods are underresourced and more impoverished than white neighborhoods.

Residential Segregation Underlies Our Most Serious Social Problems

Economic and social conditions in segregated black neighborhoods place obstacles to student performance. Children in these communities have less access to high-quality early childhood care and to afterschool and summer enrichment programs that are routine for middle-class whites. Many black children, for example, suffer nutritional deficits that impede learning because markets selling fresh and healthy food are more distant. They live in more polluted areas with poorly maintained buildings often infested by vermin, and are more likely to develop asthma that keeps them awake at night wheezing and then coming to school drowsy or sleepless. Black children are more prone to suffer lead poisoning from obsolete plumbing, toxic air, or peeling indoor lead-based paint that can cause reduced cognitive ability and self-control. Dangerous neighborhood environments and discriminatory police treatment increase stress and stimulate hormonal changes that impede both intellectual performance and behavior. African American children, on average, have poorer academic outcomes than whites; this "achievement gap" leads to large disparities in adult success. Educators try mightily to eliminate these differences, but their accomplishments are limited in the face of the enormous nonclassroom influences they try to overcome.

Poor diet, asthma, lead poisoning, exposure to violence, and other impediments in more segregated and economically impoverished communities each have a small impact on average pupil performance, but in combination mostly explain achievement gaps. If a disadvantaged child attends school where few similarly suffer, special attention might mitigate the effects of these challenges. But segregated schools, where almost every child has one or more of these difficulties, are overwhelmed by these challenges, and performance suffers.

Segregation-induced assaults on children's well-being also predict shorter life expectancies, more cardiovascular disease, and greater cancer rates than whites, including poor whites who typically live in better-maintained buildings and healthier neighborhoods than blacks with similar low incomes.

Segregation has created and sustained a dangerous black-white wealth gap. Although African American family incomes are about 60 percent of white incomes, African American household wealth is only about 5 percent of whites'. The disparity largely stems from mid-twentieth-century government policy that subsidized the purchase of suburban homes by white working-class families. These properties subsequently appreciated greatly in value, while the same federal program prohibited black working-class families from gaining homeownership and equity in the same way.

Living costs are higher in segregated neighborhoods, where black families pay more in rent than whites for apartments of similar quality, where black homeowners frequently pay higher property taxes than whites for homes of similar market value, and where groceries are more expensive (and of lesser quality). Families without wealth can't dip into savings to weather temporary unemployment or medical emergencies. In such disasters, some are pushed further down the income ladder, often forced to rely on public safety-net programs— food stamps, housing subsidies, temporary cash assistance. This greater reliance on public assistance then reinforces an image held by many whites of black men and women as less self-reliant, ambitious, and industrious.

Segregation contributes to political polarization, which is more severe now than at any time since the lead-up to the Civil War. While not entirely racial, our divisions largely track along racial lines. Whites as well as blacks pay a big price. More whites than blacks depend on food stamps, child nutrition supplements, and financial assistance for low-income mothers. But support for these programs has been weak because white voters have become convinced, falsely, that they mainly benefit black households. Some American politicians and the wealthy constituents and business executives who support them believe that there is no need for public services and want to keep taxes low. These leaders then enlist the backing of white voters to limit these programs by suggesting that they mainly exist to help African Americans. This is not the only reason that all of us have less adequate schools, health care, retirement systems, early childhood programs, environmental protections, reasonably priced higher education, roads, bridges, and public transportation than residents of other industrialized countries, but it is part of the explanation.

How can we ever develop the common national identity that is essential to the preservation of our democracy if most whites and African Americans live so apart from each other that we have no ability to identify with each other's experiences or empathize with each other's hopes and dreams?

What Can Be Done? Improve Lower-Income Black Areas and Open White Areas to African Americans

With the enormous crises that residential segregation provokes, how can it be that our nation nonetheless leaves it largely untouched? Mostly, it's because remedies are hard. When we passed ordinances denying restaurants the right to exclude black diners, the next day black diners could demand service. But if we passed ordinances that required neighborhoods to reverse their segregation and inequality, the next day things wouldn't look much different.

The Fair Housing Act now forbids unequal treatment by landlords, realtors, banks, and insurance companies—although it is a poorly enforced civil rights law. But even a vigorously imposed ban of discrimination can do little to transform racial living patterns that were established fifty or one hundred years ago. The wealth gap, for example, limits the ability to roll back segregation: prohibiting realtors from discriminating against black house hunters has limited impact when so many suburban homes, once affordable but prohibited to black families, are now priced out of reach.

What we require are actions as powerful to diminish segregation as those that created it. It requires policies and programs of several kinds:

- Improving resources—housing and school quality, available medical care, financial services, public libraries, transportation options, better retail, access to healthy food and air—in existing lower-income black neighborhoods, which were intentionally neglected by government-sponsored segregation. In housing policy, these are called *place-based* approaches.
- Effective control of urban gentrification, which too often ends with massive displacement of black and Hispanic residents from communities where they've benefited from established social networks, churches, and extended families—places they considered home.
- Opening exclusive white neighborhoods to diverse residents— with zoning reform, subsidies for African American home buyers, inclusion of housing that's affordable to middle- and lower-income families, affirmative marketing to residents of black neighborhoods, and prohibition of discrimination against renters who get housing subsidies. In housing policy, these are called *mobility* approaches.
- Protection of residential desegregation in places, including gentrifying ones, where racial diversity has a foothold, and stemming white flight from neighborhoods in transition.

Housing policy experts debate whether place-based or mobility strategies are best. Our view is that we have such a long way to go before we've taken sufficient steps toward the meaningful remedy of segregation that we can't afford to be choosey. Every little bit helps.

Only the federal government has the power and resources to accomplish these tasks. But our nation is now deeply divided about racial justice. Waiting for the president and Congress to act is an excuse to maintain the status quo. What we're missing is not so much new policy ideas but a reinvigorated civil rights movement.

Begin Locally

Several national civil rights organizations continue to do important work. They file lawsuits that represent victims of racial bias and seek to overturn programs that harm African Americans. Other groups defend the specific interests of Hispanics, Native Americans, and Asians. They advocate for national legislation to reduce racial inequality. They also analyze data to help city and state groups challenge segregation in their own communities. In low-income and minority neighborhoods, chapters of national networks mobilize residents to campaign for economic reforms and vote for candidates who promote them. Local organizations also investigate individual cases of discrimination and pursue remedies.

When we urge a reinvigorated civil rights movement, we acknowledge all these groups. However, redressing residential segregation will also require the formation of biracial and multiethnic local committees of residents whose efforts are balanced between place-based and mobility reforms, and between remedial and forward-looking campaigns.

Like any popular movement, efforts to challenge segregation will have to begin locally, with residents pressing for both public and private action in their own communities. Voting rights in 1965 were won not only by lobbying but by thousands of volunteers who went door-to-door to persuade terrified black sharecroppers to register to vote. The desegregation of public accommodations would not have happened if brave young men and women had not sat down in restaurants that refused to serve them.

Few people will play such dramatic roles in a new wave of civil rights activism, and few will be necessary. This book is not aimed at such heroes and heroines. Rather, it is aimed at their multitudes of supporters and followers who want to confront racial segregation and inequality but don't yet appreciate the levers of power they hold in their own hands. If more Americans rise to this occasion in their own neighborhoods, a civil rights movement can begin to erase this most serious of all blots on our national character, our residential apartheid.

The Color of Law recounted the unconstitutional fashion by which government at all levels created segregation. *Just Action* describes how we can begin to undo it.

Don't Minimize Other Groups' Oppression but Remember: Slavery and Jim Crow Were Unique

America is not only racially unequal but also grossly unequal economically. Many policies for which civil rights activists should agitate will benefit not only African Americans but Hispanics and others, including lower-income whites. Yet the groups are in different circumstances, and we can't be effective if we don't distinguish them. The legacies of slavery and Jim Crow are singular and should be the primary focus of racial justice advocates. Substituting a concern for "people of color" can lose this priority.

Certainly, Hispanics and Asians have also suffered from discrimination—and still do—and racial justice groups should work to end that. But African American segregation from whites remains more severe and is declining much less than the segregation of Hispanics and Asians, as the 2020 census again confirmed: white neighborhoods are becoming more "diverse," mostly because they include more Asians and Hispanics, but not blacks. Typical measures that show white neighborhoods becoming less segregated ignore the reality of continued African American exclusion. Black neighborhoods can also seem to be more diverse because of the in-migration of Hispanics and Asians, but the in-migration of whites to black neighborhoods remains minimal.

We should not confuse the segregation of African Americans with the poverty and neighborhood isolation of recent immigrants from Mexico and elsewhere in Latin America, Asia, the Caribbean, and Africa. Segregation implies both disadvantage and lack of opportunity. But in the twentieth century, non-English-speaking low-wage immigrants (Southern and Eastern Europeans, Asians, Hispanics) almost always initially chose to cluster in ethnic neighborhoods where their language was spoken, family connections were strong, and informal job networks led to employment. Indeed, in most cases these first- and second-generation immigrants could not have thrived in diverse areas. Their communities *were* places of opportunity (although they would have had much greater opportunity if we enacted economic policies that narrowed extreme inequality).

But in the English-speaking third generation and beyond, these groups usually leave immigrant neighborhoods. It is true of Hispanics today, as it was for previous low-wage immigrants. It's a mistake to deem the "segregation" of Hispanics to be comparable to the isolation of African Americans. If the census could separately report third-generation-and-beyond households, we would have a more accurate account of where Hispanics live, and we would see that their segregation is less severe than the data currently suggest. This is difficult partly because many third-generation-and-beyond Hispanics identify themselves in the census as white alone.

Although it would be cumbersome to attempt, in each case, to describe the extent to which the segregation of African Americans overlaps the segregation of Hispanics, readers should feel free to read that overlap into our analysis when they believe it is accurate and appropriate to do so.

Native Americans have experienced not only discrimination but genocide. This book does not attempt to describe how civil rights groups should press for remedies, mostly because Native Americans are geographically concentrated in different places from areas of black concentration and because programs to redress the survivors of genocide will be different from those designed for survivors of slavery and Jim Crow. Blurring such differences by grouping them together as "people of color" impedes clear thinking about how to craft remedies for the distinct harms each group has suffered.

We've Lost the Aspiration for a Non-segregated Society

A civil rights movement to challenge segregation and inequality should include African Americans and whites, Hispanics, Asian Americans, Native Americans, and others. Because African Americans suffer most intensively from residential segregation, they have the responsibility for leadership.

Many (though not all) African Americans have lost enthusiasm for integration. Their efforts have frequently involved black families unsuccessfully seeking acceptance in overwhelmingly white schools and neighborhoods. Attempts by African Americans to be good neighbors in previously all-white neighborhoods have too often been met with violence. Few whites have sought to integrate by seeking acceptance in overwhelmingly black schools and communities. After decades of this imbalanced pursuit of integration, many blacks, including leaders, wonder why they should continue to seek to live among whites who are hostile.

Middle-class African Americans who have now successfully integrated (though not fully) professional workplaces may also be unenthusiastic about residential integration because they daily suffer uncomfortable (and sometimes humiliating) interactions with white colleagues. The perpetrators may not be intentionally malicious, but when whites treat their black co-workers as a strange species, asking questions about hair, names, or food traditions, when whites refer to a co-worker as "the black guy who . . . ," implying that race is his most important characteristic—or worse, when whites assume that African Americans with whom they are not familiar must be service or clerical workers—black professionals seek safer places. Segregated middle-class neighborhoods to which they can return after working hours offer exactly that. There, cultural traditions will be honored, friends will be accepting, churches may be close by, neighbors won't assume they are breaking and entering their own homes, and schools won't track their children into classes where lower achievement is expected.

Living in such segregated middle-class black neighborhoods is frequently the only choice available. Many realtors continue to make it more difficult for African Americans to find homes in mostly white neighborhoods. Yet middle-class African Americans who do choose segregation pay a price for it. Mostly middle-class black neighborhoods almost always have higher poverty rates, schools with less adequate programs, less access to healthy food and air, more deteriorated buildings, and more aggressive policing than areas where middle-class whites reside. Residents of middle-class black neighborhoods generally live closer to low-income segregated neighborhoods than do whites with similar incomes. Sons of middle-class black families are then more likely to be exposed to and pulled into crime and violence than middle-class white boys.

Many low-income African American parents have similar fears about integration and similar comfort with familiar churches and cultural institutions. They may mistrust those who encourage them to leave: they understand that their neighborhoods are unhealthy and lack opportunity but know that many African Americans were displaced by "slum clearance" programs, only to find themselves relocated not to healthier and racially diverse neighborhoods but rather to places that were even more neglected and distant from jobs and opportunity.

Yet when low-income African Americans with rent subsidies are offered moves to higher-income and whiter neighborhoods, the waiting lists for such programs are long. In recent years, working- and middle-class black households have sought better housing in previously all-white suburbs. More African Americans now live in suburbs than in central cities. Too often, white flight then transforms many of these suburbs into newly segregated places for blacks. But the initial movement of black households suggests that a preference for segregation is not universal; we should honor the choice of these families by preserving the diversity they seek. Certainly, challenging segregation does not mean that every community should aspire to be demographically identical. In urban and suburban neighborhoods today, there are Irish, Japanese, Dominican, Armenian, Iranian, Korean, and other clusters that are large enough to support ethnic churches, synagogues, and mosques, where supermarkets offer preferred foods, and where other cultural institutions thrive. But these religious and ethnic groups are not segregated like African Americans, who more often live in concentration because other choices have been denied. Healthy metropolitan areas should welcome freely chosen African American clusters as segregation is demolished.

Some African Americans also have unfounded romanticism about the success of segregation in the early and mid-twentieth century. They recall grandparents or great-grandparents who attended segregated schools in the rural South, were well prepared for college and professional school, and used their educations for successful adult achievement. We don't doubt such accounts. For every human characteristic and institution, some perform above average (and a few far above), and some below (and a few far below). Averages themselves tell different stories. In 1950 when Southern schools were still segregated, 33 percent of African Americans nationwide had five years or less of schooling while only 9 percent of whites had so little. Of young adults, whites on average had completed high school; African Americans had only gone through eighth grade. In the 1920s, the Harlem Renaissance produced great poets, writers, musicians, and artists. But most neighborhood residents were poorly educated and underemployed. There was no golden age of segregation.

Placing "Black Lives Matter" Signs Is Not Enough

Few racial justice protests in 2020 highlighted the extent to which residential segregation contributes to police abuse of African Americans (especially young men) and the epidemic of incarceration that has disproportionately imprisoned them for the past fifty years. This is not to say that an officer would never mistreat a black youth were it not for segregation, but abuse is more systematic in cities where young black men are concentrated in segregated neighborhoods without access to good jobs or transportation to them, and where schools are overwhelmed by students' social and economic challenges. Police engage in confrontations with these young men because officers' implicit role includes keeping discontent contained so it doesn't spill over into white neighborhoods. When black youths wander into white communities, police are likely to stop them to inquire about their reason for being there. Police investigate less thoroughly and solve far fewer murders in segregated black neighborhoods than in white ones. All of this discriminatory and unconstitutional practice would diminish if residential segregation declined, and diverse neighborhoods became commonplace.

Black Lives Matter lawn and window posters signal support for actions that attack racial inequalities, but redressing segregation requires hard work and will take sacrifice from both black and white activists. We're all in this together. Let's get moving.

PART ONE

LAYING THE GROUNDWORK

How we can get started to redress segregation in our communities: forming biracial committees; ensuring that when we win reforms, African Americans benefit from them; and taking action to improve housing opportunities in black, white, and diverse neighborhoods.

Chicago map twins: When they met in 2018, Brighid O'Shaughnessy (left) assisted people with mental health challenges to express themselves in dramatic performances; she lives in the mostly white Edgewater neighborhood. Carmen Stratton (right) was a school bus driver; she lives in the African American Englewood neighborhood. Ms. O'Shaughnessy later began working with traumatized black youth and Ms. Stratton became a youth case manager for a social service agency. They got acquainted at Ms. Stratton's home and discovered they had much in common.

Chapter 1

You Should Just Do It

Forming Biracial Committees May Be
Difficult but Is Not Impossible

O ur residential and social segregation is now so extreme that many, even those who understand its harm and want to remedy it, have few personal friendships outside their own racial group. Whites and blacks now frequently interact in workplaces, retail establishments, and government offices, sometimes even in parent-teacher associations in desegregated schools, but not as often in places where they engage in conversations that go beyond the business they may be conducting. A 2022 survey found that two-thirds of white adults had not discussed a single important matter with a nonwhite person in the previous six months. Yet half of white adults wished they had a more racially and ethnically diverse group of friends with whom they could have such conversations. In the same survey, African Americans had a more diverse group of friends than whites, but even so, almost half also wished their friendship group was more diverse. This suggests that local civil rights groups have great potential to be biracial. It may take more time to develop it, but committee diversity is an essential first step that cannot be postponed. Once you have created a committee that is racially isolated, it will be more difficult, if not impossible, to diversify it later.

Where possible, local committees to confront residential segregation should have African American leadership but whites should help lead as well. In a nation where whites have greater power and influence than others, a civil rights group without significant white participation will find it difficult to develop the community, political, and financial support needed to win big victories. But a civil rights group led mostly by whites will be perceived as, and may in fact be, engaged in a misguided project to tell African Americans what is good for them. The unhealthy history of racial interaction in reform organizations has too often included deference by African Americans to whites, and whites' assumption of superiority.

Some African Americans may have to confront and demolish unconscious assumptions about their own inferiority and acceptance of racial stereotypes. Social psychologists have a term, *stereotype threat*, that describes how African Americans can sometimes reduce their effort because they have been told so often in schools, in the media, and in interactions with whites that they are less capable. These descriptions are then reinforced when African Americans observe that many fewer blacks than whites are economically successful. It may be too easy to absorb an unconscious belief that, to some extent, it is their own fault.

Whites also should work to challenge unstated racial assumptions and superiority but would be mistaken to conclude that this examination itself will advance racial justice. Certainly, we should all explore unconscious biases, racial and otherwise, and those joining biracial coalitions should especially take on this effort. Whites should seek to understand African Americans' experience of discrimination, both past and present. They should translate this understanding into creating activist groups where African Americans are leaders and equals, not subject to microaggressions, and not tasked with educating their white counterparts about their implicit stereotypes. And whites should manage feelings of guilt that may arise, without expecting their black counterparts to assuage it.

For whites, examining racial assumptions may make working across racial lines more effective, but it can allow them to dodge responsibility if it doesn't lead to action that creates more equal opportunity. A better way is for whites to interact with African Americans as peers, not merely in workplaces but in our homes and in community organizations. Because our racial divides are so great, initiating such relationships may seem like a daunting task, but it is out of such relationships that biracial and multiethnic committees to remedy segregation are most likely to emerge.

African American advocates can dodge responsibility as well. Some say, "I'm tired of explaining racism to white people." Unfortunately, that is part of the work that African Americans must continue to do, tired or not. Explaining racial inequality to white people is a necessary first step toward broadening a civil rights movement that can create real change. It is merely an initial step, and is valuable only if it leads to direct action, but it must be done, over and over again.

Anyone serious about becoming a racial justice advocate should make it a priority that their committees are biracial. There are models. We describe just a few in this chapter. You can invent your own.

Chicago's Map Twins

Tonika Johnson is an African American resident of Englewood, a mostly black neighborhood on Chicago's segregated South Side, where median income is less than half the city's. Chicago's black population is concentrated on the South and West Sides, while whites are concentrated in the north. Although the North Side has become more diverse with immigrants from Asia and Latin America, that diversity has mostly not included blacks.

As a teenager in the 1990s, Ms. Johnson participated in a school choice program to attend a racially mixed but still mostly white high school on the North Side. She was struck by how different from Englewood were the communities she observed in traveling to school. By 2018, she had become an accomplished artist and photographer. She decided to take advantage of Chicago's geography to dramatize how severely its residents' experiences and perspectives were limited by having only same-race friendships.

Chicago's unusual street layout lent itself to her project—the entire city is a grid and with few exceptions, every block is rectangular. In the center of downtown, Madison Street runs east–west, and State Street runs north–south. The intersection of State and Madison Streets has the geometric coordinates of 0, 0. If you go north from Madison on State Street, a building at 100 North State Street is as far north of Madison as a building at 100 South State Street is south of it. Every other north-south street has the same characteristic.

Hermitage Avenue is one that runs from the white Edgewater

neighborhood in the north to African American Englewood in the south. Ms. Johnson realized that if she took a map and folded it in half at Madison, a black-owned home at, say, 6305 South Hermitage would rest precisely atop a white-owned home at 6305 North Hermitage. Ms. Johnson called the residents of such homes "map twins" and proceeded to photograph their houses to illustrate Chicago's segregated patterns.

She sent letters to residents of buildings she'd photographed, describing her project and asking if they would like to meet their map twins. Many agreed. Almost all the white map twins, including those who had lived on the North Side all their lives, had never been to Englewood; most of the black map twins had never been to Edgewater.

To participate in her Folded Map Project, twins were expected to meet at each other's homes at least once and then take their twin on a neighborhood tour. Ms. Johnson recorded videos of the map twins getting acquainted, and she then displayed photos of their houses and videos of their interactions at the Loyola University Museum of Art.

Nanette Tucker is an African American seamstress who was preparing to open her own boutique in Englewood when she met Wade Wilson, her white Edgewater twin who works in a software company's finance department, and his wife, Jennifer Chan, a physician. Ms. Tucker described what she discovered as she got to know Mr. Wilson, expressing a sentiment similar to what other map twins also reported:

> I want people to know that most of us have some of the same things in common; that we are not so different. Our communities might be different, we might pay a whole lot less for our houses, but we have some of the same things that we want out of life. . . .
>
> Just step out there; meet people, meet someone that is different from you, you might meet someone that is like you. . . . He lives on the North Side and I live on the South Side. My area might not be as great as his area but we do have things in common.

Wade Wilson put it this way:

You've got to sometimes take the initiative and do the uncomfortable thing. I mean, obviously, we didn't have to do that because she [Tonika Johnson] did it for us and we're very grateful for that but I would encourage anyone who wants to help bridge the gap that we all know is there, that you should just do it . . . there are many opportunities, many events, and I would say, just get involved.

The friendships endure. Twins began regular meetings at restaurants, alternating between the north and south parts of town. During the coronavirus pandemic, Nanette Tucker sewed decorative masks and brought some to the Wilson-Chans as a gift. Ms. Tucker had purchased an abandoned Englewood lot from the city for one dollar and kept a flower garden there. Dr. Chan is also a gardener and the two now visit to exchange plantings. Another Englewood twin organized a community bike ride in his neighborhood; his North Side twin showed up, saying he thought it would be a good way to learn about a place he otherwise would never have visited.

Map twins: Englewood resident Maurice Perkins takes Edgewater residents Jonathan Silverstein and Paula Herman on a tour of his African American neighborhood.

As the cross-city relationships deepened, Nanette Tucker and Jennifer Chan came up with the idea of expanding their friendships into "block twins." The Wilson-Chans organized a group of their Edgewater neighbors to go to Englewood to assist Ms. Tucker and her neighbors as they cleaned and painted abandoned homes that had contributed to a sense of disorder and reduced nearby property values. The map twins also planted flowers to help make the area near Ms. Tucker's home more attractive. Her neighbors now call themselves the Englewood Renaissance Group; the North Side twins hosted them at a subsequent outdoor social gathering in a neighborhood backyard. Twenty-five Edgewater residents attended and expressed interest in joining the collaboration.

Then Covid intervened and made the crosstown visits less possible. The block twins began regular Zoom meetings and created a quarterly newsletter. They worked together to attract investment to a commercial corridor in Englewood. Nanette Tucker said that neighborhood beautification is only a small beginning: "We know we can grow much larger than that and make something of an impact to the people that live in Englewood, including myself and my family."

The notion has spread. The Chicago Bungalow Association includes some twenty-five thousand owners of architecturally similar houses. Members get advice about repairs, landscaping, environmental compliance, assessment appeals, and similar topics. In 2021, its director posted a message that described the Folded Map Project and asked members whether they would like to meet their map twins. Thirty volunteered; the association posted videos of some initial meetings, illustrating both the unexpected commonalities and obvious differences between other-race households. One recording shows an African American South Side couple, Cory and Tayo Martin, meeting white North Siders Rick Cardis and Julie Toole. The Martins—she's a public school counselor and he's a tech support specialist for the University of Chicago economics department—bought their home for $175,000 in 2013. The Cardis-Tooles, both public school teachers, had purchased a similar home for $340,000 in 2009. In an initial meeting that the association videotaped, Mr. Martin described how police had harassed him on the North Side; both couples described being conditioned to think of the other-race side of town as a foreign space to avoid and noted how different were the shopping and other neighborhood amenities.

Tonika Johnson did not undertake the Folded Map Project as a way to create new activist groups. Whether the Englewood Renaissance and its North Side twins will evolve to address the deeper causes of Chicago's segregation is unknown. But for those who want to devise plans to redress segregation in their own communities, she's demonstrated that taking a first step need not be difficult. You don't need a city with a folded map; as the Bungalow Association showed, there are other ways to reach across racial boundaries. As Wade Wilson said, "You should just do it."

Winston-Salem's Presbyterian Inter-Racial Dialogue

Churches, synagogues, and mosques are our least diverse institutions, and not just because African Americans and whites belong to different denominations. Churches also remain segregated within a denomination. Still, these institutions can create opportunities to establish cross-race relationships that eventually lead to committees that redress segregation.

The first segregated black Presbyterian church was founded in Philadelphia in 1807, and separate black and white Presbyterian churches continue to this day. In the 1990s, Winston-Salem, North Carolina, had six Presbyterian churches—three with African American congregations and black pastors, three with white congregations and white pastors. The black churches were smaller and less well financed than the white ones. Many white parishioners were barely aware of the existence of the black churches, and vice versa. Almost all African Americans and their churches were on the east side of town, and almost all whites and their churches were on the west.

The pastors knew of one another but had little meaningful contact with their other-race counterparts.

In 1991, Rodney King, an African American construction worker in Los Angeles, was driving drunk and stopped by police after a high-speed chase. The officers beat him severely while an onlooker filmed the confrontation. After a jury acquitted the officers the next year, African Americans in cities nationwide responded with riots, looting, and vandalism.

One of the white Winston-Salem pastors, Steve McCutchan, was troubled by television images of the rioting and his inability to understand it. His confusion was compounded by recent incidents in Winston-Salem itself. For example, a black woman had mysteriously died after being jailed, handcuffed, and gagged; four white men had been arrested for the unprovoked murder of a black transient; and four black teenagers had run over and killed a white police officer who attempted to stop them from driving a road grader they had stolen.

Rev. McCutchan called two of the black Presbyterian ministers and asked that they get together for lunch. One, Sam Stevenson, was skeptical, believing that a discussion would serve only to make the white pastor feel good about himself but accomplish nothing else. Yet they had previously done some joint Bible study, so he was willing to give another meeting a try. The other black minister, Carlton Eversley, believed that "when white people have discussed something, they'll think they've *done* something;" he agreed to meet only if there was a commitment not only to talk, but to take action that narrows racial inequality. Rev. McCutchan and his colleagues later wrote about what followed in a book called *Let's Have Lunch*.

The pastors created an ongoing discussion group they called the Presbyterian Inter-Racial Dialogue (PIRD). They understood that like Rev. Eversley, black parishioners might justifiably be skeptical that the effort would lead to anything meaningful, and thus might not stick with it for long, so the pastors made a critically important decision: PIRD would be restricted to forty members, twenty of whom must be white, and twenty black. If someone quit the group, a new member could join only if he or she maintained the racial balance. It was difficult to maintain participation. Black members dropped out because they had too many life challenges to juggle—jobs with rigid schedules, child care responsibilities, and the need for a refuge on weekends (when PIRD meetings took place) from whites who supervised their employment and disrespected them in daily interactions. Whites left PIRD because they did not think that they should accept personal responsibility for fixing problems that they themselves had not created. Black participation was higher when the meetings took place at a black church in a neighborhood they were familiar with and where they felt comfortable. The opposite was true for whites. Yet PIRD survived for twenty years.

Winston-Salem, 1992. Presbyterian ministers (left to right) Steve McCutchan, Carlton Eversley, and Samuel Stevenson met to plan a dialogue between their churches. Rev. Eversley hesitated: "When white people have discussed something, they'll think they've done something."

Its first meeting took place at a black church, the second at a white one. The dialogue began with small group discussions in which participants described their own histories and how their religious faiths had influenced their views of racial tension in Winston-Salem. They continued to meet every other month, initially to read and discuss books about race and segregation. The pastors encouraged participants to meet socially between meetings but few at first felt comfortable doing so. Most had never been to an other-race home or had an other-race friendship. The pastors attempted to overcome this by pulling names from a hat to create biracial pairs and instructing them to meet for lunch before the next PIRD meeting. The instruction was only sometimes successful, yet over time personal contact grew with picnics, other-neighborhood tours, movie nights, and pulpit and choir exchanges.

Eventually, Rev. Eversley's demand for more than talk was met. In 1993, a year after they first gathered for lunch, he and Rev. McCutchan worked together to persuade the Winston-Salem school board to revise its curriculum to include material about contributions of African Americans. The following year, white and black PIRD members met with the mayor and spoke before the board of aldermen to protest its decision to end a civilian police review program that the board claimed was "controversial and unnecessary." The board's decision was reversed. Then, when the school board proposed to terminate the inclusion of African American history in the curriculum, black and white PIRD members protested and project funding was continued. In biracial teams, they visited residents of local nursing homes. The group's youth council delivered supplies to impoverished rural schools serving African American children; it planted trees and built a bench at one of the resource-starved black churches. And in 2000, PIRD raised funds to construct the first of five Habitat for Humanity houses.

Although PIRD had been in existence for eight years, maintaining its biracial character took careful attention. Many volunteers were necessary for the Habitat fund-raising activities—car washes, bake sales, yard sales, a golf tournament, a youth group talent show—and Sue Kent, a white participant, recalls that the recruitment of black volunteers frequently had to overcome a suspicion that the whites were going to pop into their lives and pop out "because it makes them feel good that they are doing this, and nothing will come out of it." The fund-raising activities succeeded in involving a thousand people from black and white congregations. The pastors asked a rabbi and an imam to invite their congregations to participate as well. PIRD likes to boast that its initial house was the "first [Habitat] build in the world to be sponsored by three faiths and two races." All were constructed in the black neighborhoods of Winston-Salem; four were sold to black families, of which three were single working mothers—a teacher's aide, a customer service representative, and a medical center office worker. One was to a white college student, also a single mother.

As the ministers who founded PIRD retired or died, the organization withered without a racial justice program to follow its Habitat project. It is remarkable that it lasted as long as it did; the ministers' (and their successors') priority was tending to the spiritual needs of their congregants, not conducting campaigns to fix their community's segregation. For that to occur, organizers with a racial justice mission would have been necessary to supplement the pastors' efforts. Nonetheless, like the map twins, PIRD illustrates that creating interracial relationships upon which a social change movement can build is possible if the intention is present.

Debbie Layman, the successor to Steve McCutchan as pastor of the largest white church, wonders why PIRD never questioned the placement of all its Habitat houses for black families in the black neighborhood of east Winston-Salem, respecting the city's segregation.

Wilmette's Montgomery Travelers

Cynthia Barnes-Slater retired in 2017 from her job as an administrator at the Baha'i House of Worship in the village of Wilmette, an almost all-white Chicago suburb that is one of the wealthiest in the nation. She had chosen not to live in Wilmette but rather rented an apartment in nearby Evanston, a more diverse community where, as an African American woman, she felt she was not treated as an object of curiosity when she walked down the street.

Before retiring, Ms. Barnes-Slater had never been involved in civil rights activity or even been much aware of community affairs, not in Evanston, or in Wilmette, or in Oakland, California, where she had lived before taking the Baha'i temple job. But now, with free time and her children grown, she joined an Evanston-based group called HEROS (Healing Everyday Racism in Our Schools) that had organized in response to a wave of antiblack graffiti, racially derogatory comments by teachers, and other incidents at a high school that served Wilmette and other affluent white suburbs. HEROS, whose membership was about half white and half black, called upon the school board to meet regularly with its few African American students and initiate exchange programs with black schools in Chicago. They also proposed that the school district increase faculty diversity, implement a racial justice curriculum, endorse affordable housing construction in the village, and share resources with underfunded Chicago schools. Per pupil spending on the suburban high school students is twice the city's level. Except for a new monthly program to recognize people of diverse backgrounds, none of these proposals have been enacted.

In July 2018, a friend at the Baha'i temple mentioned that a documentary titled *The Long Shadow* was going to be shown about an hour's drive away. In it, Frances Causey, the white filmmaker, recounts her life in a segregated white community and attributes her family's prosperity to its having opportunities that African Americans were denied. Ms. Barnes-Slater attended and was so moved by the film that she organized a subsequent screening, sponsored by HEROS and open to the public, at the Baha'i temple. She publicized the event with Facebook advertisements, flyers left at businesses, and email invitations. She invited attendees to remain for a discussion after the screening and to come to weekly discussions over the next month.

Meanwhile, Laurie Goldstein, a Wilmette resident, organized a July 2018 trip for thirty members of her synagogue to the Legacy Museum and Memorial, which had recently opened in Montgomery, Alabama. The museum is a project of Bryan Stevenson's Equal Justice Initiative. A lawyer, Mr. Stevenson has devoted his career to challenging racial bias in the nation's criminal justice system and the too often unjustified and almost always excessive punishment meted out to African Americans. In 2014, he published his memoir, *Just Mercy*, a powerful account of racial bias in the nation's criminal justice system and of his own mission to defend the unjustly convicted.

Building on his book's extraordinary influence, the museum, along with columns memorializing the victims of lynching, illustrates America's four-hundred-year march from the slave trade through Jim Crow segregation to the mass incarceration of black men in the present day. Ms. Goldstein returned from Montgomery troubled about what she had learned and feeling an obligation to do something about racial injustice. Others on the trip were also moved, and as they described their experience to others, interest grew in making a second pilgrimage. With a friend, Sherri Simpson, Ms. Goldstein began to organize another trip for whites in Wilmette, not necessarily restricted to synagogue members. It never occurred to her to invite nonwhites; she thought that it was whites who needed to understand the history of racial injustice.

Ms. Goldstein then saw a Facebook announcement of the Baha'i temple screening of *The Long Shadow*. She attended and stayed for the discussion afterward. She recalls that:

> I talked about this trip I was planning for white people and Cynthia Barnes-Slater turned to me and said, "I want to go on your trip and I have some friends that I'm going to get too." As tactfully as I could, I told her that the idea was crazy. I said, "The best way I can explain it is, I'm Jewish and if I

were going to learn about Auschwitz, I would not want to go with a group of Germans who didn't know much about the Holocaust" and she said, "I know what you are saying, but I want to go." Slowly other black people started to say that they wanted to come too.

Soon, five African Americans joined the trip's twenty whites. Ms. Goldstein worried about the white participants unintentionally committing racial microaggressions that would offend their African American companions:

> When we asked Cynthia, she said that the white people should read *White Fragility*. So everybody got that book. We came to understand that it shouldn't be a time for white people to be going up to the black people and saying, "It's so terrible what happened, I'm so upset about it" and to be crying and looking for comfort from black people.

The excursion took place in April 2019, after which the two leaders held a post-trip workshop. "We knew this was a group that was going to stay together," recalls Ms. Goldstein. Cynthia Barnes-Slater said the trip "really changed my life. I was learning about my own history and feeling like, now I'm at this point where I've retired, I can spend some time seeing how I can give back, how can I get engaged in transformation." Sherri Simpson added that "everyone said it had been life-changing. We were calling people to action. We were brainstorming about what initiatives we could take with racial justice, and then from there great things have happened. Our group is very cohesive."

They now call themselves the Montgomery Travelers, and members who were not previously involved became active in HEROS. They have given presentations at their village library on aspects of racial injustice and then took their programming to libraries in other nearby white suburbs. They have begun investigating racially exclusive subdivision deeds in Wilmette and nearby, preparing to conduct educational campaigns about the area's history of segregation. The Travelers hope that if citizens learn how purposefully their communities became segregated they will become more willing to support initiatives to diversify them.

Several Travelers who lived in the nearby suburb of Northbrook testified to their village board to urge a new affordable-housing plan, expecting that it would help to desegregate their community. It already had an ordinance that required construction of low-income units, but only for seniors and persons with disabilities. A new regulation was adopted without that restriction; it remains to be seen whether much new housing will actually be constructed and whether Travelers and other activists will succeed in persuading African American families that Northbrook would be a welcoming place to live.

Laurie Goldstein testified to her own village board that Wilmette's history of purposeful racial exclusion means that the responsibility to fix it "has been handed down to our generation and [I] hope it will not be passed on [unfulfilled] to the next generation." Van Gilmer, a Montgomery Traveler and one of the few African Americans who live in Wilmette, told the trustees that building affordable housing was not enough; the village has to make African Americans feel welcome "beyond smiles and patronizing behavior."

Reflecting on his work in HEROS and other civil rights groups after returning from Montgomery, Mr. Gilmer says, "I reluctantly joined the predominantly white group led by Laurie and Sherri to visit Montgomery. . . . I'm sure that these words would embarrass my white colleagues, but I think that the friendships we have made, and the roads we have traveled together have cemented an intimate connection among us in a way that nothing else could have done." Bruce Bondy, a white Montgomery Traveler, says that "the greatest gift of that trip for me was my subsequent friendships with the Black members of the trip."

As Tonika Johnson's map twins, the Presbyterian Inter-Racial Dialogue members, and the Montgomery Travelers have learned, developing meaningful relationships that cross the boundaries of racially segregated neighborhoods is not impossible. As the following pages describe, to move from relationship building to action, groups will then need to educate themselves about their community's segregation and the policies, practices, and players responsible. Subsequent chapters suggest ways they can then challenge these forces, including campaigns they can wage and change for which they can advocate. Not described in these pages, but no less important, is the organizing work that is necessary to translate these cross-race and cross-neighborhood relationships into committees that can effectively challenge segregation. It takes trained organizers, resources, and thoughtful strategy to build a base of support, identify the groups' goals, and develop and then execute successful campaigns to achieve them. The groups described here offer models for beginning this process, but the work does not end there.

What About Implicit Bias?

Many schools, government agencies, and private corporations now hold training sessions that ask participants to understand, confront, and eliminate biases that perpetuate racial hierarchies and to become aware of how contemporary institutions reinforce inequality without a design to do so. In practice, however, such programs do little good on their own.

These trainings do not usually result in more diverse hiring or promotion practices. They may lead to more racially tolerant attitudes immediately afterward, but the effect frequently disappears after only a few days. The efforts may even be counterproductive if participants conclude that since they are now bias-free, they need take less care to avoid actions with a discriminatory impact.

The trainings may ask participants to read books like Ibram X. Kendi's *How to Be an Antiracist*, yet readers can overlook Professor Kendi's many warnings about relying too heavily on examining biases: "Moral and educational suasion breathes the assumption that racist minds must be changed before racist policy, ignoring the history that says otherwise." Or "[k]nowledge is only power if knowledge is put to the struggle for power. Changing minds is not a movement. Critiquing racism is not activism. Changing minds is not activism. An activist produces power and policy change, not mental change."

More important than trying to eliminate implicit bias is taking action that redresses segregation, and if the action is successful, implicit bias will wither naturally. That's because implicit bias is essential to efficient brain function. It allows us to manage our complex environment by making generalizations based on our experiences and, in many cases, our exposure to what we see in the media.

Imagine that thirty years ago you went to a doctor's office and an attendant took you to an examination room, advising that the doctor and nurse would soon come to examine you. A man and woman then walk in. You might have been a committed feminist yet most likely would have assumed that the man was the doctor and the woman the nurse. In most cases, you would have been correct because only one out of six physicians in the United States was female; you employed a useful mental shortcut. You had developed your mostly (but not always) useful implicit bias from your own observations and from your exposure to doctors and nurses in the media.

If the same thing happened today, however, you might not make that assumption. Now, more than one out of three physicians is female. Young people especially would be unlikely to commit the same error, because of their own observations (a majority of medical school students are now women) and because of what they've absorbed from the media, where women doctors and male nurses are commonplace. As experiences and observations change, stereotypes adapt.

Generalizations are essential, but sometimes they are incorrect, even terribly harmful, as is frequently the case with racial stereotypes in America today.

From the end of Reconstruction through the first half of the twentieth century, Southern states employed a system of mass incarceration that nearly perpetuated conditions of slavery. Sheriffs arrested African American men for speaking too loudly, being unable to prove that they were employed on a plantation, changing jobs without permission, loitering, and other offenses contrived for the purpose subjugating the black population. After being convicted and locked up, the men were then leased out to firms like U.S. Steel that sent them to work at the most dangerous jobs, which killed many. Most whites in the north knew nothing about this system, except that hundreds of thousands of black men were imprisoned in the South for criminal activity; they concluded that African Americans were likely to be criminals.

Today, the excessive incarceration of African American men for trivial offenses that would rarely result in the arrest and conviction of whites—from personal drug possession to a broken automobile taillight—continues the earlier pattern. The United States imprisons a larger share of its population than any other industrialized country,

Georgia, 1930s. When African Americans were, and are, convicted of phony offenses and imprisoned, whites can too easily conclude that black men have criminal tendencies.

with black men incarcerated at six times the rate of whites. As before, the imprisonment of so many African Americans reinforces the stereotype many whites hold that young black men are more likely to be criminals. Implicit bias training can help to reduce the power of this stereotype by teaching how black men were and are abused by the criminal justice system. Such training is important, but the best way to eliminate this implicit bias would be to reform the criminal justice system so police stop abusing and imprisoning innocent black men.

In the twentieth century, government, developers, banks, speculators, and realtors engaged in a massive conspiracy to deny housing to African Americans in most neighborhoods and then to charge them more than whites paid for similar residences. Higher housing costs increased the economic pressure they already felt from being restricted to the lowest-paying jobs. To pay monthly charges for their higher-cost mortgages, African Americans had to double and triple up with relatives or subdivide homes for rental income. They converted living rooms to bedrooms, often forcing family and social life into the streets. Meanwhile, local governments collected garbage less frequently and maintained roads and sidewalks less adequately. Many black neighborhoods became slums. Whites' default assumption was too often that African Americans were slum dwellers who lacked middle-class values. Implicit bias training can help reduce the power of this stereotype by teaching how government and the private sector segregated the nation's housing. But the best way to eliminate this implicit bias would be to permit black families access to housing that is safe, sanitary, and adequately spacious.

A local committee should begin by learning how we came to be so segregated. Knowledge of this history can be empowering. Once we understand that segregation didn't happen naturally or by accident, it is a small step to realize that equally purposeful action can fix it. Members can then research how their own city segregated, perhaps with help from area college and high school faculty and students.

To Get Started: Follow Segregation's Paper Trail

Marianne Villalobos is a retired high school teacher in Modesto, the largest city in Stanislaus County, California. In 2016, she was seeking a new home. Her real estate agent, Alfredo Garcia, sold her one in a predominantly white area. Unlike many Modesto real estate agents, Mr. Garcia did not steer Mexican American clients like Ms. Villalobos away from white areas, yet he had not previously sold many homes in such neighborhoods. When he examined paperwork for the Villalobos sale, he was shocked to see that the deed specified the house could not be "occupied by any person or persons not of the white or Caucasian race or by any Mexican, Filipino or Hindu." He had never before noticed such deed language, called a *restrictive covenant*. He was upset by it and felt he had to show it to Ms. Villalobos.

She also was stunned and a few months later had occasion to meet with Sharon Froba, a white retired teacher who lived with her husband, Dave, in a neighborhood of single-family homes owned almost entirely by middle-class white families, with a tiny sprinkling of middle-class African Americans and Hispanics. Ms. Froba coordinated volunteer mentors for high school students and was hoping to recruit Ms. Villalobos to participate. As their conversation was ending, Ms. Villalobos told Sharon Froba about "the strangest thing" in her deed.

Troubled about it, Ms. Froba called the county clerk to ask if there were other properties in the county with similar language. The clerk said yes; Ms. Froba and her husband went to the town hall to see for themselves. There were so many such deeds that they began to inventory all the subdivisions in Modesto with restrictive covenants. They knew they couldn't do it on their own, so they consulted with a social studies teacher at Modesto High School.

Nearly three-quarters of that school's students came from low-income families; a similar share were Hispanic; and about 10 percent were white, most of whom were in an advanced placement track that required community service. The social studies teacher invited Ms. Froba to explain her project to his advanced placement juniors. Twelve volunteered to assist; they began in May 2019 and continued through the summer; unlike most Modesto High School students, they were from better-off families and did not have to work during vacation.

The Frobas and their student researchers eventually documented that by 1950, ninety subdivisions required occupancy only by whites (or live-in domestic servants). By Ms. Froba's estimate, "at least three-quarters of homes in our city had racist restrictions on their deeds." They also learned that in 1885, Modesto was the first city in the United States to use zoning as a tool of racial exclusion: an ordinance prohibited laundries owned by residents of Chinese-origin from locating anyplace except in an area known as Chinatown; laundries owned by others could operate anywhere.

One student researcher was Darshan Vijaykumar, the son of computer engineers who had emigrated from India when he was six months old. Darshan had experienced some mild negative comments about his dark skin but mostly thought of America as an equal place. But after he spent time in the county clerk's office, he said he had an awakening. "It was hard to swallow that discrimination was not just isolated incidents but rather a component of how society functioned." He had noticed that some areas had deteriorated homes that lacked sidewalks, gutters, and sewage systems, unlike white neighborhoods; now he began to understand why.

Another researcher was Adjua Kwarteng, a black student whose parents came from Ghana. She had felt excluded when she attended middle school but was happier at the more diverse Modesto High—although only three of the more than one hundred seniors in the advanced placement program were black. She said, "This project made me think about the implications this has had for the wealth inequalities between white people and people of color." After graduating, Adjua attended college in Houston and began to volunteer in a civil rights group there.

Several students commented about how little they had previously known about the country's racial history. Jobanna Peralta, a third-generation Mexican American, says that all she had been taught in history class about race was "what Martin Luther King did, segregation that occurred with tables, seating, buses. . . . [But it was] almost kind of surprising to me how I didn't think about how segregation affected the people around me in my community." Investigating the deeds was an awakening:

> [O]ther people, their grandparents bought the house and they were able to pass that house down to their parents, their parents now own that property and they have that money, they have that land. . . . [W]e, people of color are kept in a box, a box that we can't escape because it ties back to many, many years ago and the chain just keeps on going.

A white student on the team, Clara Silva, recalled:

> In our freshman year, we were educated about redlining. It was only covered briefly in one part of one lesson on one day. . . .
>
> With redlining, most people assumed it was a Southern sin. To see that it was also in the North and in my home town, it was surprising to see how cancerous it was. I found that my own home was built for whites only.
>
> I would like it to be more widely known to the public because it could influence how they vote. There could be federal, state, or city funding to help better these run-down parks in minority neighborhoods to help the children have better places to play.

Jobanna Peralta thinks that learning this history would make people speak up when they see racial injustice—someone using a racial slur, for example. Darshan Vijaykumar said, "I feel like before we can solve these problems, we have to understand what the problem is. Then, people will ask, how can we repair the barriers that were put in place to create an unequal playing field? I don't have an answer to that yet."

The Frobas created an inventory of every Modesto subdivision, including the specific racial language that each deed employed. They put it online, so residents can look up whether their home was an instrument of their city's segregation. They teamed up with Wendy Byrd, president of the local NAACP branch, and gave public presentations to groups like the Kiwanis, the Rotary, the Church of the Brethren, the Latino Community Forum, the League of Women Voters, and the NAACP, as well as at secondary schools. At each, they distributed copies of Marianne Villalobos's deed. Most audience members were surprised; "I had no idea!" was a frequent reaction.

Every February, Stanislaus County adopts a feel-good resolution commemorating Black History Month. But after Wendy Byrd and the Frobas' educational campaign, the 2020 resolution was different. It concluded with these words:

> [T]he County Board of Supervisors and the organizational leadership of the County commit to . . . working toward solving racial inequities in housing and all areas of historical inequality for black Americans.

The supervisors, however, hadn't thought about what this might entail. It is up to Modesto activists to ensure that the county follows through with solutions that will have to include—but go far beyond—challenging a friend who uses a racial slur or fixing up parks where children in low-income neighborhoods play.

The NAACP asked Sharon Froba to chair its housing committee, which soon developed a plan to use a city-owned but unused golf course for affordable housing. The city was not supportive. The mayor and council wanted to reopen the course, convert it to a park, or use it for higher-end retail, offices, and market-rate housing. Homeowners near the golf course were vocal about not wanting low-income families nearby. Ms. Froba and Ms. Byrd recruited speakers to attend council meetings to promote their vision. They testified that "15,485 households in our county . . . need low-income affordable housing. Seventy-six percent of them are paying over half of their monthly income for rent and utilities. They are one catastrophe away from homelessness!"

We Can't Erase Our History, but Acknowledging It Is Not Enough

In her 2019 book, *Learning from the Germans*, Susan Neiman claims that Germany has done a better job of confronting its past than we have. On May 8, 1985, the fortieth anniversary of the Nazis' defeat in World War II, West Germany's president stunned his countrymen by calling it a "day of liberation." Neiman writes: "Imagine Virginians celebrating the Confederate surrender at Appomattox, and you'll have a rough idea of the effect." She meant white Virginians, of course.

In Germany, there are now more than sixty thousand "stumbling stones" hammered into sidewalks at buildings where Jews lived before the Nazis seized and massacred them. Victims' names are carved into the stones and pedestrians passing by see a reminder of the genocidal crimes of their forebears.

A few Jews in Germany survived the Holocaust, and some descendants returned. When they go down these sidewalks, should they be forced to be reminded, constantly, of their country's campaign to exterminate their forebears? How should German society weigh its interest in having its non-Jewish majority forever commit to prevent a resurgence of Nazism, against its interest in making Jews feel welcome and secure without constant reminders of the Nazi era?

Neiman, Jewish and residing in Berlin, says she would not have moved to Germany if her sons would "be forced to walk past [Nazi generals'] statues or flags flying swastikas." Such symbols would be an assault to her children's security. The stumbling stones' purpose is to confront non-Jewish Germans with evidence of crimes that were committed in their names. But they may also be too distressing for some German Jews who confront them.

In the United States, we've been removing statues and renaming schools and streets that commemorate generals, soldiers, and government officials who owned slaves or fought to protect slavery. We do so in part because the defense of slavery is abhorrent to our values and in part to avoid such symbols sending a message to African

Americans that they should feel insecure in their own country. It is not possible to preserve awareness of our history of racial subjugation without the unintended consequence of making African Americans uncomfortable. A proper balance should always be struck in deciding whether evidence of slavery and Jim Crow should be contextualized or eliminated.

The stumbling stones in Germany and Bryan Stevenson's lynching columns are attempts to strike that balance. Mr. Stevenson also suggests renaming Southern buildings to honor white abolitionists and antilynching activists. Perhaps statues to these heroes should also be constructed. This would be a different way to strike the balance—it would project less of a threat to African Americans but also convey less of the horror that whites should contemplate.

The movement to cleanse this country of the symbols of racial subjugation extends to campaigns to remove restrictive covenants from deeds. Frequently, investigations begin when home buyers like Marianne Villalobos learn that they have purchased a property intended to be racially exclusive. Many are offended to learn that they live in homes that were constructed and reserved for Caucasians only, but it's difficult for homeowners to remove these clauses. Deeds are a permanent contract among an owner, the county, and neighbors. A homeowner can no more unilaterally delete a racial clause than change a property line in a deed. Such change ordinarily requires court approval, and it is expensive to accomplish.

Several states have passed laws to simplify the process, in some cases waiving filing fees or requiring county clerks to strike through racial deed restrictions upon a homeowner's properly filed request. A bill before the Massachusetts legislature allows a homeowner to go to court and ask a judge to expunge it. The media too often portrays proposals like this as permitting the actual removal of a racial deed, but all that can happen in practice is a striking through of the offensive language, perhaps to the extent of making it illegible.

The legislator who sponsored a Maryland law that made striking through a racial restriction simpler said that constituents pressed her to do this because "[t]hey really wanted their deeds to reflect the community in which they lived and their own personal values." Some county officials have interpreted the law to allow not simply putting a line through the language but use of a black marking pen to render it unreadable. Whether there was a downside to hiding this history was apparently not something that the Maryland legislature took seriously.

This is not an easy balance to strike, but we can do it. Perhaps Germany's stumbling stones offer a hint. The stones, after all, do not glorify the Holocaust; they mourn it and remind us of the need for vigilance to ensure that it never happens again. Instead of crossing out racial language from deeds and declaring it null and void, we should staple an affirmative statement on top of the restrictive language.

Marin County, California, has done this, enacting an ordinance that permits homeowners to ask the county to certify that their deed includes illegal language that is inconsistent with the community's values. The county clerk must then attach a repudiation atop the offending clause. The county states that the program "creates an opportunity to educate, engage and assert that such racially motivated housing policies are part of our past and that the County has created an affirmative response for residents [to] acknowledge the history of the homes in which they live. It . . . is government's responsibility to address how those actions created the disparities that continue to exist in our communities today."

Such modification can convert an obscenity to a positive commitment in a way that is not possible for Confederate statues. Some opponents of removing statues suggest that we should, instead, place plaques on their pedestals, expressing shame that many whites once considered it noble to defend slavery. This is an unsatisfactory remedy because passersby may not bother to read the statement and will be threatened by the statue's message. But placing an educational statement and a commitment to remedy its consequences atop a restrictive covenant is different; it will be unavoidable and dominate the null and void language. If racial clauses had been removed from deeds in Modesto, would student volunteers in Sharon Froba's project have been as motivated to ponder how to remedy segregation? It is troubling that many activists devote more energy to symbolizing the values they want to reflect than to the more difficult and expensive actions that diversifying their communities require.

Racial clauses are only one aspect of white communities' histories of segregation and not always the most important. Many white neighborhoods employed policies and practices of segregation without relying on language in property deeds. In 1948, the Supreme Court prohibited legal enforcement of the covenants; although it did not ban their continued use, most developers ceased using them. But policies and practices of segregation continued for the next twenty years until passage of the Fair Housing Act, and frequently even after that.

An effort to educate residents about their segregation, as a prelude to taking steps to redress it, requires uncovering these other actions as well.

March 4, 1861. President James Buchanan escorted Abraham Lincoln to his swearing-in. Lincoln's inaugural address asserted that we would cease being a democracy if we gave the Supreme Court unchecked authority to decide which laws were constitutional. (Drawing by Winslow Homer)

Chapter 2

Dare to Defy
Timid Deference to the Supreme Court Blocks Racial Equality

Policies that enforced segregation in the twentieth century were so powerful that they continue to influence and often determine today's racial boundaries. While the Fair Housing Act of 1968 prohibits new acts of discrimination in the sale and rental of housing, even if it were well enforced (and it is not), a ban on future unlawful actions can do little to remedy the segregation and inequality of neighborhoods that already exist. It is a mostly empty gesture to tell black families, as the act does, that they now have the right to move into neighborhoods that have become too costly but were affordable when African Americans were excluded.

Making that right a reality requires not only an end to ongoing discrimination but racially explicit preferences and support for African Americans who seek housing in neighborhoods from which they were banned a half century ago. The segregation of this country was purposeful. Only equally purposeful policy can reverse it.

The Fair Housing Act requires government to "affirmatively further" the law's purposes, but federal agencies have not used the directive to implement and justify race-based programs that support housing needs of black families. In 1972, the Supreme Court agreed that a legitimate goal of the Fair Housing Act is the creation of integrated communities, but it did so in a case about ongoing discrimination that would maintain existing segregation. It did not say that the act requires reversing the segregation of neighborhoods that government previously segregated. A 1988 federal appeals court stated that temporary race-conscious housing remedies were sometimes permissible, but it didn't approve a specific program, nor have other federal courts done so since.

A 1976 federal law permits lending institutions to extend credit to African American borrowers on more favorable terms to remedy their historic exclusion from credit markets, including mortgages. The program, however, has been used only infrequently. On the occasions when firms have invoked the law to justify a policy intended to benefit black families, they have employed work-arounds to avert legal challenge: for example, rather than giving preferences to African American borrowers, they've targeted home buyers in areas where the population is largely black. Neither the Supreme Court nor federal appeals courts have considered challenges to the law.

Beginning in 1883, the Supreme Court asserted that the Constitution prohibits remedies for private discrimination against African Americans, effectively annihilating the clear intent of the Thirteenth and Fourteenth Amendments. Nearly a century went by while the Court blessed various impositions of second-class citizenship for descendants of the enslaved.

In 1896, it determined that "separate but equal" was acceptable in both public and private spheres; it maintained this position until 1954, all the while never bothering to question whether the separate facilities it endorsed were in any way equal. In 1926, it validated restrictive covenants and until 1948 allowed African Americans to be evicted from homes they had legally purchased in white neighborhoods.

In 1968, it changed its mind about its 1883 permission for private discrimination. The Court decreed that the 1866 Civil Rights Act prohibiting it had correctly implemented the Thirteenth Amendment's intent to ban the "badges" of slavery. In 1979, the Court took a further step and permitted remedial preferences for blacks in employment. It concluded that under the Constitution, extra opportunities given to African Americans for jobs from which they had historically been excluded could not be deemed to violate whites' civil rights. Otherwise, the Court said, policy would fail to account for African Americans' historic denial of job opportunities. The ruling stated that a ban on race-specific remedies would violate the spirit and intent of a law that prohibited racial discrimination and be "completely at variance with the purpose of the statute." But seven years later the Court concluded that while the Constitution permitted race-conscious hiring preferences, it also allowed Congress to effectively annihilate them by prohibiting the protection of those new employees from being laid off from lack of seniority, their historic exclusion notwithstanding.

Nine years after that, in 1995, the Court went further: it found it impossible to conclude that African Americans generally have been disadvantaged in the United States, so determined that the Constitution permits a remedy only for individuals or groups who themselves suffered from specific acts of discrimination. The legacies of centuries of slavery and segregation were now deemed to have no relevance for contemporary inequality.

Today, a militant Supreme Court majority is hostile to affirmative action and any programs that promote desegregation, ignoring the history of how the United States came to be segregated. In 2007, the Court declared that neighborhoods in Seattle and Louisville had been segregated *de facto*—by acts of individual bigotry, private companies' discriminatory policies, people freely choosing to live with others of the same color, and economic differences between the races—without significant government involvement. On this basis, it prohibited school districts from implementing trivial desegregation plans because, in its view, segregated attendance zones did not violate civil rights as they simply reflected naturally occurring racial neighborhood boundaries. Chief Justice John Roberts wrote that the remedies for school segregation were discriminatory because they acknowledged students' racial identities, and he called for the nation to be race-blind.

Regrettably, the Seattle and Louisville school districts did not justify their plans by citing the history of how government throughout much of the twentieth century enforced residential segregation; instead, the explanation the districts offered was "restrictive covenants and 'private codes' between landlords and realtors." The dissents by justices who approved of the desegregation plans never challenged Chief Justice Roberts's audacious claim that the neighborhoods were racially divided only because of "societal discrimination." The Court's fiction of *de facto* segregation was not seriously challenged.

In higher education, the Supreme Court has permitted admissions officers to seek "diversity" of all kinds in enrollments, not specifically of race—giving small preferences to violinists, rugby players, and African Americans, among other categories that university officials believe will enhance educational experiences for all. This permission was granted not to remedy any historic wrong, but after military and corporate leaders pleaded that the experience of diverse classmates, black students in particular, would better prepare graduates to lead their institutions. The Court also deduced that the Constitution requires that admission preferences for black students for purposes of diversity must end by 2028, with no explanation of where in the Constitution they found support for this precise conclusion.

Surely, diverse neighborhoods are as important to American democracy as diverse colleges. But there is little doubt that today the Court would strike down new public and private programs that redress the legacies of slavery and Jim Crow by taking race-targeted action to provide housing opportunities for black households.

That is no reason to avoid enacting such programs. Those we design to remedy specific past acts of unconstitutional denial of rights are most likely to win occasional lower-court approvals and powerful dissents in cases of disapproval; those dissents can later form the basis of a new consensus in favor of such policies. Some local or state governments or private groups may adopt programs of affirmative action in housing that openly defy current Supreme Court rules. Proponents may be sued, prosecuted, or held in contempt. If so, they would not be the first civil rights activists to take risks fighting for constitutional rights that courts refused to recognize.

Supreme Court Opinions on Race Keep Changing

The Supreme Court frequently reverses course, as it did on abortion in 2022. But there are few topics where it has done so more frequently and more radically than race. It is hard to argue that there is some deep meaning in the Constitution regarding civil rights, a meaning so difficult to divine that it justifies such flip-flops. These reversals are worth reiterating: In 1876, the Supreme Court said that the federal government had no power under the Constitution to interfere with a Ku Klux Klan mob that massacred more than a hundred African Americans in Colfax, Louisiana; in 1966 (more than three thousand lynchings later), the Court revised its position, saying the federal government could prosecute Klan murders if a state government was looking the other way. In 1883, it said federal laws to ban discrimination in the sale and rental of housing violated the Constitution; in 1968, it repudiated that view and said that prohibition of private property discrimination had been a reasonable exercise of congressional power. The Court in 1896 blessed keeping the races "separate but equal"; in 1954, it said this was unconstitutional. In 1926, it ruled that it was legal to use deed clauses (restrictive covenants) to bar African Americans from white neighborhoods; in 1948, it changed its mind and said that enforcing such language violated the Constitution. In 1979, the Court permitted affirmative action programs to benefit black job applicants; in 1995, it concluded that preferences that account for a history of black subjugation were unconstitutional and permissible remedies could only be for victims of identifiable recent discrimination (like practices of a particular company that excluded black applicants). In 1985, the state of Ohio enacted a program that gave subsidies to blacks who moved to white neighborhoods and to whites who moved to black ones, a policy that was then considered so reasonable that its legality wasn't even litigated—but today's Supreme Court would almost certainly prohibit it.

Such flip-flops make an absurdity of claims that the Court simply interprets the Constitution when it considers matters involving race. A more reasonable explanation is that its racial jurisprudence expresses the justices' political allegiances and, most often, bigoted personal views.

Lincoln Defied the Court's Rejection of Black Citizenship

In the 1857 *Dred Scott* case, the Supreme Court ruled 7–2 that it had been unconstitutional for Congress to ban slavery in western territories that were not yet states and that African Americans, free or enslaved, could not be American citizens, even in states that prohibited slavery. The Court defended its claim by looking back seventy years to the Constitution's adoption and concluding that African Americans then had "no rights which the white man was bound to respect." Like Chief Justice Roberts's 2007 decision to prohibit programs that intentionally desegregate schools, Chief Justice Roger Taney's 1857 ruling invented history to justify its claims. In fact, when the Constitution was adopted, although 90 percent of African Americans in the country were enslaved, sixty thousand of them were free, about half of whom were in northern states; many had full state citizenship rights and voted in numbers proportional to their populations in elections to ratify the document. Although northern states with free black residents still maintained racially discriminatory laws, African Americans' citizenship status was not in doubt. Free blacks even voted in the slave-holding state of North Carolina to ratify the Constitution. A dissenting justice in *Dred Scott* recited this unhidden history, to no avail.

Antislavery activists did not accept the ruling. They openly defied it. The Washington correspondent of the *New York Tribune*, a prominent northern newspaper, wrote that the Court's opinion deserves "no more respect than any pro-slavery stump speech." The Maine legislature declared that the decision was "not binding" and that any slave brought into the state would automatically be free; the legislature also authorized county attorneys to represent runaway slaves whose freedom was challenged. The state supreme court then reiterated the right of blacks to vote. The Connecticut legislature also confirmed African Americans' citizenship. A Pennsylvania legislative committee declared the *Dred Scott* decision "inoperative." Ohio, New Hampshire, and other states passed similar resolutions, and their courts made similar rulings. In response to *Dred Scott*, New York's legislature made enslavement of blacks a felony, punishable by up to ten years in prison. It went further: African Americans already had the right to vote in New York, but a state law required that their eligibility depended on having assets greater than those of white voters. Less than three weeks after the *Dred Scott* ruling, the state abolished the discriminatory property requirement.

Several months after the decision, Abraham Lincoln urged Americans not to obey it, based as it was on a false historical account. He said he expected the decision to be overturned in rulings that followed the dissenters' arguments and therefore it should not now be respected. Implicit in his prediction was that a future court could repudiate *Dred Scott* only if it considered new cases that arose in defiance of the earlier decision. Lincoln also declared that if he were again in Congress, he would ignore the Supreme Court and continue to vote to prohibit slavery in the territories. His first presidential inaugural address asserted that the United States would cease being a democracy if citizens conceded the right of the Supreme Court to decide which government policies were permissible.

Nineteenth-century Supreme Court justices also served simultaneously on lower courts. One of the *Dred Scott* dissenters upheld the citizenship rights of free blacks, refusing to apply the ruling when he heard local cases. During the Civil War, Congress and President Lincoln simply ignored *Dred Scott* by again abolishing slavery in the territories. In 1862, Lincoln's attorney general issued a legal opinion that the *Dred Scott* ruling denying African Americans citizenship was "of no authority" and that free blacks were citizens, no matter what the Supreme Court had said. In general, the Lincoln administration and Congress ignored the *Dred Scott* decision; for example, they permitted freed slaves to vote in Southern states well before the adoption of the Fourteenth Amendment, which formally overruled the Supreme Court's opinion that blacks could not be citizens.

Civil rights supporters today should view Supreme Court decisions of the last forty years that limited and then prohibited affirmative action in the same way that Lincoln viewed *Dred Scott*. Rulings like Chief Justice Roberts's 2007 opinion, which denied the well-documented history of African American subjugation, are firmly in the *Dred Scott* tradition and worthy of no greater respect.

When the Supreme Court ruled that school districts could not pursue desegregation, school boards and superintendents should have replied that the case was "of no authority" and gone ahead with their race-based remedies. Public and private programs that are designed to redress past segregation should be the priority for civil rights advocates and be adopted, in disobedience of a Court that may later strike them down.

No "Checks and Balances" Here

When they take office, the president, members of Congress, and federal judges all take oaths to support and uphold the Constitution. With rare exceptions, they're not lying; they mean what they say. But somehow, five Supreme Court justices have the power to decide that only their own oaths matter. They can strike down actions of the president and Congress, declaring that these elected officials aren't upholding the Constitution at all.

How did we come to this? Most Americans today assume that our Constitution gives the Court a final say over what public policies are permissible. Yet the Constitution itself doesn't give the Supreme Court such power. It has nothing to say about whose oath carries the day when justices, the president, and Congress disagree. According to the Constitution itself, justices' interpretations of what it means to uphold the document's principles have no more validity than those of the president or Congress.

Making a final decision about whether the federal government is adhering to constitutional requirements is a power that the Supreme Court assigned to itself in 1805 but it wasn't until *Dred Scott* in 1857 that the Court declared a law unconstitutional. Except for the initial defiance of that particular decision, most Americans, including public officials, have deferred to this power grab.

Supporters of civil rights and civil liberties generally consider it too risky to renounce judicial supremacy. They fear that we may need a Supreme Court to prohibit enforcement of repressive laws if a hostile Congress and president control the government; the alternative ambiguity, they feel, is too dangerous for the nation's stability. This fear ignores the fact that the Supreme Court has almost always been on the side of repressing rights, not protecting them.

There was only one brief period when the Court, led by Chief Justice Earl Warren, was more likely to protect African Americans' rights and the civil liberties of all: the fifteen years from 1954 to 1969. Before and since then, with rare exceptions, the Court has consistently enforced racial discrimination and blocked efforts to overcome it. Liberals' nostalgia for the Warren court, and a fanciful expectation that it may someday be reincarnated, have taken precedence over a clear-eyed look at the role of judicial supremacy in our racial history.

The three constitutional amendments adopted in the aftermath of the Civil War prohibited not only slavery but any expression of second-class citizenship, what the Warren court termed "the badges and incidents of slavery." Employing authority explicitly granted by the Thirteenth Amendment, in 1866 Congress enacted a law to prohibit even private racial discrimination, including in the sale and rental of property.

The Fourteenth Amendment guaranteed full legal rights to African Americans and prohibited state and local governments from treating residents unequally or unfairly. Since this recognized African Americans as citizens, the Fifth Amendment now meant that federal agencies were also banned from practicing discrimination against blacks. The Fifteenth Amendment banned voter suppression by race.

In what we can only consider a counterrevolution, the Supreme Court unilaterally annihilated the amendments' power to create a nation of racial equality. It converted the Civil War victory into a defeat in all but name by declaring discrimination in housing and "separate but equal" in all realms of life to be constitutional. Since the 1870s, racial justice advocates have protested each landmark decision but have never challenged the Supreme Court's right to subvert the Civil War's outcome. If we continue to accept the Court's authority to rewrite the amendments, an aspiration for a nation of equals can never be achieved.

Supporters of racial equality should today have no less integrity than Abraham Lincoln and northern legislatures exhibited after *Dred Scott* and press for race-based public- and private-sector remedial policies that ignore the Court's arrogant and unsupportable views. In housing, this includes public and private subsidies for African Americans to purchase now unaffordable homes from which their forebears were unconstitutionally excluded, preferences for African Americans to purchase a share of newly constructed moderate-income housing, and similar race-targeted programs.

Schoolchildren are taught that it is not undemocratic for a court to have final say. Because elected presidents nominate and elected senators confirm appointees to the Supreme Court, judicial supremacy illustrates only "checks and balances." But these disappear when one of the purportedly coequal branches asserts, without constitutional authority, the right to veto with finality judgments that the two other branches have made. That the other two branches acquiesce in this usurpation doesn't give it any greater legitimacy. In practice, when presidents appoint partisan judges at young ages to lifetime tenure, little checking or balancing is present. Justice Clarence Thomas has been a consistent vote against affirmative action for more than thirty years. More recent young appointees who are hostile to remedies for segregation may serve even longer. There is nothing democratic about this.

As a democratic society, we should abandon entirely the notion of judicial supremacy and return to the principle upon which the nation was founded: three coequal branches of government.

Learning from Abortion Opponents

While civil rights advocates today bow to the Supreme Court's authority, others harbor no such scruples. Abortion opponents, for example, adhered to Abraham Lincoln's view that defiance of the Court is the proper way to challenge Court rulings that they believe defy constitutional principles. In 2021, Arkansas adopted an abortion ban that it boasted was inconsistent with settled Supreme Court doctrine. Upon signing the law, the governor announced that the law was designed to defy "longstanding Supreme Court precedent." In the same year, Texas banned all abortions after six weeks of pregnancy, and Oklahoma followed with similar legislation in 2022. Although most public attention centered on the states' delegation of enforcement to private lawsuits, their defiance of the Supreme Court was most blatant in the six-week prohibition itself, which violated the Court's precedent that the Constitution permits abortion prior to fetal viability (or about twenty-three weeks). Mississippi took a similar step, outlawing abortion after fifteen weeks. The Arkansas, Mississippi, Oklahoma, and Texas policies followed other state laws that whittled away at *Roe v. Wade*, all enacted by legislatures and governors who claimed that the decision was not worthy of respect. Eventually they prevailed, as Supreme Court justices reread the Constitution and found a different meaning than the one their predecessors detected.

"Diversity" Can't Fix Our Problems the Way Race-Based Preferences Can

Affirmative action policies in housing should not be reckless, but carefully targeted to redress specific wrongs borne by black Americans. For other groups that have suffered from discrimination, remedial policies should also be carefully designed to remedy identifiable injustices.

In 2021, however, the Biden administration adopted remedial pol-

Greensboro, North Carolina, February 1, 1960. Ezell Blair Jr., David Richmond, Franklin McCain, and Joseph McNeil, freshmen at North Carolina Agricultural and Technical University, ordered coffee at a Woolworth's lunch counter. Company policy, protected by law, was to serve whites only. Sit-ins spread across the South, with hundreds arrested. College students picketed northern stores in support. The 1964 Civil Rights Act finally banned segregation of public accommodations. Today, a tradition of nonviolent resistance to discriminatory laws has disappeared; instead, racial justice advocates wait for the Supreme Court to tell them what they can and can't do.

icies that were careless and indefensible. In one case, it attempted to extend loan forgiveness to farmers who are "Black, American Indian/ Alaskan Native, Hispanic, Asian and Pacific Islander" and defended this as a remedy for "a well-documented history of discrimination against minority farmers in Department of Agriculture loan and other programs." There is certainly clear evidence of federal farm loan discrimination against African American farmers. But when a federal court blocked the program, it observed that "Asians, Native Hawaiians, and Pacific Islanders [are] groups for which the evidence of prior discrimination by the [government] in farm loans, programs and services appears to be exceedingly thin." The government offered no facts to the contrary. By including all but white farmers, the program made its blockage by the courts inevitable. If the program instead had focused with more discipline on remedies for African Americans whose discriminatory treatment has been substantiated and the Supreme Court then prohibited it, federal officials would have been in a stronger position to ignore the Court's ban and proceed to implement a justifiable remedial program.

The administration also authorized post-pandemic grants to restaurant owners that gave priority to those who were in the above categories as well as veterans, women, and those in "lesbian, gay, bisexual, transgender and queer (LGBTQ)" categories. This, too, was indefensible and blocked by a federal appeals court; there is no consistent pattern of discrimination in federal small business loan programs against other groups that compares to the exclusion of African Americans. By including in its favoritism every category of restaurant owner except white heterosexual males who had not served in the military, the administration guaranteed that courts would block the program. Advocates thereby surrendered an opportunity to extend aid to African Americans whose lack of wealth and ability to engage in business was demonstrably attributable to unconstitutional federal policies of the past. The program also seemed to reflect a politically suicidal mission of rejecting any possible support of white male voters.

Liberal constitutional lawyers have also hobbled their ability to make the long-term case for the redress of segregation by two short-sighted compromises. One was acceptance of the brief (and unlikely to last for long) Supreme Court tolerance of universities that claim they seek only student body diversity, not affirmative action for African Americans. Courageous public and private university leaders should have risked judicial contempt and continued to grant carefully designed preferences for black applicants.

A second compromise has been the stance of civil rights advocates that the appropriate remedy for violations is to respect rights in the future. In 1954, after the Court finally acknowledged in *Brown v. Board of Education* that school segregation violated the Fourteenth Amendment, lawyers and activists focused efforts on getting court rulings, including a second Supreme Court decision, that required districts to move more quickly to desegregate. Advocates filed no cases and conducted no campaigns that sought compensation for students who had received inferior educations because of their unconstitutional segregation. It is doubtful that the Supreme Court would have granted such relief, but lawyers and activists lost opportunities to build cases that might, eventually, have led to the capacity to remedy racial injustices of which we have now become so aware.

Achieving Racial Equality Requires Defiance and Reform of the Supreme Court

We recognize that this discussion will be controversial. Few advocates of racial equality have considered alternatives to judicial supremacy, and we have not presented a fully developed alternative. For those who want to examine it further, we recommend Eric Foner's book *The Second Founding*. It asks us to confront the Supreme Court's radical antidemocratic counterrevolution after the Civil War and to recognize the Court's successful attempt to ensure that we could never become the racially egalitarian society that the amendments promised.

President Biden created a commission to review the role of the Supreme Court. For a summary of the Supreme Court's long history of undermining democracy and annihilating the country's promise of civil rights, we also recommend the testimony of Harvard Law School professor Nikolas Bowie.

The commission made no recommendations. Alternatives it considered, short of abandoning judicial supremacy entirely, include requiring a supermajority of justices to declare a law unconstitutional; making greater political balance on the Court more likely by instituting term limits; granting each president the right to appoint a share of justices proportionate to his or her term in office; and permitting a subsequent supermajority vote of Congress to overrule a Supreme Court opinion that a law is unconstitutional.

The Constitution already gives Congress the right, by simple majority vote, to prohibit the Supreme Court from considering specific topics. When he was an assistant to the attorney general in 1981, Chief Justice John Roberts wrote a memo for President Ronald Reagan pointing out that the Constitution explicitly authorized Congress to pass laws overruling both *Roe v. Wade* and *Brown v. Board of Education* and then forbidding the Supreme Court from hearing appeals of challenges to these new laws. If the president had persuaded Congress to follow Roberts's advice, not only would the right to abortion have then been revoked but the "separate but equal" doctrine that enforced segregation would have been restored.

Congress has never used this expressly granted power to remove a topic from Supreme Court review. Elected officials won't prohibit the Supreme Court from deciding the constitutionality of remedies for segregation without a more powerful civil rights movement that installs senators and representatives who support reform programs and understand that the Court's record on race has no legitimate basis.

Until then, achievement of greater racial equality will almost certainly require defiance of both Congress and the Supreme Court.

Citizen activists in New Orleans developed a fair housing plan that led the city to reform its restrictive zoning. Above, Tulane University architecture students volunteer to help construct a multiunit affordable-housing project that previously would have been prohibited.

Chapter 3

Make a Plan

Using the "Affirmatively Furthering Fair Housing" Rule

The 1968 Fair Housing Act is the closest we've come to adopting a race-conscious remedy to segregation, but it falls short. The act requires communities to affirmatively further its purposes, which civil rights advocates interpret as including both combating future discrimination and undoing segregation already in place. But the law provides little guidance on how to do this.

In 2015, the Obama administration adopted the Affirmatively Furthering Fair Housing rule to define this obligation. It called for cities and counties to analyze the extent of their residential segregation, identify policies and practices that contribute to it, and establish remedial strategies—for example, by building opportunity in high-poverty neighborhoods and opening other areas to blacks and Hispanics who have been excluded. The rule required "robust" community participation to create a plan.

New Orleans was one of the first cities to comply with the 2015 rule, designating the Louisiana Fair Housing Action Center to fulfill the community participation requirement. Like fair housing centers elsewhere, the Louisiana organization investigates complaints of housing discrimination, audits realtors and landlords to identify bias, conducts training sessions in the community about nondiscrimination, litigates violations of fair housing practices, and advocates for tougher enforcement policies. It receives both federal and private foundation funds for its work.

To engage the community, the center enlisted individuals and groups that were not usually involved in government deliberations. It publicized the planning process and recruited participants, using newspapers, radio, television, and social media. The center held training sessions on fair housing. It taught attendees how to comment on the city's draft plan and helped them write up and submit their feedback. To ensure that trainings and community meetings were easy to attend, the center provided child care, food, and translation services. It also made modest payments to organizational leaders who attended and gave gift cards to all who came. It held meetings on weekends and in convenient locations, including community rooms of low-income housing developments. It hosted a dinner meeting for residents of publicly supported housing. The center mobilized participants to attend city council, housing authority, and building resident meetings.

These were occasions for an organization of the formerly incarcerated to explain how criminal background checks make it difficult for those with arrest or conviction histories to find housing. An organization of day laborers and other low-wage workers, like those employed in seafood-processing plants, urged that the plan include ways to resist gentrification that priced members out of their neighborhoods. A member of a Latin American immigrant rights group noted that the housing authority needed more bilingual materials and staff to help Spanish-speaking clients.

An organization that advocates for the rights of persons with disabilities proposed that the plan should include job creation and higher-wage goals, because workers could not otherwise afford housing in all areas of the city. Transportation advocates wanted the plan to include public transit routes that connect workers living in the central city to jobs in surrounding suburbs. Environmental justice activists insisted that the plan should solve the plight of African American residents of Gordon Plaza, a development built on a former dump; the city had been sued for toxic conditions but failed to buy out the homeowners so they could afford to move elsewhere.

Members of public housing resident councils and other tenant associations also took part. The fair housing center hired public housing residents to canvass buildings and distribute information about opportunities to engage in the process. Many who were eligible for government rental subsidies (Housing Choice Vouchers, commonly termed Section 8) called attention to the limited list of landlords provided to recipients and the difficulties faced by those hoping to rent in low-poverty areas. They also pressed for better maintenance standards in public housing and in units rented to voucher holders.

The final New Orleans Affirmatively Furthering Fair Housing Plan includes ten goals and more than fifty strategies for achieving them. Each has a time frame for implementation, ways to measure success, and identification of the responsible agencies.

The city pledged to use public land and resources to develop affordable housing in higher-income communities and to address restrictive zoning codes that prevent this development. The city also committed to conduct campaigns to increase public awareness of nondiscrimination practices and tenant rights, provide funds for fair housing groups, and expand help-line capacity to respond to discrimination complaints. It also promised to perform an annual assessment of local banks' investments in low-income communities.

Community input about substandard conditions in rental housing resulted in the plan's proposal for a rental registry on which private landlords can verify that their units meet basic safety and habitability standards. Public comment about limitations of the Section 8 voucher program led to the housing authority's agreement to study how to increase access to more costly neighborhoods.

Under the Obama administration's rule, if the city and its public housing authority had not followed through and grappled with the plan's goals and strategies, the center and its allies had the right to challenge how federal funds were distributed in New Orleans. Although the federal government rarely withholds funding from jurisdictions that fail to implement their fair housing obligations, it has such authority. Local activists could have used this threat as leverage to ensure that public officials follow through on desegregation goals and that candidates for office also commit to implementation.

The Trump administration withdrew the rule, yet New Orleans continues to make strides on many goals that the process highlighted. The housing authority has held focus groups with landlords and implemented their suggestions to ease participation in the voucher program, such as allowing electronic signatures on rental documents. It also started a program that increases voucher amounts in areas with higher rents and another to help voucher holders move to middle-class areas.

The plan is only as strong as elected officials' resolve to stand up to those who oppose it. White homeowner groups have resisted placing affordable housing in their neighborhoods and local leaders have acquiesced. New Orleans activists have their work cut out to counter this opposition. Because of their input into the plan, other strategies they helped craft are moving forward while they focus on this resistance by supporting specific proposals for affordable-housing development in higher-income neighborhoods and advocating policies to address the obstructionist tactics of homeowners' groups in these areas.

The Biden administration has proposed to reinstate the rule, with modifications based partly on what worked so well in places like New Orleans. Activists elsewhere can follow that city's example, with its robust community participation. Even with no rule, community organizations can duplicate the process; local officials and foundations can voluntarily support them to do so. As in New Orleans, they should recruit a wide range of voices and ensure that it's easy for them to take part by being thoughtful about when and where meetings are held and addressing obstacles to participation. A coordinating group, the National Fair Housing Alliance, provides training to local organizations in other cities that also want to engage in the affirmatively furthering process.

PART TWO

EXPANDING HOUSING OPPORTUNITIES EVERYWHERE

How we can improve conditions for African Americans in black, white, and diverse neighborhoods: by increasing access to homeownership and making certain that all communities are affordable to families of all income levels.

Kaiden, age eleven, was excited about his room in a house that his mother, Markita Bryant, purchased in 2021. She did so with down payment assistance from a private real estate company that provides grants from a share of its profits to African American homebuyers. The firm's executive, Lisa Wise, looks on.

Chapter 4

Is Homeownership the Answer?
It's Complicated
Buying Property Is One Way to Increase African Americans' Wealth. But It's Not Always the Best Way

The black-white wealth gap is enormous. Median African American household wealth is about 5 percent of whites', a 20-to-1 disadvantage. It impedes black families' ability to buy homes in higher-opportunity neighborhoods, weather health emergencies or temporary unemployment, retire in comfort, pay for children's higher education, and then gift or bequeath what remains to children and grandchildren, perhaps for down payments on their own homes.

Twentieth-century discrimination in employment and education contributed to this disadvantage, but most powerful were actions of federal, state, and local government, in concert with banks, insurance, and real estate firms, to exclude black families from homeownership in both urban and suburban areas.

Giving more black families the opportunity and means to own homes supports stability. Less subject to moves that a landlord might force, homeowners are more rooted than renters. They have more connections to neighbors, are more invested in area improvements, security, and resources, are more likely to be involved in children's schools, and are more active in political and community affairs.

When the economy collapsed in 2008, foreclosures took homes from a disproportionate share of African Americans because banks targeted them for fraudulently marketed loans. The terms included sudden large interest-rate hikes that many found unaffordable. Reduced homeownership rates are associated with a decline in voter participation. If not for the housing collapse that left African Americans less stable and less invested in their communities, election results since the financial crisis might have been different.

The history of whites' gains in property value makes it tempting to conclude that increased black homeownership is also the main way to close today's wealth gap. It's one way, but not the only one, and it cannot close the gap alone.

Homeownership Can Generate Wealth

A family that purchases a home with a mortgage and remains in that house for many years will accumulate equity even if its property value doesn't increase. Most mortgages today are "amortized," meaning that monthly payments remain the same over the entire loan period. Each payment includes part that reduces the amount owed and part that's interest on debt that remains. At first, almost the entire payment is interest. But as years pass, the interest share decreases because less is owed; to keep monthly payments constant, the remaining debt declines. If the home retains its worth, paying down the debt increases the family's share of its home value owned outright. In effect, a mortgage is a forced savings plan. Wealth accumulates faster the longer the homeowner remains.

Homeownership can also spur voluntary savings when a first-time home buyer's monthly housing costs are less than his or her previous monthly rent. Even if this is not immediately true, a mortgage payment remains constant for the life of the loan while rents almost always rise during that time, so homeowners may spend less on housing over time than they would have spent by continuing to rent.

In the twentieth century, many white working-class families gained wealth in both ways; they paid down amortized mortgages and obtained federally subsidized suburban housing for which monthly costs were less than rent they had previously paid in cities. They also had a third route: their property values rose, giving them equity that was more than the house was originally worth, even after adjusting for inflation.

For example, if you bought a home thirty years ago for $100,000, made a down payment of $10,000 and had a thirty-year mortgage of $90,000, you are left with $90,000 in wealth (on top of the $10,000 you initially invested) once you paid off your loan. If your house is still worth $100,000, then $90,000 is all the wealth you've accumulated from the forced savings built into your monthly mortgage payments. If your house is now worth $300,000, you've gained an additional $200,000 in wealth without having done anything to earn it. This has been a more frequent experience of white than of black homeowners.

Homeownership Doesn't Generate Wealth for Everyone

These days, about 40 percent of African American and 75 percent of white households own homes. The ownership gap narrowed a bit by 2000 but widened after the housing bubble burst in 2008 and is now greater than it was sixty years ago. You might think that if racial differences in homeownership was the most significant cause of the wealth gap, the white-black wealth ratio would be more like 2-to-1 (75-to-40), not 20-to-1. A good part of the explanation is that most African American owners have homes in neighborhoods where property values haven't skyrocketed the way they have in white neighborhoods.

Driven by pandemic-induced high demand, low mortgage interest rates, and a national housing shortage, most homeowners saw a rapid increase in home values between 2020 and 2022. While this benefited both black and white homeowners, it only exacerbated the wealth gap, since fewer African Americans owned homes and benefited from this surge in value. The resulting high costs made homeownership even less attainable for those who didn't already own.

African Americans who do own tend to buy less expensive homes with more debt, buy their first homes later in life, and are less likely to sustain long-term homeownership than whites. These characteristics limit the wealth accumulation potential of owning a home.

More than a century of discriminatory zoning policies in black neighborhoods have permitted nonresidential uses, such as industry and even toxic dumps, to be placed in many black areas. When they could, highway planners routed interstates through black communities, not white ones. A long history of discriminatory income policies has resulted in placement of lower-quality retail outlets in black than in white neighborhoods. Buyers will pay more for houses in neighborhoods with good supermarkets and without toxic dumps or traffic noise.

Of course, increased African American homeownership will contribute more to narrowing the wealth gap if new black homeowners are fortunate enough to buy homes in neighborhoods where property values will rise more rapidly. But we can't know in advance which neighborhoods those will be. If it could be known, speculators would purchase homes in those neighborhoods, making it more difficult for African Americans to do so. And, indeed, speculators are now doing that in neighborhoods that are beginning to gentrify in Denver, Nashville, New York City, Los Angeles, and elsewhere.

There Are Other Ways to Close the Gap

If we are concerned about the wealth gap, as we should be, we must pursue a variety of economic reforms in addition to African American homeownership. Making voluntary saving easier is as important as making involuntary saving (with a mortgage) easier. This requires policies that narrow income inequality. Black households are more than twice as likely to have student debt than white households, resulting in less ability to save in adulthood. Making community college free would narrow the racial wealth gap for families of low- and moderate-income students who are disproportionately enrolled in two-year institutions. Black workers earn lower average wages than whites and so can save less from their paychecks. Initiatives that support earnings in occupations in which African Americans are heavily represented would also permit voluntary savings; these include increases in the minimum wage and facilitating unionization.

We could strengthen our retirement systems to reduce the incentive for white families to rely on property values as insurance for their old age. We could enact universal health insurance with lower copayments and deductibles so that lower-income black families don't have to dip into their savings for medical emergencies. We could tax inheritance more severely to reduce incentives for families to build up excessive wealth that gives many white children an unfair competitive advantage in life.

These national economic reforms to boost black savings are among the most powerful tools to narrow the racial wealth gap. Yet achieving them is beyond the reach of local activist groups. Advocates can, though, make a small dent in black homeownership rates that are decreasing and expected to continue doing so. With African Americans likely to experience the biggest declines in coming decades, these efforts will be worthwhile. While no panacea, helping African Americans buy property is one of many ways to narrow racial inequality.

Many Black Home Buyers Lack Inherited Cash to Get Started

Many African Americans who've never owned homes could qualify for mortgages, especially in the frequent cases where monthly charges (including taxes and insurance) are not much different from rent payments. These potential homeowners can demonstrate good credit but don't have savings for a down payment.

Banks may require borrowers to pay as much as 20 percent of the purchase price in cash. If the Federal Housing Administration backs the loan, the down payment can be as low as 3.5 percent, but borrowers then have higher monthly charges to cover a mortgage insurance premium that's a condition of the government program.

White home buyers are more than twice as likely as African Americans to get down payments from equity retrieved when they sell a previous home. With the black homeownership rate barely half that of the white one, this option is less available to African Americans, who are more likely to pull money from retirement accounts, putting their future security at greater risk. White young adult home buyers often use parental gifts that were generated by equity gained from years of previous homeownership; African Americans are less likely to have this option.

One obvious solution is to subsidize down payments. This could begin to compensate for decades of discrimination that depressed black homeownership and wealth. Many such initiatives exist. Civil rights groups can advocate to improve them if assistance is inadequate or does not reach African Americans. Where there are no programs, they can press public and private institutions to initiate them.

A concern about such programs is that buyers who do not contribute the full down payment themselves are more likely to default. Actually, they face foreclosure no more frequently than similar households that don't get help, partly because the assistance reduces their debt and keeps families from exhausting their reserves, allowing them to weather emergencies and still maintain mortgage payments.

Down payment assistance can lose its effectiveness when interest rates rise, as they did in late 2022. In such circumstances, prospective homeowners who lack wealth for deposits but can afford regular mortgage payments may no longer be able to meet the new higher monthly charges. House prices, however, should decline when interest rates go up, although this may take time. It's not possible to predict when economic conditions will make down payment assistance programs most effective; groups promoting such aid should be prepared to increase their efforts when overall financial environments offer the best opportunities.

Savings Support Plans

Some nonprofit organizations administer a federal initiative that helps low-income families build assets for home purchases, education, or starting businesses. It matches up to four dollars for every dollar the applicant saves. Participants also get financial counseling and help to secure appropriate mortgages.

Another federal program helps families save for home buying if they receive government rental assistance. Recipients normally contribute 30 percent of their incomes toward rent. If their earnings rise, they pay more toward rent and need less subsidy. For participants in the savings program, public housing agencies keep the subsidy unchanged but deposit the foregone reduction in a savings account that the families can use for a down payment. Most local authorities resist doing this—they have their hands full administering their basic program—but a city's housing officials may not appreciate the great benefits, both to households and to their communities, of increased homeownership. Racial justice groups should urge housing agencies to consider participation.

Public Down Payment Assistance

Every state has a housing finance agency that makes below-market-rate loans and provides down payment assistance to lower- and moderate-income home buyers. Repayment is often not required until the borrower resells the property.

A few examples: Iowa requires borrowers to complete a home-ownership education course and provides up to $5,000 as a loan or $2,500 in a grant to those who purchase homes in low-income neighborhoods. Georgia offers up to $7,500 to lower-income families who either are first-time homeowners or purchase in a low-income neighborhood. To be eligible, borrowers must come up with $1,000 of their own money. Arizona will loan up to 5 percent of a property's purchase price and forgives loans entirely for borrowers who live in the house for at least three years.

The federal government also has eleven regional Home Loan Banks that offer down payment and closing cost assistance as well as counseling for low- and moderate-income first-time home buyers. The San Francisco Home Loan Bank matches four dollars for every dollar a home buyer saves, up to $22,000. The Cincinnati bank gives $5,000 grants, and the Dallas bank offers up to $10,000 to home buyers who contribute at least $500 and complete a homeownership counseling course.

Many cities and counties have their own programs. Madison, Wisconsin, provides no-interest down payment loans to lower-income households, repayable, along with a share of the home's appreciation, upon resale or refinance. Loans can be up to $20,000; buyers have to contribute 1 percent of the purchase price from their own savings. Washington, D.C., offers no-interest loans ranging from $16,000 to $80,000, also repayable when the house is resold or refinanced.

These efforts by state, federal, and local governments are presently race-neutral, but some programs use criteria that, while not openly race-based, are designed to narrow racial inequality. For example, some efforts give priority to households that have been displaced from low-income black neighborhoods as rents and land values have escalated. Others give preference not to first-time home buyers but to those who are first-generation purchasers. Since African Americans have a lower homeownership rate, they are more likely to qualify because they have parents who never owned a home. Yet even black parents who have owned are less likely to have enough equity to offer sufficient assistance to their children. Some programs overcome this obstacle with preferences for applicants who live in historically redlined neighborhoods—places that for much of the twentieth century, banks and the federal government barely served because they had black populations. This doesn't exclude nonblack applicants, but a large share of those who qualify are likely to be black. Yet initiatives like these don't help blacks buy homes in neighborhoods that weren't redlined and do little to redress their segregation.

The best way to make public down payment assistance a tool to narrow racial inequality and segregation is to target assistance explicitly to moderate- and lower-income black home buyers and not limit where they can buy. Absent that, it is to recruit more black potential homeowners to use current programs. Black families may be unaware of these programs and, even if aware, may be mistrustful. Community organizations have a big role to play by helping to overcome this reluctance and lack of information.

Private Down Payment Assistance

Banks, realtors, developers, and other housing industry firms bear responsibility for the low homeownership rate and limited wealth of African Americans and should contribute toward a remedy.

Wells Fargo was one of the banks that marketed the risky loans to African American and Hispanic homeowners and buyers that helped contribute to the subprime mortgage crisis of the early 2000s; the Department of Justice sued. A settlement included bank finance of interest-free, forgivable down payment loans to home buyers in communities where this discrimination was most widespread.

The Justice Department also won a settlement with Bank of America. It resulted in the bank offering down payment grants up to $10,000, and up to $7,500 in closing cost credits to its mortgage holders who are low-income or are purchasing a home in a low- or moderate-income neighborhood. The bank subsequently added another program that requires no down payments from lower- and middle-income applicants who seek properties in predominantly black or Hispanic communities.

Other banks that now express remorse for their participation in segregation should also offer down payment assistance. Civil rights activists should press them for aid that's substantial enough to enable black households to get into homeownership. They should also attempt to block programs that may target underserved areas but have eligibility requirements that most people who already live in the areas cannot meet.

The largely unused 1976 federal law that allows financial institutions to offer race-conscious lending products requires they demonstrate that the programs meet the needs of an economically disadvantaged group. This should not be difficult to do, but few banks have been willing to try. Activists can pressure banks in their communities, especially credit unions and other locally based lenders, to use this authority to implement down payment assistance programs targeted to African Americans.

Real estate firms and associations also pledge to remedy their past practices; down payment assistance is one way to do it. California's and New York's state associations of realtors offer such programs but more should.

Jasmin Shupper, an African American real estate agent in Pasadena, California, founded the Greenline Housing Foundation in 2020 to provide down payment grants to African Americans and Hispanics. In its first year, it made three grants—$42,000, $50,000, and $100,000—with funds raised from her personal contacts. The foundation awarded at least seven grants in its second year, after more widespread fund-raising efforts. The owner of a mortgage broker firm contributed funds. Two churches, one diverse and one mostly white, pledged annual donations. A media company agreed to match donations made by its employees. A wealthy white family committed annual gifts. A few realtors send funds when their transactions close, and Greenline urges others to do the same. A real estate investment company plans to sell some distressed properties it rehabilitates to Greenline grantees at below-market prices.

Greenline's grants help recipients who have some savings as well as those whose incomes qualify them for a mortgage but have no cash to put down. Grantees receive home buyer education and can buy homes in any neighborhood. Initial grantees have mostly been local, but the foundation has made a few grants in Georgia and Oregon. Ms. Shupper hopes to expand even more, perhaps with partners elsewhere.

Flock is a high-end property management company in Washington, D.C. After George Floyd's murder in 2020, its white chief executive, Lisa Wise, researched the powerful role that realtors played in creating racial inequality and was disturbed by what she learned. "I either didn't want to be affiliated with the industry or I really wanted to challenge the industry," she says. She created a plan that offers down payment grants of $5,000 to $15,000 to black and Hispanic first-time home buyers who can qualify for a mortgage but may not have savings for a down payment. Initiated in 2020 with $215,000, the fund can provide help to only a few buyers, but for those who benefit, it can be the difference between getting into a home or not.

Markita Bryant, a federal government paralegal and single mother, is one of the initiative's first grantees. She saw her neighborhood changing and was worried about being pushed out by rising rents. When she was a teenager, her family had become homeless, and she wanted to save her eleven-year-old son from the same experience. She decided to pursue buying a home and enrolled in a home-buying education course that covered money management skills that she hadn't learned from her family. It taught, for example, how to improve loan eligibility by requesting a credit report, checking it and disputing any errors it contained, opening credit accounts to establish a payment history, and diversifying credit types. Ms. Bryant applied for a city program that requires developers to include homes priced low enough for moderate-income households like hers. She won a lottery to purchase a two-bedroom town house in an affluent neighborhood for $249,000 (the area's median home price was over $700,000).

Ms. Bryant qualified for about $20,000 in a deferred interest loan from the city but still couldn't assemble enough for a down payment. A friend told her about the Flock initiative; she applied and it awarded her $10,000. With this grant, the city's loan, and $3,000 of her own savings, she was able to close on the home and retain a small reserve. Ms. Bryant and her son moved from their one-bedroom apartment into their new home in September 2021. "I feel like I can exhale now. I won't be put out on the street," she says.

Other realty companies can follow this example but are unlikely to do so without pressure from community organizations and activists. Most down payment assistance schemes, public and private, offer too little aid to dent the black homeownership deficit. But in some markets, modest grants along with minimal savings from home buyers may be enough to purchase homes using a government-insured mortgage. In these cases, institutions offering aid can make their efforts more workable if they provide additional help to offset the Federal Housing Administration's insurance premium. For conventional loans, a modest subsidy will not be enough, so pressing banks and realtor groups to offer higher subsidy amounts is needed.

Home-Buying Education and Counseling

Many initiatives we've described require homeownership education courses or one-on-one counseling to prepare participants for purchases and avoid delinquency and foreclosure. The programs cover financial literacy and budgeting, including how to select a mortgage and home, assess readiness to purchase, identify scams, avoid discrimination, and maintain a home and finances for the long term. First-generation home buyers, who have not learned the ins and outs of homeowning from their parents' experience and are disadvantaged when starting the buying process, can especially benefit from such programs.

Home buyers, both first time and repeat, who participate in such education and counseling are less likely to default than those that do not. By increasing the likelihood that homeowners will sustain homeownership, these programs also contribute to neighborhood stability. The federal government has certified and funded homeownership education and counseling services since the early 1970s. There are several thousand government-supported providers nationwide.

NeighborWorks America provides grants and technical assistance to several hundred local housing and neighborhood stabilization nonprofits. One, for example, is the Portland Housing Center in Oregon, which also gets financial support from local banks and the city. It offers low down payment mortgages, down payment assistance, matched savings plans, one-on-one home buyer assessment and counseling, and a Home Buyer 101 course to first-time home buyers. The course teaches participants about shopping for a loan, available financial aid for first-time home buyers, and searching for, inspecting, insuring, and maintaining a home.

In 2010, Portland administrators noticed that while black households were overrepresented in their target population of median-income, first-generation home buyers, they made up few of its home-buying clients. The center attributed this to African Americans not thinking of themselves as homeowners because renting was so much more common in Portland's black neighborhoods. The center then developed a financial fitness course taught by African Americans that challenged the stereotype.

The course addresses how homeownership contributes to inter-generational wealth transfer and what this implies for narrowing racial inequality. Participants learn among people who have similar experiences around homeownership and money management. They also meet with African American graduates of the program who became homeowners, receive ongoing counseling, and can join a social network to share advice about maintenance, city services, and property assessment issues. The course has led to increased savings, decreased debt, improvement in credit scores, and more financial confidence. After a few years of offering the course, the center saw nearly a doubling of African American clients and a corresponding increase in those who completed a home purchase. It illustrates the importance of aggressive outreach to African Americans who could become homeowners and of consumer education that confronts the history and ongoing practice of racial housing discrimination head-on.

Credit Scoring Hurts African American Home Buyers; Here's How We Can Fix It

When banks decide whether to make loans, they evaluate how likely borrowers are to repay. These days, banks don't usually make this judg-ment themselves. Instead, they follow standards set by Fannie Mae, a government-regulated agency that buys mortgages it deems safe. In this way, Fannie Mae replenishes funds that banks have lent and enables them to finance new home buyers. The Fannie Mae evaluation of borrowers' default risk considers how faithfully consumers have repaid past obligations. Called *credit scores*, these reports are generated in secretive calculations by three private companies. Higher scores give borrowers a better chance of getting new loan approvals and lower interest rates. Lower scores can make them impossible.

If mortgage applicants haven't been good borrowers—if they've defaulted on car loans or been late paying credit card bills—their scores will be low. Applicants are also penalized if they use more of their available credit. Upper-income households, frequently offered higher credit limits than they need, will have more unused credit eligibility as a result. Their scores will be higher than those of moderate-income families whose debt is closer to their allowable limits, even if both groups pay their obligations on time. Those who haven't taken out many loans or whose payment records (like rent) don't count will have lower scores, no matter how faithfully they've paid what they owed. A system is bound to increase inequality when it is based on the principle that the more you have borrowed from banks in the past, the more you are entitled to borrow again.

African Americans, on average, have lower credit scores than whites. They are more often first-time home buyers without previous opportunities to improve their records with on-time mortgage payments. If they can get home loans, they probably will have higher interest rates. Banks' use of scores to evaluate credit worthiness may not intentionally discriminate by race, but it's discriminatory in effect. Unless financial institutions adjust to account for this, use of credit scores for mortgage eligibility should be deemed to violate the Fair Housing Act. Yet the law is only weakly enforced, so it is up to civil rights activists to press local banks to be more sophisticated in how they determine if a borrower can be counted on to repay.

Even if community groups succeeded in winning such changes, there's another challenge: many low-income workers live in neighborhoods with few retail banks and don't have regular bank accounts. Instead, their communities have more high-interest financial services. Residents sometimes live from paycheck to paycheck; in advance of receiving wages, they may borrow short term from payday lenders, whose fees are high. Repayment of these advances takes great discipline, but lenders who issue them report only if borrowers default, not if timely payments are made, so evidence of responsibility doesn't help their credit scores. African Americans use payday loans more than twice as frequently as others.

Middle-class households get credit cards and overdraft protections, for which lower-income workers can't qualify. Prompt repayments of storefront advances don't count toward credit scores that boost eligibility for home buying.

Also, low-wage workers in a pinch may take out short-term loans from storefront lenders (with names like Cash-N-A-Flash), using automobile titles as collateral. Interest rates are exorbitant (over 100 percent), and if borrowers can't repay, they lose their cars. The terms are so onerous that a few states prohibit them, while others set limits on interest that can be charged. These companies don't report faithful borrowers to credit agencies either. Borrowers who use such services might be acceptable customers for mortgages that could reduce monthly housing costs and make urgent loans less necessary. Payday, title, and other nontraditional sources of credit are more prevalent in lower-income neighborhoods, disproportionately African American.

Regular utility and cell phone payments may also demonstrate that consumers are likely to fulfill mortgage obligations. Not paying these bills can harm credit scores if utility or phone companies refer delinquent users to collection agencies, but paying bills on time doesn't improve a score. Credit-reporting firms could, with little difficulty, collect this information from utility and cell phone companies and the government could require them to provide it. For now, only pressure from local activists can get banks to consider this reasonable evidence of financial responsibility, to supplement what they receive from credit bureaus.

Some noninstitutional payments would also provide evidence of good credit, yet they too don't count. Prompt alimony or child-support payments, for example, might be evidence that a mortgage applicant is a low risk; banks don't consider this either.

One way to know that mortgage applicants will be low risk is whether they've made regular rent payments of similar amounts, but credit-scoring firms do not collect this information. Missed payments to large property managers are often available for credit scoring because there are court records of collection proceedings. Evidence of timely payments doesn't leave a similar public trail. Credit-scoring firms could easily collect the information from corporate landlords.

Many black working- and middle-class neighborhoods have buildings with two or three units, sometimes because they were constructed that way and sometimes because homeowners who needed rental income subdivided what had once been single-family structures. Payment histories of such tenants are also typically ignored in the credit evaluation process.

A nonprofit lender in Indianapolis now considers applicants' rental payment history to determine their future likelihood of default. When it announced the program in 2021, hundreds of potential home buyers inquired, and the lender began working with fifty of them using this approach.

Habitat for Humanity's affiliate groups acquire land—by purchase, gift, or bequest—and build homes for lower- and moderate-income families. Construction costs can be contained, because some building materials may be donated and volunteer labor assists professional contractors. Still, the groups must help applicants obtain mortgages to purchase the houses, even if Habitat subsidizes the sale by requiring a first mortgage of less than full market value (affordable based on the buyer's income), and supplementing it with a second loan for which payment is not required (and is sometimes forgiven) until the homeowner sells. In some cases, Habitat groups issue mortgages themselves; in others, they work with local banks to do so. But whether directly or with a bank's collaboration, Habitat's credit evaluation can be more creative and supportive than that of typical banks. Affiliates consider not only conventional credit history but also timely utility and rent payments (obtaining letters from landlords, for example). If Habitat can be flexible in this way, local banks can adopt similar policies, and civil rights activists should press them to do so.

Public housing residents frequently have incomes that are high enough to support homeownership; many would qualify for mortgages if regular rent payments were counted in credit scores. For renters in public housing or with Section 8 vouchers, banks and Fannie Mae have no reasonable excuse for not considering their histories in evaluation of risk. The information could be collected from public housing agencies that administer both their own units and Section 8 vouchers. Neither Fannie Mae nor credit agencies bother to get it.

For renters of private dwellings, Fannie Mae made no effort until recently to include their payments in its risk evaluations. There was no good explanation for this because in some cases, it's not hard to discover if rent payments have been timely: renters' monthly checking account statements make this clear, and loan applicants could sign authorizations for their release. For years, fair housing advocates have pressed Fannie Mae to develop a simple way for apartment dwellers to get credit for responsible behavior. Then, in 2021, Fannie Mae learned that investigative journalists were about to issue a report denouncing this failure. The agency then changed its risk formula to permit banks to include regular rent payments of home seekers for whom the information was accessible, a long overdue reform.

It won't be easy to implement; whereas large corporate entities (like holders of previous mortgages) supply most credit information electronically to credit-reporting agencies, the new Fannie Mae policy allows applicants themselves to supply personal checking account statements or other proof of timely rent payments. This is needlessly burdensome. Fannie Mae could require renters' banks to certify that their payments were made, without disclosing full bank statements or needing applicants to give express permission. It could also require corporate landlords to report good credit records of tenants.

Announcing its new policy in 2021, Fannie Mae reported that in the previous three years almost one in five applicants who had been deemed ineligible for mortgages would have been approved if rent payments had been considered. Preventing these families from owning homes violated the Fair Housing Act, because the policy disproportionately affected African Americans, more likely than whites to be renters. Fannie Mae's new policy did not include an offer of compensation to the potential home buyers it had rejected.

Civil rights advocates could seek to identify these families in their own communities and assist them in pressing for compensation. Perhaps local banks and mortgage brokers should now grant preapproval for loans to these families and offer payment of damages for previous denials. The institutions undoubtedly will claim that the discriminatory policy wasn't their fault and that Fannie Mae should fix it. In our complex economic system, finger-pointing will always be the first line of defense for institutions called upon to redress segregation. Yet, just as there are many collaborating participants in every significant system of racial discrimination, many actors should also take part in the remedies.

The affluent, mostly white city of Petaluma, California, requires developers to sell 15 percent of units at prices affordable to lower- and moderate-income households. Teachers, first responders, and city employees can now live in the city they serve. In 2020, Lisa Windham (right), a paralegal, was the first African American to buy a reduced-price condominium in the new Brody Ranch subdivision. With her in a three-bedroom home are her daughter and grandchildren, who attend school nearby.

Chapter 5

Mix 'Em Up!

Creating Racially and Economically Diverse Communities

When the Montgomery Travelers moved from the study of segregation to its remedy, they campaigned for affordable housing in their affluent white Chicago suburbs. When Sharon Froba and her NAACP housing committee wanted to reverse Modesto's segregation, they proposed using an abandoned golf course for affordable housing.

But *affordable housing* is a troublesome term. Most advocates have in mind subsidized apartments for low-income households, usually financed by a federal program that gives tax breaks to developers. The projects frequently house those with extremely low incomes: almost half have annual earnings of less than 30 percent of their area's median, with a low of about $13,000 in Mississippi to a high of $28,000 in Maryland.

These are families badly in need of good housing, but they are not the only ones facing affordability crises. In much of the nation, adequate dwellings are also too expensive for lower-middle-class households—those that earn between 60 and 120 percent of their area's median income, which nationally is about $40,000 to $80,000, also with big state-by-state variation. These are teachers, nurses, police officers and firefighters, bus drivers, clerical and office employees, factory workers, laborers, and many others. Most African Americans are not poor; they are part of this middle-income group.

The private sector is now often incapable of providing homes for this "missing middle." Land scarcity in many urban areas has pushed prices so high that most homes are out of reach. Government insists that construction be safer than it once was, with fire codes, plumbing, heating, and structural standards, as well as environmental regulations (such as insulation requirements), all of which contribute to house prices that are beyond the means of working-class families. These are justifiable regulations, but others are unreasonable: excessive off-street parking requirements accompany refusals to invest in good public transportation, and overly complicated permitting adds months to construction while interest on builders' loans accumulates. In many places, opponents of residential projects delay them for years by filing meritless challenges and lawsuits, often claiming to oppose new construction to protect the environment, but actually from a desire to exclude working-class and lower-income residents. All of these obstacles, both the sensible and the abusive, can make it unprofitable for private-sector contractors in many places to build for any but higher-income households.

Meanwhile, tax credits to construct units for low-income families are by far the largest federal subsidy for housing. Developers who want to create homes for the missing middle can only try to cobble together scarce subsidies from state and local government with some obscure federal aid plans. Making finance of missing-middle housing even more daunting, users of federal support must obey a law that requires construction workers to be paid union-scale wages. This enables them to stay out of poverty and afford the homes they build but increases costs.

Learn from the Past: Don't Construct Housing That Isolates the Poor

Typical middle-income African Americans reside in areas with more poverty than typical low-income whites. We should be concerned as much with expanding middle-class African Americans' access to better housing as with needs of the poor.

History has a lesson: public housing was originally for families who required no subsidies. Initiated in President Franklin Roosevelt's New Deal of the 1930s, it was for moderate-income (mostly white) households who could afford to rent apartments but couldn't find any because construction activity had slowed in the Great Depression, resulting in a housing shortage.

Beginning in the late 1940s and into the 1950s, and with the best of intentions, public housing officials evicted middle-income families, reasoning that the poor were in such desperate need that it was wrong to allow tenants to remain if they could find private housing. Projects soon concentrated the most disadvantaged families and had to be heavily subsidized. Without middle-class neighbors, residents lost political influence, maintenance declined, young children and adolescents lost friends with middle-class ambitions and adult role models who were economically successful, local schools faced greater and soon insurmountable challenges, and quality grocery and retail businesses fled. Violence and crime increased; many public housing projects deteriorated into such dysfunctional slums that, beginning in the 1970s, cities began to demolish them—and continue to do so.

The suffering of low-income households in desperate need of safe homes is immediate. The costs of isolating them from better resources and reinforcing segregation are longer term and harder to see. Because we provide inadequate public support for housing, advocates and officials face an unacceptable choice, usually opting for more segregated housing for the poor rather than mixed-income housing that requires spending scarce funds on discounts for the middle class.

Moderate-Income Households Also Need Affordable Housing

The lack of government subsidies for moderate-income housing is not the only reason that so many housing advocates seem interested only in "affordable" units for the poor. Another explanation is that too many whites, including some housing experts, retain the stereotype that black and poor are almost the same thing.

Yet only about one-sixth of African Americans are poor. That's more than triple the white rate, but still only a small share of blacks. One in eight African American workers are private-sector business managers. Another one-fifth are professionals in fields like health care, education, and computer technology.

Over one-fourth of black families have incomes too high for subsidized housing but too low to afford market-rate homes in many urban and suburban areas, especially if they lack wealth for down payments.

Another fourth have higher incomes but can't afford to purchase a home in an increasing number of metropolitan areas.

The country's growing isolation by income as well as race reinforces the misconception that we can undo African Americans' segregation with housing for the poor. Not only do few whites have meaningful social contact with blacks, but most Americans also lack connections with those of another social class, except in workplace or service relationships. College graduates are more likely than before to marry partners with similar educations—mostly because more women are now highly educated. Affluent families are more likely to live among other affluent families. Thirty years ago, nearly two-thirds of Americans lived in middle-class neighborhoods. Now only half do, and the trend—a growing likelihood of living either in a rich or a poor neighborhood—shows no sign of abating.

When the wealthy live only with others in similar circumstances, their higher property taxes can purchase better resources—schools, parks, and libraries—that compound their advantages and those of their children. Affluent residents then resist sharing their resources, blocking the less fortunate from joining them. Our racial and class isolation becomes self-perpetuating and makes it even more difficult for us to come together, undermining our ability to forge a common national identity.

Lower-income families, particularly African Americans, are also more concentrated than they were before the civil rights victories of the 1960s and '70s. With the Fair Housing Act's passage and the growth of a more diverse professional class, many middle-income blacks have left poorer neighborhoods to find better housing elsewhere, leaving their low-income neighborhoods more uniformly distressed.

Daryl Carter, an African American real estate developer, summarized this complex story on his website. When he was young, his father had a job at a General Motors plant in Detroit, close to home; like many other autoworkers, he picked Daryl up from school on his daily walk back. "The neighborhood had no crime or gang problems, and families from different backgrounds—from autoworkers to doctors—lived side by side," Mr. Carter wrote. But in the 1970s and '80s, auto companies moved to the suburbs. Mr. Carter's father then commuted about twenty miles to his factory, no longer able to pick his son up from school. "The neighborhood changed—and not for the better." Most black workers were unable to follow jobs that far and became poorer, leaving communities like Daryl Carter's areas of concentrated poverty.

Mixing Only Rich and Poor Is No Formula for Successful Desegregation

When planners and developers try to avoid isolating the poor, they frequently do so by choosing affluent neighborhoods in which to place subsidized housing. Or they create projects that they term *mixed-income*, which include market-rate units, affordable to higher-income families, along with units for the poor. Frequently, this means developments that accommodate the most disadvantaged black households along with much wealthier whites, with nobody between.

Some development experts believe that bringing together people of such different racial and economic classes will increase their mutual respect and understanding. But might the opposite be the case, with greater contact making us less tolerant of one another?

At first glance, the evidence seems contradictory. Sometimes, closer interracial contact can reinforce stereotypes. At other times, contact can challenge them—when people of different races have more exposure to one another, they can come to appreciate they have more in common than they'd thought. That's what Tonika Johnson's map twins discovered.

In the 1970s, federal courts ordered school districts to desegregate by busing white children to predominantly black schools and vice versa. In practice, politically powerful white parents sabotaged the two-way design; busing mostly dispatched black children to predominantly white schools. This set up fraught situations in which black children were subject to abuse and discrimination at their destinations. Many African Americans felt that busing was degrading, with black children chasing after whites who didn't want them.

Even where the abuse was not intended, it was hurtful. A journalist interviewed Boston busing participants as adults, two decades after their high school graduations. One recalled that when the curriculum turned to slavery and Jim Crow, her white classmates turned to stare at her to see her reaction. "Turn around," she told them. "I wasn't there. I'm trying to learn this, too."

Nonetheless, despite frequent microaggressions, white and black busing veterans reported greater understanding, respect, and tolerance for the opposite race, and these attitudes persisted into adulthood. Twenty years after court-ordered busing ended in the early 1980s, sociologists interviewed more than five hundred adults who were sent to distant high schools for desegregation. In Texas, a white graduate recalled how much more comfortable he felt than his wife (who had not been bused) in the rare occasions when they were in non-segregated settings: "We walked into a movie theater and we were in, definitely racially in a minority, and it kind of startled my wife. She had not grown up in a desegregated setting, and I felt sorry for her. . . . I remember feeling 'I'm so glad I went to [a diverse school] for that reason right there.'"

Many black adults expressed gratitude for the busing experience, despite the abuse they encountered. One in New Jersey reported, "I would say it makes me feel comfortable that I can go anywhere and not feel intimidated. I just always feel like I belong, and it didn't matter who was in the majority or minority, that I knew how to deal with all of them." A black lawyer said her colleagues feel defensive around white lawyers and judges whereas she is able, because of her experiences, to be in control when dealing with white peers.

Exposure doesn't always lead to tolerance, though. In the early 2000s, Chicago demolished high-rise public housing projects and replaced them with developments that included for-sale and rented homes, town houses, and apartments. The complexes were called mixed-income but mixed only two groups. Some units were sold or rented at expensive market rates, while others were subsidized for low-income households.

Planners expected that from living around higher-income whites, the low-income black residents would develop habits—a stronger work ethic, greater respect for property, and more restrained public behavior—that would help them get better jobs and escape poverty. Officials thought these were characteristically middle-class habits, although there is no evidence that lower-income families have less respect for property or a weaker work ethic than middle-income families, provided jobs are available. When the economy improves, poorly educated young black men tend to join the labor force more rapidly than similarly educated whites. Many deeply subsidized families who moved to these developments worked multiple jobs and inconvenient shifts to make ends meet.

Project managers had no program to challenge affluent whites' negative view of public socializing—to help them develop better understanding of how it was a response to having lived in overcrowded apartments in dense segregated neighborhoods. The market-rate occupants thus acquired little incentive to question their stereotypes of black neighbors or make efforts to engage with them.

When the two groups came in contact, results could be unpleasant. Affluent whites pressed management to prevent what they regarded as lower-class lifestyles by installing fences around internal parks, locking community rooms, or issuing warnings for too many guests or too much noise, for example. The tensions broke down along class lines, not just racial ones. Affluent black market-rate residents often had similar attitudes. Some occasionally engaged in friendlier intraracial socializing, but others felt that subsidized residents had incompatible habits. One black homeowner complained that "when I come home from a hard day's work or an easy day of work, I really don't want to see people hanging out on the front porch."

The lower-income African Americans rejected these criticisms. Several said they had made efforts to interact with higher-income families but were rebuffed: "Say, like you are getting on the elevator. People are coming off the elevator. You speak . . . you just say good morning, good afternoon. People walk right past you . . . like you're not even there."

Project rules prohibited residents of the subsidized units from having pets or barbecuing, both of which were permitted for market-rate owners. One low-income resident referred to a white homeowner in the project who "would always call the police on them for barbecuing in the park. Isn't that where you're supposed to barbecue at? In the park?" Yet another observed that "when the [white] condo owner down the hall [is] playing music and smoking pot [and is] just as dysfunctional as everybody else; just got a little more money . . . no one complained to [the project management]. . . . So I think it's a different way that people deal with [the former public housing residents], which I think, is unfair."

So-called mixed-income projects are usually mixed in name only, segregating low-income and higher-income residents. In 2015, New York City sponsored a mixed-income building of 219 luxury apartments that sold for $25 million each, and 55 subsidized units for low-income families that rented for $850 a month. The developer planned a separate entrance (a "poor door," as it became known) for the rental units, evoking comparisons to apartheid in South Africa and twentieth-century legal segregation in the American South. Bad publicity led the city to prohibit separate entrances, yet the ban did not prohibit developers from locating low-income units on separate floors. Nor did it prevent other New York builders from continuing to construct different buildings for subsidized units within larger market-rate developments.

The owner of New York's "poor door" project defended his design by arguing that low-income tenants did not object—there were 88,000 applications for the 55 rental units. This wasn't surprising: African Americans living in poverty prefer segregated housing to no housing at all.

Developers may say that it's impossible to finance mixed-income buildings without internal segregation. Subsidized units are easy to rent because low-income black households are desperate for good housing and waiting lists are long. A family that obtains one is not likely to give it up, so turnover is low. Vacancies in market-rate units are more frequent. Potential occupants have other housing choices and are more mobile. Default risks for loans covering market-rate units are higher. Builders often get separate loans for the construction of market-rate units, with more onerous terms than loans for building the tax-credit apartments. The developers call this "condominium-izing" the project and they claim that the financial terms require physical segregation of market-rate units. This is untrue. Separate financing need not require that income groups be physically separated on different floors or buildings. Some successful projects have spread market-rate and subsidized families throughout.

When developers segregate tenants by income, they do so not because desegregation is financially impossible, but from deference to the race and class prejudices of potential affluent residents, reflected in the reluctance—and, frequently, the refusal—of lenders to finance desegregated units. It is easier to rent or sell market-rate apartments that are physically separated, and easier to charge more for them, because realtors can appeal to customers' elitism.

Housing the Missing Middle

When greater interracial contact leads to greater understanding, it usually occurs when the social class status of blacks and whites is not radically different. Mixing races only at the extremes of social status can have an opposite effect, reinforcing stereotypes, not diminishing them.

Universities that have enrolled racially and economically diverse student bodies have lessons for housing policy. The most affluent white college students are the least likely white group to interact socially with black classmates. The lowest-income African Americans are also unlikely to have interracial relationships. Upper-middle-class and middle-class blacks, however, are most likely to have interracial relationships as well as engagement with lower-income African Americans.

A healthy community that can sustain a common national identity is one where affluent, middle-class, working-class, and low-income families of all races and ethnicities have access to the same resources and whose children attend the same schools. This should be the aspiration of civil rights activists.

There are a few examples.

Bart Mitchell, president of a Boston-based housing development firm, the Community Builders, wanted to find a way to create truly mixed-income and mixed-race projects. An obscure financing source he found was the federal New Markets Tax Credit. It's not designed for housing but for commercial projects that would attract other investment to low-income neighborhoods. A rarely utilized provision allows the program to finance residential construction if at least 20 percent of project revenue comes from nonresidential sources. A builder can put retail stores on a ground floor to generate that 20 percent and apartment units on upper floors. It can sell some of the residential units at market rate, finance some with a federal subsidy for low-income families, and create units for middle-income households using the New Markets program.

One project that the firm created with this finance combination is Avondale Town Center in Cincinnati. Located in a low-income neighborhood, it attracts renters who are racially, ethnically, and economically diverse, in part because it's within walking distance of hospitals that employ health care workers at many wage levels.

In 2016, Massachusetts created a Workforce Housing program

that offers low-interest loans to build homes to sell or rent to families who earn too much to qualify for federal low-income subsidies, but too little to afford market-rate housing in high-priced neighborhoods. Developers who use the credit to subsidize moderate-income households must also reserve one-fifth of their units for lower-income renters. Some projects also include town houses, providing homeownership opportunities for first-time home buyers. By the spring of 2022, the Workforce Housing program had thirty-two projects in operation across the state, with another twenty-four under construction.

One completed building is The Watson in Quincy, a close-in commuter suburb of Boston. Of its 140 apartments, about one-fifth are subsidized with the federal subsidy for low-income households, another fifth are sold at market rate, and three-fifths are mildly subsidized by the state initiative for missing-middle households.

The Watson managers protect its permanent mixed-income character: they do not evict tenants in the Workforce group if their incomes increase above the eligibility limit. They remain but their apartment gets reclassified as a market-rate unit, while reserving the next vacant market-rate unit for a moderate-income household. The balance of middle- and market-rate residents then continues. Residents of the low-income units are similarly protected if their income increases to the middle level. If a household's income declines so it can no longer afford its Workforce unit, management reclassifies it as subsidized for low-income tenants, and the next available low-income unit is made available to a new moderate-income resident. The policy works because all units are of equal quality and are distributed throughout the project, not segregated.

The Watson is also racially mixed. About two-thirds of the market-rate units are occupied by whites, with African Americans in about a fifth of the units. Market-rate occupants generally have six-figure incomes and work in Boston's financial district or as lower-level corporate executives. About half of the Workforce residents are whites, with African Americans and Asians each having about a one-fifth share. They are emergency medical technicians, technology workers, chefs, telemarketers, and paralegals. African American households rent almost half of the low-income subsidized units; whites are the next largest group, followed by Hispanics, Asians, and Native Americans. Households in these apartments mostly have jobs as retail or supermarket employees.

The Watson includes a coffee bar, a gym, and a clubroom, which opens to an outdoor patio with social gathering areas and grill stations, available to all residents. These have led to tenant interactions that include interracial and interclass exposure. One moderate-income renter has been Chazzie Henderson, an African American fifth-grade math teacher with a daughter. When she relocated to Boston from Florida, she searched fruitlessly for a safe, clean, and affordable apartment, not so far from Boston that she'd be unable to get her daughter to school and herself to work on time. From The Watson, Ms. Henderson could have a short commute to her job at a private Episcopal school.

Before the onset of the pandemic, she and her daughter participated in community activities that the building hosted. She was unable to tell which people she met were in market-rate, moderate-income, or deeply subsidized units. She speculated that three Asian-American college students she befriended were paying market rate, that an African immigrant couple next door were probably in a moderate-income unit, and that an elderly white woman's rent was deeply subsidized, but Ms. Henderson couldn't be certain of any of this.

The Watson design is encouraging but only suggests the potential of truly mixed-income, mixed-race housing. With only one- and two-bedroom apartments, it attracts mostly younger recent entrants to the

Quincy, Massachusetts, 2019. At The Watson, an artist instructs black and white tenants of varied income levels at an annual "paint night."

workforce, single parents with small families, and childless unmarried couples. This reflects a significant share of today's working-class families, as single-parent households become more commonplace for whites as well as for blacks and as couples marry later in life and have fewer children. Yet to house larger moderate-income families, bigger units than The Watson offers are necessary, and the state's subsidy is too small to support their construction.

Financial backing for missing-middle housing should come from local jurisdictions and employers as well. Some municipal governments are concerned about their towns' safety if firefighters, paramedics, and police officers can't afford to live close to where they serve. A few school districts, mostly in California, have built subsidized housing to permit teachers to live in the expensive communities where they teach.

Community activists should not assume that nothing can be done for the missing middle. In Massachusetts, they might focus on pressing their state legislature to expand the subsidy to support construction of larger units. Elsewhere, they should mobilize to persuade both local and state governments to create new programs that permit truly mixed-income and mixed-race projects.

PART THREE

INVESTING IN SEGREGATED BLACK NEIGHBORHOODS

How we can challenge practices that sap the resources of segregated communities and instead improve investments in them, while protecting residents from displacement as neighborhoods become more desirable and unaffordable.

Deborah Johnson (right), her partner, and their three children got an eviction notice during the pandemic when they fell behind in rent. Ms. Johnson, an auto-parts store clerk, had to quit because she could find no adequate child care options when schools shut down. Her partner also lost his job during Covid. Legal Aid attorney Lauren Hamilton (left) represented them at no charge under Cleveland's right-to-counsel policy and got social service agencies to provide $17,000 in rental assistance; the landlord then withdrew his eviction notice. On September 8, 2022, lawyer and client reviewed settlement terms.

Chapter 6

Invest in Place
Increasing Housing Opportunities in Low-Income Segregated Communities and Ensuring That Current Residents Benefit

O ur housing patterns segregate people, but they also segregate resources, leaving some areas wealthy and others impoverished. While people remain segregated by race, it is unconscionable not to narrow the ongoing economic segregation of our neighborhoods.

More investment is necessary in low-income segregated black areas, including: construction of higher-quality low- and moderate-income housing, more African American families owning their own homes, home-improvement grants, better retail outlets, reformed policing, well-maintained parks, upgraded school facilities and curriculum, well-funded early childhood and afterschool and summer programs, access to good jobs, clean air, better public transportation options, supermarkets selling fresh foods, local bank branches, and responsive public services. But these improvements have a cost.

Improved Conditions in Low-Income Areas Can Attract New Residents and Bring Added Resources. But Not Everyone Benefits

When lower-income areas become more attractive, middle-class households (including whites) will also want to move in and may displace long-term residents in the process. Landlords who seek wealthier tenants will remodel buildings, raise rents, and evict families who don't leave voluntarily. When houses appreciate, higher property taxes can make neighborhoods unaffordable for longtime homeowners, even those who have paid off mortgages and own their residences, free and clear. We call this process *gentrification*.

In some places, gentrification is not a consequence of urban neighborhood improvement; rather, it is the cause of added investment when younger white adults, attracted by low housing costs and commercial rents, move into low-income urban areas. They've repudiated common racial stereotypes of their parents' generation and purposely seek diverse communities in which to live. The new arrivals usually have incomes and education levels that are higher than those of their new neighbors. They start businesses and attract higher-end retail to the area, making it more attractive to other middle-income movers. In the process, rents increase and many black and Hispanic longtime residents and small shop owners are priced out. Those who own homes have a rare chance to get a high price by selling to newcomers. Existing community members who cannot afford these higher costs must now look elsewhere for homes.

One way to prevent that is to keep the neighborhood poor and undesirable for middle-class households. This is not a solution we should accept. The challenge is to improve amenities so a neighborhood diversifies and strengthens economically, while preserving existing residents' ability to remain in sufficient numbers that cultural characteristics and social networks of the community are not undermined. This requires place-based strategies to prevent the displacement of African American residents as conditions improve.

Some African Americans reject the goal of stable racial diversity that can result from gentrification. They hope to improve neighborhood quality while simultaneously maintaining an area's African American cultural and racial homogeneity. This aspiration is reinforced by public officials and housing and urban development experts who convince themselves that more investment in low-income black neighborhoods can transform them into places with equal opportunity while preserving their racially exclusive character. But this is a contradiction: it is impossible, however attractive the idea may seem. "Separate but equal" doesn't work any better for neighborhoods than it did for restaurants, buses, or schools. Inferior community resources and racial isolation cannot be separated. Wherever we may succeed in improving conditions in underinvested black neighborhoods, middle-income families, black and white, will move in. Aggressive policy can ensure that large numbers of African American households remain as the neighborhood becomes diverse.

Another contradiction arises from the importance of narrowing the black-white wealth gap that underlies so much of our social and economic inequality. African American homeowners in gentrifying neighborhoods who want to retire and downsize or move for other reasons, and whose properties have appreciated in value, cannot reasonably refuse to sell to the highest bidder—who may be a white home buyer or a developer. Sellers may feel conflicted, knowing that such a sale will contribute to their community's gentrification, a trend that may have troubled them. But it also allows a future bequest to children and grandchildren, something that few black families had an opportunity to provide during the era of forced segregation.

Conscientious Gentrification

Although they choose diversity, new middle-class residents in urban neighborhoods are rarely prepared to make the behavioral adjustments that diversity requires. Successful gentrifying areas need community organizations that educate white newcomers about how to adapt to neighborhoods in which they reside. The groups should intervene when whites' behavior undermines healthy racial coexistence.

Luke Davenport, a forty-five-year-old data consultant to school districts, grew up in the affluent white Boston suburb of Hingham. He recalls that "when the time came to leave home, I was ready to live someplace more diverse, and more representative of the country as a whole." He spent his adult life living in gentrifying neighborhoods, first in Columbia Heights and Adams Morgan in Washington, D.C., then Washington Heights in Manhattan and Prospect Heights in Brooklyn. Like some (but not enough) gentrifiers, he was troubled by how he, and others like him, were destroying some admirable characteristics of their new communities. He wrote a pamphlet he called "Becoming a

Conscientious Gentrifier in 8 Easy Steps" and circulated it to friends. Here is a much-abridged summary.

1. **Shop at older businesses**. When new residents arrive, local businesses struggle. Even if the bodega doesn't sell the gluten-free pasta you want, there's probably other things you can buy there. Don't just go to the new cocktail place, go to the neighborhood bar. You might feel awkward—that's okay. Almost always you and your dollars will be welcomed.

2. **Join, volunteer, and donate.** Join local groups that serve long-term residents. Look at what they've done—not the quality of their website. They're the ones who started the night youth programs and senior meal delivery service, beautified the local park, or rallied to insist landlords make needed repairs. They might meet in a church basement or someone's living room. You'll get to better understand issues facing your neighbors so you can advocate for them.

3. **Learn**. Learn your neighborhood's history. Newer buildings may have been opposed or supported by different community groups. Their accounts will help you understand the concerns of long-term residents.

4. **Be friendly.** It sounds simple, yet many don't do it. Say hello to the older woman you see sitting on her stoop. Or the guy you see walking his dog in the park. Not everyone will be friendly, but that's okay—most will. You can meet some great people. Participate in local events open to the public. Shop at the church's holiday market or school's bake sale.

5. **Worship.** Attend a local church service and make a donation. It's likely a bedrock of the community, but at risk as long-term residents move away. You can help breathe new life into it. Don't worry if it has a different vibe than one you grew up with—focus on what you share.

6. **Educate.** Got kids? Send them to the local public school. Look at its impact, not just test scores that have little to do with instructional quality. Visit it and form your own opinion. Does it seem warm and inviting? Are the teachers enthusiastic and cre-

ative? Do children get individual attention when needed? Join the local PTA to advocate for all children, not just your own. And keep in mind the enormous advantages your children will gain from attending a diverse school and making friends with others from different backgrounds.

7. **Be bold but humble.** Don't be afraid to be the only new resident in the room. Curious stares won't kill you, and mostly people will appreciate that you're trying to support the community. Support, but don't take over. Follow before leading—or just follow!

8. **Advocate.** You don't have to be a radical activist to make a difference. Call on local elected officials to support policies that would best serve your neighbors. But there's one form of advocacy you should be careful with: calling the police. A violent crime or unsafe situation is one thing; a noisy party on a holiday weekend or a loud conversation on the street is another. Before calling, ask yourself if someone's safety is in jeopardy. If not, just let it go; if it's really unmanageable, try politely speaking to the person or people yourself. A polite request will probably be met with a polite response.

In some places, gentrification has advanced beyond the time when preventing massive displacement is possible—for example, parts of New York City, San Francisco, Oakland, Washington, D.C., Boston, and Austin. In cities like these, African Americans have sometimes been forced by rising rents and property values to move to more affordable suburbs. The challenge in these areas is to ensure that displaced households have healthy communities in which to resettle, without finding themselves in newly segregated and poorly resourced places.

The gentrified cities from which they came, and whose policy failures resulted in their displacement, have generally taken no responsibility for the welfare of their former residents. Activists in these gentrified communities can take up this cause.

Oakland has been enriched by the higher property taxes of its new middle-class households and relieved of some need to finance support services required by a low-income population. It should assume a role in fixing the difficulties faced by its displaced residents who now face hours-long commutes from distant suburbs to get to work.

In the San Francisco Bay Area, tech companies use fleets of luxury coaches to ferry employees from outlying suburbs to Silicon Valley work sites. The buses speed through in designated lanes, bypassing commuters who are stalled in rush-hour traffic. At a minimum, Oakland should provide a similar service for the restaurant, construction, and hospital workers who've been displaced from the city but continue to serve its residents.

Many employees of Oakland's unionized public and health care sectors earn good blue-collar wages but still cannot afford to rent or purchase decent housing reasonably close to their workplaces. Should these public and private institutions accept an obligation to subsidize (and build, if necessary) moderate-income housing in Oakland itself? A union representing some of these African American and Hispanic government workers, including janitors, cafeteria workers, nursing assistants, and nurses, has begun to demand that housing allowances be considered as mandatory a subject of collective bargaining as health care. Unions elsewhere should consider something similar.

In most cities, resources in traditionally black neighborhoods have not improved so much that gentrification has begun and residents can no longer afford to remain. These places suffer from lack of investment, not too much of it. As assets increase, policies and practices should be put in place that create opportunity for a racially and economically diverse community where longtime residents can preserve cultural familiarity and residential security.

Housing experts are aware of policies that can prevent displacement from gentrification. But knowing the solutions is useless without mobilized activists who build the power to insist on their implementation.

These policies include inclusionary (mixed-income) zoning, rent control, prohibition of evictions except for just cause, prevention of security deposit theft, limits on condominium conversions, support for community land trusts, regulation of phony home sales, and property tax freezes. An impediment to advocacy is that state governments have constitutional authority to prohibit municipalities from enacting them. In states that do prohibit one or more of these actions, city officials will have to press for state permission before proceeding.

Inclusionary Zoning

As lower- and moderate-income black and Hispanic neighborhoods gentrify and more affluent households arrive, developers may buy and demolish existing properties to construct more expensive market-rate buildings. As these accumulate, there is less housing for longtime residents. Eventually, the area can flip from a low- and moderate-income segregated community to a wealthy (and increasingly white) one.

Local officials can limit this displacement by requiring that new market-rate projects set aside some units in urban gentrifying neighborhoods for low- and moderate-income households. As the area changes, this policy, called *inclusionary zoning*, can preserve housing for those who would otherwise be pushed out.

Hundreds of cities have such regulations. They have produced more than one hundred thousand affordable units. However, some states, like Kansas, Indiana, and Tennessee, prohibit localities from adopting inclusionary requirements. In those that permit it, racial justice groups can campaign for ordinances that specify varied affordability levels for set-aside units. Rules should stipulate whether the provisions are for rentals or ownership units, if all developments must comply or only those in certain locations, and how long the set-aside units must remain affordable. Community groups should press for as much protection for existing residents as their organizational strength permits.

- Most programs mandate that 10 to 25 percent of a development's units should be offered at below-market-rate rents or sale prices. The higher the share, the less community displacement can result, but the harder it may be for a developer to make a profit. Cities can support more affordability with incentives to offset the rules' costs, such as greater allowable project sizes, relaxed development or design standards, lower local fees, and subsidies or tax breaks.

- Developers will usually prefer to reserve units only for the lowest-income tenants, because there are more federal subsidies available for these. Inclusionary zoning ordinances should be designed to meet the housing needs of moderate-income families as well.
- Regulations should authorize racial preferences for the below-market-rate units and consider priorities for households that have been displaced from the community by rising rents or building demolitions.
- Some cities permit developers to meet their inclusionary requirements by constructing separate buildings for subsidized households and sometimes by placing these in different neighborhoods. City officials should insist that affordable apartments are integrated within otherwise market-rate projects in gentrifying neighborhoods. They should deny developers the right to place units for lower-income families in disadvantaged neighborhoods that are not undergoing gentrification. To permit such placement would only reinforce a city's segregated patterns.
- Some cities permit developers to meet their inclusionary requirements by paying a fee instead of making affordable units available. This does not fulfill the anti-displacement goal of an inclusionary zoning policy, unless the fee goes to a fund that's specifically designated to subsidize mixed-income and mixed-race projects in gentrifying neighborhoods and is large enough (which it often isn't) to finance such construction at a reasonable level.
- The policy should prohibit poor doors and other similarly discriminatory approaches. Units for households of different income levels should be externally indistinguishable and distributed throughout developments.
- To create mixed-income and mixed-race communities, inclusionary zoning policy should apply citywide. It would be reasonable to make the affordability provisions tougher for projects constructed in neighborhoods where displacement is occurring.

Chicago's inclusionary ordinance aims to balance the goals of creating mixed-income developments with increasing affordable housing in high-cost areas and gentrifying neighborhoods. It has different set-aside and affordability requirements based on a development's location. Those in low- or moderate-income neighborhoods must set aside up to 10 percent of their units for low-income households. Projects in targeted areas (neighborhoods with a lack of affordable housing or where displacement is occurring or residents are at risk of being priced out) must set aside 20 percent of units at a mix of affordability levels. At least one-quarter of the set-aside units must be provided on-site. For rental developments, this is a requirement. For owned homes, builders face a financial penalty if they do not comply. In gentrifying areas, off-site affordable units must be located within one mile of the market-rate development and not in a low-income community.

Rent Regulation

Even in neighborhoods that are not gentrifying, lower- and moderate-income households find it difficult to come up with monthly rents because for the past forty-five years, real wages have been stagnant, with nominal gains wiped out by inflation. While maintenance costs have grown and landlords have raised rents to protect normal investment returns, tenant earnings have not kept pace. From 2001 to 2019, renters' median incomes rose only 3 percent while their rents rose 15 percent. After the pandemic, rents rose even more and became one of the biggest causes of runaway inflation in 2022.

Housing policy can't fix this. It requires higher minimum wages, more and stronger labor unions, and reforms in retirement, early childhood, and health policy that can protect lower-income families from having to divert earnings from housing to care for their young and elders, or to cover medical emergencies. Rent increases that seem to be housing crises are also failures of national economic policy. Protecting apartment dwellers requires action on both.

Community groups may not be able to reform the country's labor market and child welfare programs, but they can work to protect tenants from rising rents. A tough approach that would do the most good

*For two years, New York City tenant organizations protested
Signature Bank's lending to landlords who push out lower-income
renters and replace them with higher-paying households. On April
25, 2018, Luz Rosero, a tenant leader, addressed demonstrators
outside the bank's shareholder meeting; other protesters went into
the meeting to call for reform. Signature Bank then committed
to refuse loans to landlords who predict higher revenues than
current rents and adequate maintenance costs would support.*

for black and Hispanic families promotes neighborhood stability along
with apartment dwellers' security. It limits annual rent hikes to a standard percentage, not only for existing tenants, but for new ones who
then inherit rates previously set. New York is the only state that permits such limitation.

A less adequate method does not maintain previous rates for new
tenants but limits how much they can rise when previous occupants
leave. New Brunswick and Camden, New Jersey, for example, impose
such a restriction. Los Angeles and Oregon (statewide) place no cap on
new charges when a unit vacates. In both regulatory types, rent control
resumes for the next household, starting at the higher amount; existing
residents are protected but community character can change as households turn over and housing prices go up.

No regulatory system can offer tenants much protection if it permits rents to rise excessively. Rules frequently authorize annual
increases equal to inflation plus an additional premium. The premium
may be based on additional landlord costs, such as expenses for rou-

tine and preventive maintenance, that grow faster than wages. But if incomes aren't keeping up, then such reasonable allowances for owners can price tenants out of apartments. If increases even beyond these are allowed (and they usually are), rentals can become less affordable.

Strong regulation requires strict enforcement of building and safety codes to prevent landlords from skimping on compliance to extract higher profits, but it also can lead to rent increases to cover the expenses. For this reason, some advocates for the poor protest code enforcement measures. It's a difficult choice, with no easy solution.

Sometimes regulation provides less protection to tenants than it seems to promise. When cities allow exceptions to stated rent limits, the regulatory purpose may be undermined. For example, owners may claim that replacement of functioning appliances with higher-quality models justifies increases. But then, the apartments will be less affordable and their occupants less able to remain. Whether the upgrade was necessary is difficult for enforcement officials to judge and it's easiest for them to accept a building manager's explanation. In places where rules permit rent increases for new occupants when residents leave, landlords may provoke their departures by skipping normal upkeep to make units unlivable, forcing occupants to move and creating opportunities to remodel and then recruit higher-paying residents. Owners may charge extra for keys, internet wiring, or add other non-rent costs. These evasions of the rules are difficult to monitor, especially with small agency staffs, but only tougher enforcement can prevent such abuses.

It's Mostly a Myth That Rent Regulation Reduces Housing Supply

Because African Americans are less likely to own homes than whites, regulations that limit how fast rents can rise are one way to redress racial inequality. But developers, landlords, and realtors have powerful lobbies that persuade state legislatures to prohibit cities from enacting even the most token rent regulation. In thirty-two states, legislatures ban restrictions of any kind; in another four, cities can limit rent increases only with state permission and it has never been granted. In others, state law ensures that regulation will be weak.

Rent control's opponents cite economists who claim that it discriminates against the poor. Tenants who live in rent-restricted apartments are less likely to move, so units turn over more slowly. This protects families who are lucky enough to have one, but fewer vacancies harm the less fortunate who can't easily find shelter. This is true, but the argument reflects an overall housing shortage, not a problem provoked by controls. If unregulated rents rise and cause more rapid turnover of apartments, the number of occupied units won't change. More affordable-housing construction, not more rapid turnover, is what's needed to protect vulnerable households, especially those in urban African American and Hispanic neighborhoods.

These economists also argue that if landlords aren't free to charge whatever the market can bear, investors will hesitate to finance apartment construction. Housing shortages will increase, so rent regulation harms those it intends to help. This argument has only some truth. Rent regulation does not inhibit builders from creating new housing from which they expect to make normal returns on investment; even the strictest controls do not specify prices that landlords set when they open units to their first tenants. Regulation always permits increases in subsequent years to allow reasonable but not exorbitant profits, so it will not discourage new construction in stable neighborhoods.

Speculators, however, have a different plan and may be inhibited by strong rent regulation from adding to the housing stock. These are builders who expect an area's land values to escalate rapidly and higher-income households to move to the formerly poorer community. These developers set low initial rents for existing residents but plan to evict them and attract more affluent households. When apartments turn over, bans of rent increases above the previous tenants' caps do inhibit construction for this speculative purpose. And they should.

But even if arguments in opposition have some merit, they account only for monetary costs that economists measure. They do not put a value on families' and communities' stability, something that regulation aims to preserve. When rising rents force lower-income households to leave neighborhoods they call home, their stress and alienation also have costs, but the economists who oppose rent control don't account for them. In a narrow economic sense, it may be efficient to force families to move, but it may also reinforce segregation if they must depart for distant, unfamiliar, and inadequately resourced places.

We can't be certain whether well-designed rent regulation can support family and neighborhood stability without impeding growth in housing supply. Too few communities have enacted controls to draw firm conclusions, although limited evidence makes it reasonable to attempt regulation. Most research on rent control uses data from New York City, Cambridge (Massachusetts), San Francisco, and the state of New Jersey. These are not typical, and even in these places, existing rules are too weak to indicate whether more effective policies would function as hoped.

As a first step, community groups that press for rent regulation almost always must persuade state legislatures to give cities permission to try it.

Just-Cause Evictions

Even in the absence of rent controls, regulation can prohibit landlords from removing tenants except for just cause: nonpayment of rent, illegal activity, property damage, or sustained failure to follow reasonable rules regarding late-night noise, trash disposal, or use of common facilities like laundry rooms. Rules should mandate revocation of eviction orders if families make up back rent within a reasonable period. Tenants should have the right to challenge pretexts; for example, a landlord might not ordinarily evict a tenant for a late rent payment but do so if the tenant had complained to the city about code violations.

A city's just-cause policy should not remove an owner's right to reclaim an apartment for a family member, although it should require that the owner give longer notice than for other permissible evictions. Landlords also, again with reasonable notice, should be able to repossess a unit to engage in major reconstruction to comply with building or health code requirements.

Any lease a household has signed should provide for automatic renewals, except for just cause. Like other rent control rules, a just-cause eviction policy should survive a building sale and require new owners to honor tenancy rights of existing residents.

Several cities and states have just-cause eviction rules, but because failure to pay rent is always considered a just cause, they offer little protection unless combined with rent regulation. Some jurisdictions have weaker rules that provide assistance to tenants who are evicted but don't prohibit evictions that have no good justification. These cities require building owners to pay relocation assistance and give lengthy notice in cases where they order an eviction without a tenant failure to pay rent or a violation of reasonable building policies. Rules like these provide a starting point, and advocates can press local government to build on them. Once passed, effective ordinances require community organizations to monitor and enforce them.

Tenants' Right to Counsel

Tenants often may not know they have an eviction order until a court hearing has passed. Tenants who challenge evictions need volunteer attorneys to represent them in housing courts, which in most places otherwise rubber-stamp landlord requests.

In the 2010s, Cleveland had nine thousand evictions annually, costing the city millions of dollars in homeless shelters and services. Children of evicted families had worse school performance and greater rates of lead poisoning. Landlords who filed eviction orders usually had legal representation at housing court hearings, but tenants almost never did. Hearings were almost always perfunctory, with judges approving multiple uncontested eviction complaints each minute. Most evictions were for nonpayment of rent, but in many cases, tenants had rebelled against paying for apartments that had not been kept in habitable condition.

In 2019, Cleveland enacted an ordinance giving tenants a right to free legal counsel in eviction proceedings. It was one of the first cities to do so; others have followed since. The Cleveland Legal Aid Society provides the attorneys, and United Way of Greater Cleveland sponsors and supports the program. Philanthropies and nonprofit housing developers supplement the city's modest funding and also provide rental aid to families in need.

The law requires landlords to include information about the availability of free legal help in tenant eviction notices. The housing court gives weekly lists of pending evictions to United Way, which then sends letters to the affected tenants telling of their right to a lawyer. The charity runs radio spots to advertise the service and leaves flyers at food banks, public libraries, and social service agencies. Although in most cases lawyers obtain financial help for clients to pay rent due, often tenants don't want to remain in apartments where essential maintenance has been lacking. Regardless, lawyers' ability to negotiate with landlord attorneys to win reversals of formal eviction rulings is critical, because future property managers will frequently reject applicants with prior eviction records.

Cleveland's program is minimal; the guarantee of free representation applies only to families with children who are enrolled in Cleveland's public schools and whose income is below the poverty line. Most clients are African American single mothers. Other cities have more generous programs—New York provides free legal aid for evictions to families below twice the poverty line; San Francisco has no income limitation. But social policy is easier to enact in these liberal coastal cities; Cleveland's early adoption of the right to counsel is more remarkable.

In 2021, the first full year of the policy's implementation, 90 percent of tenants who sought legal aid saw their eviction orders revoked. But uncounted others did not know about the program or lacked the confidence to take advantage of it. What Cleveland needs now is a community group that organizes tenants and contacts those in need of help. It should also press to increase the income eligibility cutoff; many lower-income tenants above the poverty line also face needless evictions.

Cleveland once had tenant organizers. In the 1970s and '80s, the Cleveland Tenants Organization mobilized rent strikes at poorly maintained buildings and connected members with social services. In one case, after fifty tenants withheld about $8,000 (adjusted for inflation, about $40,000 in 2022 dollars) in rent, their landlord caved and sold the building to a firm that then signed a contract to invest $100,000 ($500,000 in 2022) in repairs to settle the strike.* But this citywide

---

* Henceforth, when we report actual prices from the past and where information about its current inflation-adjusted value is useful, the amount in 2022 dollars will appear in parentheses, without further explanation.

tenant organization folded in 2017. Lower-income tenants can't pay much in dues, and activists never developed the support of suburban racial justice supporters who could have helped provide a financial base. Dependent on philanthropic funding that ebbs and flows with the whims of foundation executives (and who may have boards with members from the real estate industry), the group was unable to maintain the needed staff. Contemporary community organizers should engage middle-class supporters of racial justice whose financial help can avoid such obstacles.

A tenant organizing effort in Richmond, Virginia, recently failed, also from lack of resources. In 2020, volunteer members of the Richmond Tenants Union went to the courthouse to look up addresses of households who had pending eviction complaints and then hand-carried notices of court hearings to persuade the tenants to attend. The group hoped to impede the process by clogging the housing courts. But there were too few volunteers, and they recruited too few tenants to succeed. With no just-cause ordinance or legal right to counsel, those who showed up had little defense and almost all were evicted. The volunteers had a good idea, but inadequate organizational preparation or suburban support.

Baltimore has one of the highest eviction rates in the nation. Tenants lack just-cause protections but have the authority to file papers to put rent in escrow if their refusal to pay is based on landlord failure to maintain apartments in safe and habitable condition. But without legal representation it's an empty right, and judges have not often turned down eviction requests based on claims that units were not code compliant. In 2020, the city followed Cleveland in enacting a right-to-counsel ordinance. Whether it can succeed will depend on the ability of community organizations to supplement the program with the mobilization of renters to take advantage of the new aid.

Prevent Security Deposit Abuse

A company that markets home-repair services recently conducted an unscientific poll of landlords and tenants and reported that 25 percent of the five hundred landlords interviewed admitted that they unfairly withhold at least some portion of security deposits when renters depart. Although it's hard to believe that landlords would admit to criminal theft, even to a confidential surveyor, the report called attention to the power imbalance between landlords and tenants. Renters may leave apartments clean and in good repair but have no way to force owners to return deposits they improperly retain.

States minimally regulate security deposits. Some limit them to one, two, or three months rent. Some require landlords to place them in a separate account, notify tenants of where they are deposited, and return them with interest within a month or less of a rental's end.

One way to minimize disputes over whether landlords accurately assess damages is to place security deposits in a third-party-administered fund, operated perhaps by a community foundation. A small portion of the interest earned should be sufficient to cover administrative costs. If the fund establishes a reputation for integrity, many landlords might participate voluntarily. A nonprofit group could recruit landlords to participate and press reluctant ones to do so. A further step, more difficult to achieve, is for a city itself to establish and administer an escrow account.

In Great Britain and Northern Ireland, a consumer advocacy group conducted a survey and found so many tenants not getting deposits returned that Parliament created a public organization to hold them. Landlords must either register the amount with the department or hand over security deposits to it. If an apartment owner fails to return the deposit at the end of a rental, the agency pays the household directly and takes responsibility for collecting it from the owner. The agency also makes decisions about how much is owed: if a landlord claims damage, and the renter disputes it, the government investigates and makes a binding decision. There are five million tenants in the country, and the bureau resolves thirty thousand disputes annually.

The system is generally regarded as fair, and landlords who initially resisted the idea now mostly support it; they no longer have the aggravation of arguing with former tenants about return of funds. Arguments have also diminished because landlords must now be more attentive than they were. Before the agency's creation, many building managers hadn't conducted a careful inspection or inventory before renting an apartment. With the new system, landlords can't withhold part of a deposit without evidence to support their claims.

A related problem is that tenants can owe deposits for new units before their security fees are returned from previous residences. A state government in Australia has set up a fund that lends new deposits to tenants, with repayment due when they get back their previous one.

Without similar public programs in the United States, private companies offer landlords an alternative to up-front deposits. One charges tenants a nominal monthly fee and when there are claims for damages, it reviews them and bills renters if they were at fault. Another company allows tenants to authorize it to withdraw funds from their bank accounts, up to the amount their security deposit would be, if they cause damage beyond normal wear and tear. Renters don't have to come up with cash for deposits but may lose some legal rights to dispute charges by entering into agreements with private companies rather than engaging directly with their landlords. These firms all collect nonrefundable fees from tenants and require landlords to sign up for the service.

As in Australia, nonprofit or public agencies here could better play this role. Systems they establish could be more accountable and impose lesser charges on tenants than the current for-profit alternatives.

Regulation of Building Sales

No policy can force a building owner to remain in business. If one chooses to get out and cannot find a buyer who will pay a fair price and maintain regulated rent levels, a city should purchase the building at that price, effectively turning the rent-controlled building into public housing until it finds a new buyer. This has never been done, but it should be.

When landlords want to leave the rental business and convert their apartments to condominiums, existing tenants lose housing. Cities have the power to limit the number of licenses in any neighborhood for this change. Washington, D.C., allows tenants an option to purchase their apartments before they are put on the market and provides assistance to lower-income households to do so. Proponents of similar policies elsewhere have been unsuccessful in getting them adopted.

Freeze Property Assessments

Throughout the nation, home values are increasing and property taxes may rise as well. Even with fair rent regulation, landlords are allowed to pass the higher tax burden on to tenants, who can then be priced out of their neighborhoods. To prevent this, cities can freeze property taxes so that building owners continue to pay on the assessed value established when they assume ownership. New building owners who assume the rent control obligations of previous landlords can retain their assessments. If the building owner later sells the property at a profit, or to a purchaser who does not assume the rent control obligation, the city treasury can recoup the lost tax revenue at that time.

When only a few cities regulate rents, we can't expect that racial justice advocates will be able to prevent most tenants from being displaced. But even if it is unreasonable to expect comprehensive protection for renters in the near future, any of the reforms we've discussed will slow the displacement, even slightly. And that's something worth fighting for.

Tenant protection policies, if enacted, will not be self-enforcing. They need community groups to create and support aggressive advocacy and legal aid organizations to monitor violations and take actions to prevent them. Existing government-supported legal aid and fair housing advocates do some of this work but are inadequately financed and set up mainly to respond to complaints. They require racial justice activists, and their middle-class supporters, to do more.

Ban the Box

Young black men live in more strictly policed neighborhoods than young whites. They attend schools where on-site police officers can arrest misbehaving students. Police stop African Americans more frequently than whites but then find more whites than blacks with illegal drugs. Young African American men don't use or sell drugs at greater rates than young white men but are arrested three times as often for drug use or sale and then are charged, convicted, and sentenced for drug crimes. White and black motorists change lanes without signaling, but police are more likely to stop African Americans for doing so; the drivers are then more likely to be caught up in the penal system, including jail time for inability to pay fines.

Partly as a result, African Americans are arrested at a rate more than double their population share. By age twenty-three, half of black men have arrest records. One in three will eventually serve prison time, compared with one in seventeen white men. African Americans make up more than a third of those in jail, in prison, on probation, or on parole, close to three times their share of the population.

Landlords frequently assume that applicants' criminal histories make them more likely to commit new offenses and have the seemingly reasonable belief that it's prudent to refuse rentals to tenants with arrest or conviction records. This may sometimes be true. Renters have the right to be safe in their homes. But if our arrest policies are discriminatory, excluding applicants with such records will deny housing to many African Americans who could be no less desirable as tenants than whites with similar past behavior, but who don't have records to show for it.

For public housing and the Section 8 voucher program, the government prohibits denying rentals to those who've been arrested but not convicted. For those with convictions, it allows local agencies to make their own policies, urging them to make individual assessments of tenants' suitability and probability of re-offending.

Private landlords, however, are free in most cities to refuse rentals if a household member has an arrest record, even if it never led to conviction. If we believe in the principle that one is innocent until proven guilty, this basis for refusing to rent is unjust. Going a step further, excluding those who've been convicted and made restitution, either with fines, jail, prison, or community supervision, might not be reasonable if we believe that those who've paid their debts to society should then be free to lead normal lives.

Some tenants with criminal records may pose a danger to fellow residents and property owners. But refusing to rent to all who have such records probably poses even greater dangers to the community. Stable housing reduces the chance that those who have previously been convicted will re-offend. They already have great difficulty in accessing medical and mental health services, getting jobs, and gaining educational opportunities that they need to remain out of jail or prison. Not having secure lodging makes these challenges nearly insurmountable.

Men and women recently released from jail or prison, especially African Americans, may often begin by being homeless. They are then at higher risk of being arrested, jailed, and convicted, as many cities now enforce "quality of life" offenses, like sleeping in public spaces. Homelessness and unemployment can lead to more crimes of necessity, such as theft, keeping the revolving door of incarceration turning.

Instead of refusing to house all those with a criminal history, landlords should examine the context of the conviction, considering such things as the nature of the crime, how long ago it occurred (re-arrests of those released from prison decline rapidly over time), the tenant's age (older people tend to commit crimes less frequently than the young), completion of drug or alcohol treatment programs, and participation in educational and civic activities.

Several cities and states have limited landlords' use of criminal histories to make tenancy decisions. The rules were modeled after restrictions on employers' use of those records to make hiring decisions. The ordinances are usually called *fair chance* or *ban-the-box* rules because they curb landlords' right to require applicants to check a box if they have been convicted or arrested. San Francisco's ordinance requires landlords to determine a tenant's other qualifications before considering criminal history and then make an assessment that takes evidence of rehabilitation into account. But the regulation applies only to government-subsidized, not to private housing.

New Jersey's Fair Chance in Housing Act of 2021 is the country's most comprehensive ordinance yet. It applies to all public and private housing in the state and prohibits landlords from asking about criminal history until after accepting a tenant; they can then consider serious convictions from the previous six years and may reject the application only for good reason. The law imposes fines as high as $10,000 on landlords who repeatedly violate it.

Most landlords won't know how to evaluate applicants' criminal histories to decide if they will be suitable renters. But the alternative, allowing a landlord to deny housing to anyone with a record, is unfair. Civil rights activists should advocate ordinances that provide guidance, such as limiting the look-back period for previous convictions and judging which are grounds for refusal. Portland, Oregon, gives employers a list that details the types of convictions that can make job seekers ineligible, including how long ago they occurred and which warrant individual assessments. Other cities can develop similar guides for landlords, and fair housing groups can educate them on what criminal history is appropriate to request from applicants and what should be grounds for denial.

Some state courts issue certificates of rehabilitation to the formerly convicted, helping employers make better-informed decisions. In Ohio, job seekers with a criminal record can petition a court to certify that stable employment will help them become successful members of the community and not pose a public safety risk. In practice, many firms don't know these certificates exist and many applicants don't present them. Whites with this documentation have mostly the same chance of getting a callback for a job interview as those with no criminal history, but African Americans' chances aren't improved. If activists can succeed in winning similar certification for housing searches, community groups will have to monitor the process to reduce racial bias in its application. A test of landlords in Columbus, Ohio, found some whose willingness to rent to an applicant with a criminal record increased if the apartment seeker had a formal sign of rehabilitation, like an employment certificate. Far more said they were willing if individuals produced informal signs of rehabilitation, such as letters from friends or family.

Some states that offer certificates require long waiting periods after release from prison before applicants are eligible. Ohio's is one year; Vermont requires five years. This long delay prevents the certificate from helping with employment or housing in the critical first years of reentry.

The stigma of incarceration is difficult to erase. Court documents may help, and advocates can push for their adoption, but their impact will likely be limited. Trusted community organizations should also vouch for prospective tenants and present letters from friends, family, religious leaders, and employers. The best way to improve housing access for the formerly convicted is to address the stigma of criminal records directly, by educating landlords and passing and then enforcing ban-the-box ordinances for public and private housing.

Crime-Free Ordinances Are Discriminatory; They Go Too Far

While a few communities have adopted ban-the-box housing rules, many others have done the opposite. More than two thousand municipalities have passed "crime-free housing" ordinances, police-sponsored programs that encourage or even require landlords to exclude and evict tenants with arrests or convictions. A policeman in Arizona has created an association that helps departments nationwide to adopt such laws. It trains officers to assist landlords and property managers to exclude tenants with any past criminal involvement and promotes crime-free leases that require eviction of tenants who had any contact with law enforcement or are suspected of engaging in any criminal activity, whether or not it led to arrest or conviction.

Kansas City, Missouri, has seven full-time officers who monitor alleged criminal activity in rental properties. The department encourages landlords to evict tenants who have been arrested as well as those who have merely been accused of committing crimes. Drug activity of tenants, their family members, guests, and any other "affiliated" person (a term left undefined), whether on or off the property, is grounds for eviction. The department urges property managers to advertise that they check criminal backgrounds of every applicant—not only convictions but also pending charges.

Orlando certifies property managers as crime-free and then permits them access to a database of all city arrest records, including misdemeanor and juvenile arrests, regardless of whether they led to charges or convictions or how long ago they occurred. Property managers can use the information to deny rentals and evict current tenants.

Some communities adopt such policies to stem the influx of non-white residents. Faribault, Minnesota, for example, adopted a crime-free ordinance in 2014 after its black population nearly tripled with an influx of Somali refugees. The police chief told the city council that concerns about rising crime rates were unfounded and that the proposed ordinance was based on a biased view of "problem tenants" and cultural clashes resulting from a "very large diverse population, often observed standing in groups." But the council went ahead anyway and adopted a crime-free ordinance that makes a landlord's failure to evict problem tenants a misdemeanor. In the first three years after the ordinance was adopted, ninety problem tenants were evicted, six landlords were placed on probation, and one was jailed. The ordinance succeeded: some of those evicted left Faribault to seek housing elsewhere.

In communities with crime-free ordinances, activists should collect information about those who have been unreasonably evicted or denied tenancy, and publicize their stories to build support for repeal of the laws.

Community Land Trusts Can Create and Preserve Affordable Housing

Two young white women moved to Durham, North Carolina, forty years ago to be community organizers. The rigidly segregated city was then using federal funds to refurbish homes only on the eastern, white side of town. Lorisa Seibel mobilized African American homeowners to protest at the city council; it conceded and began paying for repair of homes in black neighborhoods as well.

Susan Levy went door-to-door on the west side to identify black tenants' most serious problems, like landlords' failure to perform necessary upkeep and high late-payment fees that compounded to excessive debt. She helped tenants picket the worst-offending real estate agencies but was unable to win concessions. She then pursued a graduate degree in planning to learn more about housing reform. Her parents contributed funds for a down payment so in 1986 she was able to buy a house in the Burch Avenue neighborhood, not far from Duke University, for about $35,000 ($93,000). The area was then about half white and half black.

The neighborhood had problems—excessive litter in the streets, abandoned or poorly maintained buildings, too much crime, and no safe play area for children. One child had been killed by a car. The two young organizers, led by Herbert Dark, a retired African American teacher, his wife, and his brother, canvassed the area, recruiting residents for neighborhood cleanups and encouraging them to believe they could work together to improve the neighborhood. One opportunity stuck out: an unfulfilled promise by the city, made ten years earlier, to turn a vacant lot into a park. The Dark team persuaded families to create an organization that sent a broadly supported petition to the city council. Convinced it could not make the protest disappear, the city created the park, giving the newly formed Burch Avenue Neighborhood Association its first victory and inspiring members to believe they could accomplish more.

A new threat was on the horizon. Like many urban universities, Duke was expanding its enrollment, which increased the need for student housing. Investors began to buy nearby property, and it seemed that gentrification might soon displace many of the African American residents. The association invited an expert to explain how a land trust could keep housing affordable.

Trusts can acquire land when cities donate abandoned residential or commercial properties or through purchases supported by private donations, local and state affordable-housing grants, or a small percentage added to the property tax rate. Once trusts own the land, they can sell the buildings that sit atop it, retaining ownership of the ground underneath. Because rising land values are the most important cause of increasing unaffordability of housing, selling only the home makes it less expensive than if both structure and ground were included in the price.

After hearing how land trusts work, the Burch Avenue neighbors decided to create one. In 1987, Susan Levy obtained start-up money for a trust from a local foundation; neighbors formed a board of directors, with Ms. Seibel as president and Ms. Levy as executive director. A federal agency gave the fledgling Durham Community Land Trust funds to buy run-down properties before outside investors could gobble up too many. The trust then refurbished two vacant houses, mostly with volunteer labor. In 1993, the buildings were put up for sale; the trust kept ownership of the land underneath.

Linda Hunt, an African American nurse, was the first buyer. She had contributed to her future home's upgrade with sweat equity: the trust's construction director taught her to remove doors, then sand, refinish, and install them. She bought the house for $50,000 ($104,000), much less than the cost of property nearby, where sales included both dwelling and land. Ms. Hunt scraped together a down payment from savings and gifts from friends. Meanwhile, the trust persuaded skeptical bankers to issue an unusual mortgage for her house-only purchase. She eventually got a zero percent interest loan from a city program, packaged with a bank's low-interest mortgage.

Some of the organization's properties had a *rent-to-own* program. Tenants paid rent, and the trust set aside a portion in a down payment fund. When it was large enough, the trust worked with the city and banks to issue a building-only mortgage and it sold the renters the house.

Linda Hunt became the trust's first resident board member. She studied how to read budgets and understand technical requirements of government housing programs. Ms. Hunt then became the first trust resident to assume its presidency. Reflecting on her thirty years of experience, she says, "For the land trust to be successful, it shouldn't give people a home. It should teach people how to own a home. I had the benefit of land trust leaders who educated me."

Most early board members were white. As black families began to purchase or rent-to-own houses, they joined the board, creating a healthier racial balance. Like that of trusts elsewhere, the organization's policy is that owners or renters of its units compose one-third of its board, other neighborhood residents another third, and the rest are lawyers, bankers, or other experts. For twenty-five years until retiring in 2022, Selina Mack, an African American who started out as the trust's budget analyst and business manager, was executive director.

Even with retaining land ownership, the Durham trust could keep homes affordable to lower-income working families only if it restricted resale prices when occupants chose to move. Its rule limits the sale price to the original purchase amount, plus a portion (from 25 to 45 percent) of the house's increase in value. The range is based on how long the owner has lived in the house before reselling: those with longer ownership keep a greater share.

This *shared equity* is a compromise between the trust's commit-

*Durham, North Carolina, 2018. Volunteers helped Habitat
for Humanity build a house on land owned by the community
land trust. Paul Joyner (left), a development expert, was a
land trust board member, as was Thomas DelViscio (right), a
neighborhood resident. At completion, the home was rented
to a formerly homeless African American family headed by
a recreation aide at a Salvation Army children's program;
her earnings were below 50 percent of the area median.*

ment to keeping the neighborhood affordable and its desire to give its homeowners an opportunity for wealth accumulation. As home sellers' share of house values increase, land trust homes become gradually less affordable to lower-income families as successive ownership accumulates.

Early on, the Durham leaders proposed a permanent affordability model in which homeowners who resell could do so only for the price they originally paid (the value of the house itself, not including the land, adjusted for inflation). But several black church leaders objected. Whites, they said, gained wealth from sale of homes and land that had appreciated well beyond inflation. By preventing blacks from benefiting in the same way, the Durham plan was discriminatory, they argued. The shared equity model responded to these objections.

Successive owners have gained partial equity. Trust houses now sell for about $150,000 to income-qualified families. In this gentrifying neighborhood, similar nearby properties sell for $500,000. Still, $150,000 is more than the $50,000 ($104,000) that Linda Hunt paid thirty years ago—too much of a reach for lower-income families. These days, when homes come up for sale, the Durham trust frequently buys them itself for conversion to affordable rentals. For its few remaining home purchases, it has raised income eligibility limits to find buyers. Working-class households who still qualify are no longer low-income and less likely to be African American.

Over time, the Durham trust's holdings have grown in neighborhoods where black populations are threatened with displacement as land prices begin to escalate. The trust is now increasing density on its existing holdings, building accessory dwelling units, duplexes, or triplexes—mostly rental units—on its single-family lots. The trust's portfolio now contains about 350 homes, mostly rentals but with a small group of the early-model shared appreciation houses.

Durham's was not the first land trust in the country but was an early one. Today, more than two hundred exist. Selina Mack gets several queries a week from activists wanting advice about how to start a land trust in their own communities. Most come from areas that are gentrifying, and she tells callers it is too late if land prices have already escalated beyond what a trust with limited resources can afford. Yet many African American neighborhoods are in cities and towns (and even in neighborhoods within expensive metropolitan areas) where land prices haven't taken off so much that a land trust can't succeed. For those, the slow careful work—of Herbert Dark, Lorisa Seibel,

Susan Levy, and Linda Hunt—to win support from local government, banks, and foundations is a model.

The challenge that the Durham trust faced on how to balance permanent affordability with wealth accumulation is one that all trusts grapple with, and they arrive at many different solutions. Others are more successful than Durham's at preserving long-term affordability by employing stricter limitations on home resale prices. Some trusts have considered establishing a maximum resale price as one that moderate-income households—frequently those with incomes at or below 80 percent of the area median—can reasonably pay. Some cap the resale price at a fixed appreciation rate; others link sale prices to inflation. Some may use growth in area median family income as an alternative. Others provide additional subsidies if shared appreciation has made a resale price unaffordable to its intended home buyers.

Land trusts are not a cure-all. The Durham trust can't expand beyond city neighborhoods because suburban land is too expensive; no government program will supply funds to help land trusts buy high-cost lots. So the trust is forced to make another compromise, trading desegregation of those outlying communities for urban affordability.

Linda Hunt recalls that when she first arrived there was only one white resident on her street, and many blacks were renting from slumlords. It now has a few whites but is still mostly black because the trust owns most of the units, and prices haven't skyrocketed like those of other nearby properties. But adjoining blocks where African Americans previously paid exorbitant rents for inadequate maintenance are today mostly affluent and white because the trust could not buy and refurbish housing fast enough to stay ahead of gentrification.

Englewood neighborhood, Chicago, 2021. Plaques identify houses sold on contract to black home seekers in the 1950s and '60s.

Chapter 7

Stop the Fraud

Contract Sales Continue to Cheat Many Black
Families out of Home Ownership

In 1959, Ruth and James Wells, black migrants from Mississippi, bought a duplex in the Lawndale neighborhood of Chicago, then in transition from white to black. The seller charged them $23,000 for a property he'd purchased the previous month for $13,500. But the couple hadn't purchased the house. They had participated in what's known as a *contract sale*, in which the speculator kept the mortgage and the Wellses received no ownership rights. When the seller in 1968 charged them a new $1,500 fee for "insurance," Ruth Wells realized something was amiss—their monthly charges already included this coverage. The couple had limited means—James Wells was a foundry worker—so Ms. Wells figured the seller added this phony and unaffordable cost in the hope that she would make a late payment for the first time. The contract gave him a right to evict the Wellses if they were ever overdue. He could then keep the Wellses' down payment and the value of the remodeling they'd paid for and then find another African American family, desperate for housing, to sign a similar contract and make another down payment.

Clyde Ross, an army veteran, had also escaped Mississippi for Chicago, where he found work in a Campbell's Soup factory. In 1961, he and his wife, Lillie, contracted for a nearby home. The seller had recently purchased it from a white family for $12,000; the Rosses' price was $27,000.

Clyde Ross's brother-in-law, Charlie Baker, another Mississippi migrant and army veteran, also worked in the Campbell's Soup factory. He and his wife, Charlene, got their Lawndale home in 1960 for $26,500. After they moved in, the city declared it unsafe. The Bakers' contract, unlike a regular mortgage, required no prior inspection and absolved the seller from all responsibility for repairs. Mr. Baker took a second job driving a cab to pay for the work that needed to be done on the house and avoid eviction.

Alabama-born Saul Banks worked as a welder, and his wife, Henrietta, was employed at a printing firm when they paid $25,000 on contract for a Lawndale home in 1961. Four years later, the legal owner sold it to another speculator who charged them $3,000 to remain.

Ruth Wells, Clyde Ross, Charlie Baker, and Henrietta Banks met Jack Macnamara, a white Jesuit seminary student who'd come to Lawndale as a community organizer. With his guidance and the support of a larger group of volunteer seminarians and students, the four organized the Contract Buyers League, soon representing more than three thousand victimized families. They demonstrated at speculators' offices and homes and distributed leaflets at outlying rail stations to inform the white commuters that a fellow rider was a slumlord. They picketed banks that financed contract sellers, even one in suburban Cicero, where residents were notoriously hostile to African Americans. The exploitation of contract buyers was so egregious that passersby expressed sympathy.

League members went on "strike," putting monthly payments in escrow accounts. They hoped to force sellers to reduce debts to reasonable levels or convert contracts to legitimate mortgages. Owners had strikers evicted. When sheriffs carted their furniture outside, supporters carried it back. When private security agents occupied a home to prevent this, a group of league members surrounded the house until the force left peacefully. In several hundred cases the tactics got sellers to renegotiate contracts and reduce debts, but with other exploitative terms unchanged. Some sellers agreed to convert contracts to mortgages but only for the full exorbitant amounts that the original contracts had called for.

The Contract Buyers League filed two federal lawsuits against the sellers, alleging civil rights violations, conspiracy, and fraud. The league

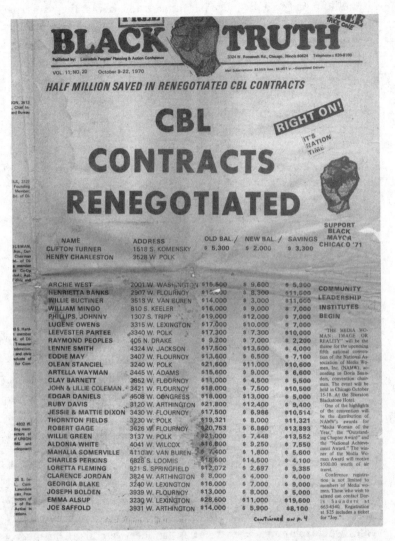

Chicago, 1970. The Contract Buyers League engaged in direct action against speculators. On one occasion, after sheriffs carted family belongings outside, league members deposited the furniture at City Hall in protest. The campaign eventually led some owners to settle, reducing buyers' debts. A community newspaper announced the victory.

lost both. In one case the judge permitted evidence that there was no discrimination against blacks on account of race because speculators also preyed on a few mixed-race couples and Hispanics. The foreman of the all-white jury boasted that he'd voted to end "the mess Earl Warren made with *Brown v. Board of Education* and all that nonsense."

During the 1950s and '60s, some 85 percent of all black-owned homes in Chicago were bought on contract. Most contract sale victims never received even partial justice.

Contract Sales Were Once the Only Homeowning Opportunities for Many Black Families

In the mid-twentieth century, banks and the Federal Housing and Veterans Administrations almost always refused to issue or insure mortgages to households in black neighborhoods. African Americans had few opportunities for homeownership, although families with similar incomes and credit records in white neighborhoods had no difficulty qualifying for a mortgage. In other cities besides Chicago, such as Baltimore, Detroit, and Cincinnati, real estate agents took advantage of black home buyers by purporting to sell homes to them while in actuality they were not. African Americans thought they had purchased homes but the contracts they were offered provided none of the security and equity of a conventional, FHA, or VA loan. With a mortgage, if an owner falls far behind in payments, lenders can foreclose, but the family first has a chance to bring payments up to date. If an owner sells, he or she can retrieve cash from a prior down payment and the principal portion of monthly charges paid. The owner also gains from a property's value appreciation.

Realtors who perpetuated the contract sale fraud sometimes initiated it by *blockbusting*, terrifying white residents that their property values would plummet because black families were about to move nearby. It was untrue: property values were likely to climb when African Americans became neighbors, because they were almost always willing to pay more than whites; they faced such a small selection of homes on offer. Nonetheless, terrified owners sold out to blockbusting realtors at prices far below their true values.

As in Lawndale, realtors then charged prices far above market value to African Americans desperate for housing. Interest rates on contract sales were exorbitant, much higher than what whites with mortgages had to pay. Speculators sometimes entrapped black buyers by pretending to represent them in negotiations without disclosing that they themselves were the owners. Contract sellers formed syndicates of white professionals—lawyers, doctors, businessmen, and politicians—to finance the speculators' operations by purchasing portions of their portfolios of contracts. These investors reaped large profits that made their way into white middle-class inheritances, which now contribute to the white wealth advantage.

Real estate salesmen misrepresented properties' deteriorated condition and colluded with building inspectors, who then required expensive repairs that victimized families could not afford; it became an excuse for eviction, after which operators could perpetuate an identical fraud upon another black family in need of housing. Collusion of building inspectors wasn't often needed; contract sellers frequently tacked on additional monthly maintenance charges that were not part of contracts and for which they provided no explanation. Failure to pay was also an excuse for eviction. Black contract buyers' higher housing costs were accompanied by lower wages because most occupations were closed to them. The ever present fear that a single late payment or sudden unexpected surcharge could make them homeless caused many to subdivide houses so rent could supplement their incomes. Relatives sometimes moved in, also contributing toward monthly payments. Black neighborhoods became overcrowded. Contract selling wasn't the sole cause of these conditions, but in several cities, it shared great responsibility.

Agents who participated in these schemes purchased properties with mortgages from the same banks that refused to finance African Americans for the same houses or, indeed, for homes anywhere. The real estate agencies, brokers, banks, and syndicate partners that colluded in this system of exploitation have, in many cases, identifiable institutional successors today. In no case have they taken responsibility for black neighborhood impoverishment or developed plans to compensate residents of communities that their predecessors exploited. It can be difficult to identify these contemporary firms. But persistent local researchers can do so.

Bankers Colluded

Contract sellers hid their roles by resting ownership of the properties in accounts that were not in their own names. Many were placed at the Chicago Title Land Trust Company. It continues to flourish today, advertising its services like this: "We can help consumers protect their private information by allowing home buyers the opportunity to purchase real estate confidentially by using a Chicago Title Land Trust. This affords our clients the peace of mind that comes with knowing their personal information is safeguarded." A trust can be a useful service for legitimate homeowners who wish to use the legal device to designate heirs and avoid probate when they die, but it also offered a way to hide contract sellers' identities. It has never been held accountable.

Chicago's First Mutual Savings bank participated so heavily that it collapsed. During the 1950s and '60s it issued loans to contract sellers in amounts that were greater than the prices that these speculators had paid for the properties. This violated a federal rule prohibiting mortgages that exceed 80 percent of an actual purchase price. Pocketing the extra cash, the brokers then sold the houses on contract to African Americans with typical markups of 84 percent, even before adding bogus charges.

At first, contract sellers had no difficulty keeping current on First Mutual loans because payments from African Americans were so much higher than interest that speculators owed the bank. When black occupants couldn't keep up, contract sellers evicted them. But if too many contract buyers fell behind at once, the speculators could default on their own mortgages. The bank could then resell the same properties to other (sometimes the same) speculators who began the process anew with another black family.

Some contract sellers got greedier, piling on more excessive charges to buyers in a growing portfolio of contracts. Households began to default and risk eviction soon after occupying their properties. Contract sellers no longer had the cash flow to pay off their mortgages. Banks repossessed the properties but since they could sell the homes only for amounts far less than what speculators owed, their balance sheets eventually suffered.

No bank officers or contract sellers were prosecuted for this conspiracy.

In 1968, the federal government forced the sale of First Mutual to Bell Federal Savings and Loan. Bell absorbed only First Mutual's profitable assets; it took no responsibility for defaulted mortgages, leaving those for the government to dispose of. Bank regulators did so, reselling the same properties to contract sellers at bargain prices. Taxpayers made up the difference. Bell Federal's assets and liabilities are now part of Bank of America.

Another Chicago-area bank that partnered with contract sellers was General Federal Savings and Loan—this was the bank that the Contract Buyers League had picketed in Cicero. Bank officers led black home buyers to believe they got real mortgages, not contracts, even having victims come to bank offices to make payments. Judges blessed the theft, lecturing home buyers that they should read contracts more carefully. General Federal has been absorbed by a succession of other institutions and is now part of PNC Bank. Like Bank of America, it's one of the nation's largest. Other banks in Chicago that participated in financing contract sellers included Lawndale National Bank (now part of Huntington National Bank), Exchange National Bank (now also part of Bank of America), and Cosmopolitan National Bank (now part of USBank).

A Memorial to Victims of Contract Sales

Executives at Bank of America, PNC, and other contemporary financial institutions may today be unaware of how their predecessors impoverished black Chicagoans. Tonika Johnson, the artist who introduced the map twins, may enlighten them.

She's photographed dozens of Chicago homes sold on contract and is placing plaques in front of many, describing how, in this location, predatory realty operators and banks robbed families of their savings and security, and calling for the perpetrators to fund remediation. Each display has a QR code that identifies the speculator who sold the home, the price he paid for it, how much he sold it for, the bank that financed him, and the black family he exploited. Ms. Johnson is now seeking a grant to purchase one of the houses to create a museum dedicated to the victimized residents.

She hopes to develop public support to place similar plaques in downtown Chicago, in front of the banks whose antecedents underwrote the exploitation. Activists can then lead campaigns to press these institutions to make amends

Those Who Gained the Most Should Lead with Remedies, but Do Not

By the mid-1950s, more than half of all black homeowners in Baltimore bought their homes on contract. The most active speculator was Morris Goldseker, who used fifty company names to disguise his operations. An unusual Maryland law permitted Goldseker to own and then rent the land that lay beneath houses he sold. Even if buyers had bank mortgages on their homes and were current on their payments, the rental contracts on the land had legal priority, permitting Goldseker to seize homes if rental fees were late. Goldseker did so in about one-third of the more than a thousand contracts he issued.

To finance his purchases, Goldseker spread business across more than a hundred banks. His assistant sat on the board of one, Jefferson Federal Savings and Loan, most of whose mortgage lending was to Goldseker himself. Another board member was Marvin Mandel, speaker of the state's House of Delegates; he resigned his bank board position only after becoming governor in 1969. Jefferson Federal subsequently became part of M&T Bank, an institution based in Buffalo, New York, which continues to do business in Baltimore, with ten branches in that city.

In 1973, Morris Goldseker died and left about $11 million ($65 million) to a foundation whose stated mission includes "community development, education, and nonprofit capacity building." Its website makes no mention of how the source of its wealth contributed to the impoverishment of Baltimore's black community. By 2021, the Goldseker Foundation's assets had more than doubled to $160 million, of which it distributed only about $4 million that year, mostly in small amounts to Baltimore neighborhood groups. Only a few of the grants improved housing opportunities; for example, $30,000 was given to a homeownership counseling project.

But the charity's biggest efforts went elsewhere. It pays its executive director about $400,000 annually, more than the total of all grants it made for housing Baltimore's black population. Of seven board members, five are Goldsekers, one of whom, Sheldon (Morris's nephew), receives more than $100,000 as chair.

The foundation should come clean on its website about the source of its funds and bring onto its board and leadership legitimate representatives of neighborhoods that Morris Goldseker exploited. Activists could conduct a campaign to persuade the charity to put its dollars to better use by providing more homeownership for those who were denied the opportunity by its benefactor.

Contract Sales Today: The Greed and Exploitation Have Returned

Contract selling in black neighborhoods diminished after 1968, when passage of the Fair Housing Act caused the Federal Housing Administration to consider African Americans and neighborhoods in which they lived eligible for its mortgage insurance. Banks followed (though not always).

But contract sales, again exploitative and again largely unregulated, are back.

During the run-up to the Great Recession of 2008, banks and mortgage companies marketed subprime refinance loans discriminatorily to black and Hispanic homeowners. Sales representatives offered deals on less favorable terms than they offered to whites. Banks gave bonuses to salespeople when they sold loans with interest rates higher than victims were entitled to pay. Some bankers referred to refinance products as "ghetto loans" or advised agents that black and Hispanic homeowners weren't "savvy" enough to bargain for the same terms as whites. Marketers showed up at black churches on Sundays to entice parishioners to refinance mortgages but engaged in no similar activity at white churches. Subprime loans frequently had teaser rates, low initial interest charges that skyrocketed after a few years, and onerous penalties if borrowers attempted to refinance again when new rates took effect. With the new higher finance costs, many victims were unable to make monthly payments and defaulted.

In retrospect, even many regular mortgages turned out to have been too risky for prudent banks to issue, because lenders assumed that unrealistically high housing prices would continue indefinitely and borrowers could refinance at will. Bankers assumed that home-owners who ran into unanticipated difficulty—loss of a job or divorce, for example—could take out cash from increasingly pricey homes and pay off their original mortgages.

Banks were also reckless because the quasi-government agency Fannie Mae bought mortgages from them to funnel new funds for the banks to lend. Fannie Mae also was careless because it, in turn, sold loans to Wall Street investors who realized, too late, that many mort-gages they'd purchased were likely to default, and then stopped buying any more of them. Fannie Mae and the investors were left in posses-sion of thousands of foreclosed houses. These were disproportionately located in black and Hispanic neighborhoods, because subprime lend-ing was more prevalent there and because homeowners in those places with regular mortgages were more likely to suffer unemployment and an inability to keep up their monthly payments.

In white neighborhoods, Fannie Mae maintained foreclosed prop-erties in better condition. In black and Hispanic areas, it allowed them to fall into disrepair, contributing to further losses in home value for nearby residents.

Fannie Mae auctioned off its foreclosed and unoccupied prop-erties for prices far below what was owed or what houses had been worth before the market collapse. From 2010 to 2014, Fannie Mae unloaded twenty thousand abandoned homes, picked up by specula-tors. But unlike the 1960s, when small-time operators bought handfuls of houses in default from local banks to resell on contract, twenty-first-century purchasers were private-equity investors who purchased thousands of poorly maintained houses in distressed communities.

National firms that bought the auctioned properties concentrated their acquisitions in black neighborhoods and marketed them on con-tract, with exploitative terms like those of the 1950s and '60s. One characteristic is worse: in the twentieth century, real estate operators typically sold houses on contract for prices that were up to twice what they had paid for them; in the twenty-first century, prices are fre-quently four to six times what the firms paid.

In other ways, patterns of fifty years ago are repeated:

- exorbitant interest rates that, in actuality, are higher than what sellers disclose;
- buyers falsely told that contracts are mortgages;
- homes "sold" without inspections and in poor condition for whose repair buyers are fully responsible;
- evictions after a single late payment, with households losing any investments they had made, including the value of repairs;
- contracts that fail to disclose existing liens or past-due utility bills and taxes that become the buyer's responsibility;
- churning of properties, with recruitment of new victims after evictions of prior ones;
- alleged property tax charges that are higher than actual taxes owed;
- tax payments allegedly placed in escrow, with sellers failing to pay taxes due, leading to evictions.

In a recent year, 75 percent of contract sales in the Chicago region were in majority-black neighborhoods, with another 15 percent in Hispanic areas. In Detroit, a majority-black city, more homes were sold on contract than with mortgages. Investors who gobbled up these properties did not plan to sell them legitimately. They understood that families who had lost previous homes to foreclosure had credit histories that no longer qualified them for mortgages. And they understood that even home seekers with good credit were finding it nearly impossible to buy homes because banks had tightened up mortgage qualifications from fears of lending to families who might possibly default, even if unlikely to do so.

The largest predator this time was Harbour Portfolio Advisors, a contract seller based in Dallas. It raised more than $60 million from individual investors to become the largest purchaser in Fannie Mae's bulk auctions. As of 2016, it had purchased nearly seven thousand foreclosed properties, mostly in midwestern states. Another large buyer was Vision Property Management, based in South Carolina. Vision also made at least one bulk purchase at a tax lien sale in Detroit, where African Americans were more likely than whites to lose homes for falling behind in property tax payments. Other firms did the same.

Are These Rentals or Owned Homes?

Investor exploitation of black households is not limited to contract sales. Some investor groups purchased Fannie Mae properties and rented them. Yet they still require tenants to take responsibility for repairs, a violation of ordinances that require landlords to shoulder that responsibility. Although investor groups bought houses at auction for a pittance, they rent them at market rates, extracting huge profits.

In 2021, almost one-third of all single-family homes that came up for sale in majority-black neighborhoods nationwide were purchased by outside investor groups, not households seeking places to live. Real estate speculators were much less interested in nonblack communities. In some African American areas, the share bought by speculators was even higher. In Lithonia, Georgia, a nearly all-black city just outside Atlanta, 53 percent of all home sales were to speculators. In the mostly black Oakdale North neighborhood of Charlotte, North Carolina, speculators purchased a similar share.

The companies may sit on these properties, expecting prices to rise, or rent them, typically charging more than local landlords would do. The speculators also have less regard for tenant interests, sometimes willing to evict after a rent payment is late only by a day.

The largest landlord of single-family houses for rent is the Blackstone Group, which buys homes in bulk at auctions of foreclosed properties. The firm's largest investors are public pension funds, which generally resist rules that prohibit investment in socially irresponsible enterprises. Pressure from activists rarely succeeds in changing pension fund behavior. But it's not impossible, so attempts to end such public investments are worth the effort.

State and local laws generally require rentals to be safe and up to code; to evade these rules, investment firms claim to be selling, not renting. But state laws require sellers to be licensed and sales to be recorded, with titles properly transferred, and subject to foreclosure procedures that include opportunities for buyers to remedy payment deficiencies. To evade these rules, the companies claim to be renting, not selling.

Speculators do not hide their intent to avoid regulation. Vision Property Management explained to investors why it did not report buyers' on-time payments to credit agencies. It might seem puzzling why firms would needlessly pile on this additional abuse and prevent victims from building up records of their faithful loan repayments. Vision explained that failing to report credit worthiness helped it to escape notice of government agencies by flying "below the radar of being a 'regulated lender.'"

Not every contract sale is predatory. Investors may repair homes before selling them. Some lower-income families may turn to a contract seller because banks won't lend money for inexpensive properties. Sellers may permit contracts to mature so buyers can convert them to real mortgages. Community groups that hope to protect victimized families will have to examine contract sales case by case in order to learn which are unfair.

Pursuing the Speculators

Local advocates should conduct community education programs to protect home seekers from unscrupulous contract sellers and to expose provisions and risks of contract sale agreements that victims may not understand. Activists may also conduct campaigns that seek compensation for exploited contract buyers, like those of the Contract Buyers League a half century ago. But first, they'll have to identify the sellers.

Harbour Portfolio Advisors no longer exists. It divided its holdings among dozens of investors; no public record names them. But if community groups identify victims of the Harbour scheme, examination of titles to their properties may identify the owners, and perhaps the chain of previous predators who collected contract payments. The state of Pennsylvania identified seventy-eight of Harbour's contract buyers and sued its principal and successor owners responsible for those contracts. A settlement banned Harbour, its main owner, and these successors from ever again doing business in the state; Harbour paid restitution of $500,000 to be divided among the seventy-eight victims, about $6,000 per buyer on average. This is a pittance compared to the damage Harbour did to these households but more than any other state has attempted to achieve.

In Cincinnati, a lawyer sued Harbour on behalf of a single victim and won for his client both damages and clear title to her property. The

local legal aid society and the city filed other suits and obtained settlements with similar provisions, as victims of both Harbour and Vision
came forward. Then, in 2018, Cincinnati adopted an ordinance that
requires contract sellers to certify that properties they "sell" are up to
code and habitable and to record all future contracts with the county,
much as regular sales are recorded.

Vision Property Management remains in operation. National civil
rights organizations have sued over its practices in Detroit, stating that
its predatory lending scheme violates the Fair Housing Act, the Truth in
Lending Act, the Equal Credit Opportunity Act, and other regulations.
A federal judge has rejected Vision's attempt to have the case dismissed,
but it has not yet gone to trial. However, even successful lawsuits cannot
undo harm the speculators have done and continue to do.

There is not usually a local representative for activists to pressure.
National firms and individual speculators that engage in this contemporary form of contract selling typically advertise their homes
for "sale" on the internet or with lawn signs (mostly in black neighborhoods). Potential buyers apply online and receive lockbox codes
to allow property visits. The speculators don't commission formal
property inspections, and the home seekers may walk through houses
when electricity and water service have been disconnected; it's not
until they have signed contracts and moved in that they learn of burst
pipes, dangerous wiring, and nonfunctioning fixtures and appliances,
repair of which is now their responsibility. Without ever meeting
employees of the contract sales firms, victims sign contracts, have
them notarized, and return them by mail. Local agents install the
lawn signs and lockboxes but have nothing to do with the sales. Activists might pressure these realtors or other professionals, who understand that tasks they perform are unethical, to name those for whom
they are working.

Legislation Can Help to Rein In the Abuses

Some states permit municipalities to regulate contract sales; in others,
activists could press to get the right for local government to do so.

To date, twenty-one states and cities have such rules—in many
cases, weak ones. Only Virginia and a few cities, like Cincinnati and

Toledo, require that homes sold on contract be safe and in conformity with building and health codes.

Regulations everywhere should classify all contracts as either rentals or purchases. In addition:

- If classified as rentals, local governments should enforce requirements that the properties be safe and code compliant and prohibit landlords from charging the cost of repairs to renters.
- If the properties are classified as purchases, buyers should not be permitted to waive independent inspections without safeguards that ensure their decisions are made knowingly—not in the small print of sale agreements. All purchases should involve a transfer of title to the buyer who should have all the rights of bank-issued mortgages. State licensing agencies should make certain that contract sellers register as mortgage originators and that buyers can lose their homes only in regular foreclosure processes.
- In some cases, buyers may want a *contract for deed* sale, in which monthly payments count toward a defined time when title is transferred, at which point the buyer does become responsible for repairs. Such agreements should be permitted only if a certified inspection discloses to the buyer what the likely cost of repairs will be and if regulations are enforced that prevent evictions on trivial pretexts just before the transfer date.
- If a contract has a rent-to-own provision, it should be considered a rental until the date of conversion, and buyers should have rights of property ownership after that.
- In no case should buyers or renters be responsible for past-due utility bills or taxes or for other liens in existence when they sign contracts or for prior bills that become delinquent after signing.
- States, counties, and cities should enforce existing laws that penalize sellers who misrepresent loan terms, including the true interest rate being charged, the time required to convert a rental to ownership, and the property's actual appraised value.

Most local governments have the authority to inspect properties and ensure enforcement of provisions like these. Activists can pressure municipalities to use the powers they possess.

In 2016, Jack Macnamara, the Jesuit community organizer, met with surviving supporters and activists from their long-ago campaign. He asked who would lead the next contract buyers league. It was the right question, and one not yet answered, not in Lawndale, not elsewhere in Chicago, and not in other cities where contract sales are again a scourge.

Two Milwaukee houses, sold within six weeks of each other in 2022. The property in a black neighborhood (top) sold for $59,000 and had an assessed value of $76,400: 26 percent more than its market value. The property in a white neighborhood (bottom) sold for $192,000 and had an assessed value of $141,500: 26 percent less than its market value. The owner of the home in the black neighborhood was paying property taxes at an effective rate that was 72 percent greater than the owner of the home in the white neighborhood. Overall, black property owners have a higher effective tax rate than white property owners in the city of Milwaukee.

Chapter 8

What's a House Worth?

*How We Calculate a Property's Value
Disadvantages African Americans*

African American homes are overassessed and underappraised. Assessors are local government officials. Appraisers are private agents of banks. Both, though, have a similar responsibility—to determine how much a house is worth. Homeowners pay higher property taxes if their assessed value increases, so they want their city or county to say their house is worth less. Home buyers may want an appraiser to say a house is worth less because that might help them negotiate a lower purchase price, although they may want a higher one because that will justify a bigger mortgage. Once they own a home, they want an appraiser to say it's worth more because that will qualify them for a bigger refinance loan as well as increase their bargaining power when they choose to sell.

Assessments and appraisals are entirely separate; homeowners can appeal assessments they think are too high and appraisals they think are too low. Most appeals of assessments are successful: it is less expensive for local government to make a small adjustment than to fight a voter. Most appeals of appraisals are unsuccessful: banks don't want to spend the money to commission a second appraisal or risk making a loan that is too difficult for a borrower to repay. Black homeowners are usually less successful in appealing both assessments and appraisals; community organizations could provide assistance but few, if any, do.

The only time to know what a home is actually worth is at the moment it is sold—the sale price is its true market value. Since few assessments or appraisals are conducted at this precise moment, they involve guesswork that leaves open the possibility of racial discrimination. When we say that the sale price is a property's "true" value we don't mean its "fair" value. The sale price might reflect racial bias, an unwillingness of buyers to pay more for a property because it is in a black neighborhood.

If African American homes are assessed higher and appraised lower than comparable white homes, and if this is due to buyers' unwillingness to pay as much for a home in a black neighborhood as they pay in a white one, reform of assessment and appraisal systems can't fix the problem. But if assessments or appraisals are themselves racially biased, and if they themselves depress sale prices, reform is urgent.

It is difficult to determine whether assessment or appraisal discrimination is commonplace in a community or whether the value assigned to a particular home is unfair. But this doesn't mean the issue should be ignored.

Assessments—Conducted by Governments to Set Tax Rates. Black Homeowners Pay More, Whites Pay Less

Once government and private businesses collaborated to establish neighborhood segregation in the twentieth century, policies and practices today can deepen that segregation, even without trying to do so. Seemingly race-neutral policies that intensify segregation have a disparate impact on African Americans—they discriminate in effect if not necessarily in intent. The Fair Housing Act of 1968 makes it possible to challenge policies that harm African Americans more than others, even if that is not the stated purpose of those practices. The courts, however, have made it difficult to win such cases. To do so, civil rights lawyers must prove not only that a policy intensifies segregation but that a less discriminatory policy could achieve the same purpose.

With courts mostly unwilling to call for the redress of practices that discriminate without stated intent, the only recourse of civil rights groups is to engage in protest and political organizing that forces public officials to act differently.

Most cities and counties rely heavily on property taxes to fund schools, libraries, parks, fire departments, and other public services. In most cities and counties, African Americans pay more than their fair share of property taxes because assessors' valuations are discriminatory in effect but not intentionally—although if white homeowners had been paying more than their fair share of property taxes, the system probably would have been reformed long ago.

It is not possible to know precisely how much excessive property tax African American homeowners pay, and social scientists who have tried to calculate it vary in their estimates. But all agree that it is severe. One recent nationwide analysis finds that the poorest homeowners, disproportionately African American, pay property taxes at about twice the rate of the richest homeowners, who are disproportionately white. Considering homeowners of all income levels, black homeowners pay about 13 percent more in property taxes than whites whose homes have similar market value. Hispanic homeowners pay about 7 percent more than whites. The more segregated a black neighborhood, the greater are its excess assessments. In the most segregated black neighborhoods, property assessments are about 50 percent higher than assessments for homes of similar market value in neighborhoods where few residents are black.

That is a very large race penalty, in some cases leaving families unable to pay their excessive taxes. In many counties even small amounts of unpaid taxes can lead to foreclosures and owners losing their homes and any equity they had gained. In other cases, homeowners who can't afford to pay their property taxes have little alternative but to sell if they can or face foreclosure if they default on mortgages.

All homeowners in any jurisdiction pay property taxes that are the same percentage of their homes' assessed values, set usually by the official assessor, who is often an elected official. If the assessor underestimates some home values, those owners pay less tax than they should. If the assessor overestimates values, those owners pay too much. One example: during a recent ten-year period in Chicago, homes that sold for $100,000 (more likely located in black neighborhoods) were assessed at an average of 50 percent *more* than their sales prices, while homes that sold for $1 million (more likely located in white neighborhoods) were assessed at an average of 35 percent *less* than their sales prices. Since the tax rate (percentage of assessed value) is the same for all homeowners, African Americans in Chicago pay more taxes per dollar value of their homes than whites do.

In a recent period, Columbus, Ohio, and St. Louis, Missouri, had ratios of assessed to market value for their lowest-priced homes that were four times the ratios for their highest-priced homes. In Charlotte, Kansas City, and Milwaukee, the ratio was nearly twice as great. In Rochester and Denver, it was about 25 percent greater. And so on. In a handful of cities—Houston, Raleigh, and Madison, for example—systematic discrimination against lowest-priced homes does not exist, but this is unusual.

With few exceptions, the methods that cities use to calculate and collect property taxes have racially discriminatory effects that have persisted for years. In 2019, reporters from an online newspaper in Syracuse, New York, demonstrated that homeowners in that city's lower-income African American neighborhoods were paying more taxes than they lawfully should and that those in white neighborhoods were paying less. Syracuse had not conducted a citywide property reassessment for twenty-five years. During that time, market values of homes in white neighborhoods rose more than market values of homes in black ones. As a result, white neighborhood homes were assessed at considerably below their current market values while black neighborhood homes were assessed at closer to their current market values.

To establish a tax rate, the total of budgets for all agencies funded by property taxes is divided by the total of all assessed values in a community. Homeowners then pay a tax amount that's calculated by multiplying the rate by the assessed value of their homes. Because the total amount collected must equal the total of all agency budgets, when some homeowners (in this case, typically whites) pay less than they should, other homeowners (typically black) must pay more than they should. The city of Syracuse owes homeowners in black neighborhoods substantial refunds for the excessive taxes they paid over the nearly twenty-five-year period when property values in white neighborhoods escalated faster.

The state of Delaware, whose counties haven't reassessed property for forty years, and Detroit, which until 2017 hadn't updated its assessments for sixty years, are extreme cases. But because property values in white neighborhoods everywhere have typically increased faster than in black ones, African American homeowners in any location that lagged its reassessments even by a few years are likely to have been similarly exploited.

After the collapse of the housing market in 2008, home prices recovered more slowly in segregated African American neighborhoods than in white areas. This created tax disparities nationwide similar to those in Syracuse. As the rebound from the Great Recession proceeded, in the absence of timely annual reassessments, property values in white neighborhoods diverged more from their assessed values than property in black ones.

In some states and localities where property values appreciated rapidly, legislatures responded to political pressure from mostly white homeowners and capped the amount by which property taxes rise each year. By doing this, legislatures were requiring that assessments diverge from home values more in rapidly appreciating neighborhoods. In the short term, such caps may benefit African American homeowners in gentrifying areas, but over longer time periods they benefit whites more than blacks because property values have increased more rapidly in white than in black communities. The cap would be a more reasonable response to the plight of homeowners facing rapidly rising tax bills if those homeowners were required to return the foregone taxes when they later sell their homes and reap large capital gains. But no jurisdiction has required such a recapture.

Lagged or capped reassessments are not the only reason that African Americans frequently pay higher property taxes than they should.

For any reassessment, even a timely one, tax officials must find ways to estimate the value of homes for which they don't have sale prices. In some cases, they may assume that homes with similar physical characteristics—square footage, number of bedrooms or bathrooms, construction type—have similar value. But in more affluent white neighborhoods, homes may have more expensive bathroom fixtures, more updated appliances, higher-speed internet wiring, or smaller repair backlogs. Assessors can't know this because they don't enter houses they evaluate. But prospective buyers do walk through the house and know its internal amenities when deciding how much to offer. The result: homes in white neighborhoods with internal remodeling are more likely to have similar assessed values but higher market values than homes with similar external physical characteristics in black neighborhoods.

White neighborhoods are also more likely to have better amenities than black ones—schools with better-trained teachers, nearby parks, popular retail outlets, restaurants, gyms, supermarkets selling fresh food. These varying characteristics also cause differences in home market values. In the slower recovery of housing prices after the Great Recession, neighborhoods of black homeowners were more likely to have more boarded-up and abandoned homes than those of whites. Properties in black neighborhoods that were maintained in immaculate condition had lower values because nearby houses were eyesores, or even dangerous. A well-maintained house surrounded by boarded-up properties is less desirable, and proper assessments should reflect this.

Racial prejudice of reluctant white purchasers also depresses the market values of homes in black communities. Many whites are willing to pay more for a house in a white neighborhood than for a physically identical property in a more diverse place. Because of this, when assessors determine the market values of homes in African American neighborhoods by comparing them with similar buildings in white areas, they overassess the black-owned homes.

Many states permit homeowners to exclude a portion of their assessed value from taxation. The exemption amount varies from state to state but it is not automatic; taxpayers must know how to apply for it. First-time homeowners who are unfamiliar with the process do so less frequently. They are more likely to be African American, so for this reason as well blacks have higher tax burdens than whites do for homes of similar value.

Also in some states, taxpayers who move from a home to a more expensive one can claim a limit on their tax increase. Since African Americans are more likely to be first-time home buyers than whites, this provision has a racially discriminatory effect, causing black homeowners who are less able to take advantage of it to pay higher taxes than whites with homes of similar value.

Homeowners can appeal assessments and many do; when they do, assessors frequently agree to make reductions. But the appeals process requires skill and research and sometimes hiring a lawyer: not all homeowners are able to assemble and present evidence that their assessments were too high in comparison with similar properties. Not surprisingly, more educated homeowners who are not afraid to challenge bureaucrats and are able to hire lawyers are more likely to dispute assessments. When homeowners, including African Americans, appeal, their chances are good of winning adjustments that reduce taxes owed. But black homeowners are less likely than whites to win, and when they do, they get smaller adjustments. The result is that the appeals process further disadvantages homeowners in black neighborhoods.

Refunds Are Due, but Not Forthcoming

In Cook County, Illinois, assessments have had a racially discriminatory effect for at least fifty years. Fritz Kaegi, its assessor, has created a web page where homeowners can appeal their assessments without a lawyer's assistance. It is too soon to know whether this will have any significant benefit for African American taxpayers. While necessary, such reforms do nothing to compensate black homeowners for overpayments they've made in past years.

It is impossible to calculate the exact amount owed to each African American homeowner for overassessment. Therefore, this injustice cannot be remedied with lawsuits filed by homeowners. The most that lawsuits can accomplish is an order for a county to fix its assessment system. In Delaware, for example, civil rights groups sued over outdated assessments; the counties settled in 2021 by agreeing to a onetime reassessment but made no commitment to do so regularly in the future.

Still, it is indisputable that African Americans are entitled to approximate recompense because they were harmed by the failure to conduct timely and accurate assessments. Mr. Kaegi, the Cook County reform assessor, acknowledges that

> low-income homeowners—particularly those in Black and Latino communities—have not been treated fairly due to the

actions of past assessors across the country. . . . If past assessors overassessed one family or business, then by definition,
they underassessed another to account for the whole pie.
Whether the causes are malpractice, bad data, or poor gover-
nance, these are actions that must stop. Those who should be
made whole have the right to demand as such.

Yet, when pressed for proposals for how Cook County should make
black and Hispanic taxpayers whole, Mr. Kaegi had none. His sugges-
tion was that the government should increase education assistance to
low-income school districts to reduce the need for property taxes to
pay for schools. More federal support is a good idea but does nothing to address the years of black homeowners' excessive payments. Mr.
Kaegi offered no thoughts about the responsibility of Cook County
jurisdictions to compensate these victims or to collect additional taxes
to pay for that compensation from white suburban neighborhoods
whose taxes were too low.

Mr. Kaegi has organized a group of fifteen fellow urban assessors
to press the federal government to make its data on home sale appraisals available to assessors. Since the government-sponsored enterprise
Fannie Mae buys a large share of bank mortgages, its data could inform
assessors' estimates of true home value variations by neighborhood
and eliminate some unfairness. But, again, his proposal would address
assessment practices only in the future, not what's owed to homeowners who have been overassessed for years.

In Detroit, Mayor Mike Duggan acknowledges that tens of thousands of Detroit homeowners were overassessed for many years. For
some, the burden was too great, and they lost homes to foreclosure. In
2020, Mr. Duggan proposed that the city give preferences to those who
paid excessive taxes; for example, he suggested that they receive discounts on properties purchased in city auctions and be given priority
for city employment, job training, low-income housing, and summer
jobs for their children. A local reporter estimated that Detroit homeowners had paid more than $600 million in excess taxes, but these pro-
posed preferences would cost only about $6 million. The city council
defeated his plan as inadequate, but neither the mayor, the council, or

Michigan's governor came up with anything better, and nothing has been done since.

One partial remedy would be for assessors to establish a compensatory system for a number of years into the future. Assessors could artificially but openly overvalue homes in neighborhoods (disproportionately white) that had historically been underassessed and likewise undervalue homes in black neighborhoods. Of course, this would be unfair: white homeowners would be taxed at rates for which they hadn't budgeted; recent home buyers in white neighborhoods would pay penalties to offset benefits they never received, while new buyers in black neighborhoods would receive benefits to offset penalties they never experienced. As a society, we are always more sensitive to unfairness experienced by whites when it is designed to remedy unfairness experienced by blacks. It would take public education and a vastly intensified public commitment to the redress of segregation before political support for such action could begin to emerge. The debate would be similar to that over affirmative action programs in higher education. Unless the public understands the harms that were suffered and begins to accept an obligation to address them, it is unimaginable that it would support these remedies.

Only civil rights activists' carefully planned campaigns can win remedial payments in Chicago, Detroit, and other cities with records of overtaxation. Opponents may acknowledge that past assessments were unfair, but rightly claim that it's impossible to calculate the precise amount owed to each homeowner or even to black homeowners on average. But disagreement among statisticians over the exact debt owed should not be an excuse for refusing to enact remedies that are approximately reasonable. Their size in any city will depend more on the strength of activists' campaigns than on calculations of social scientists.

While victims of property tax discrimination are more likely to be black than white, black homeowners are not the only ones affected. For similar reasons, homeowners in lower-income white and Hispanic neighborhoods also pay more property taxes than they should, although the disparity is not nearly as great as it is for African Americans. To rectify this injustice, a civil rights movement led by African Americans can also enlist others, increasing its political power.

*Appraisals—Commissioned by Banks to Evaluate Mortgage Risk. Black
Home Buyers' Appraisals Are Lower and Whites' Are Higher*

Lenders contract with appraisers to help decide whether to finance or
refinance mortgages; banks seek assurance that they are not lending
more than a house is worth and that they will not risk a loss if they
foreclose and have to sell a property for less than the remaining loan.
For owners, a disappointingly low appraisal would force them to settle
for a smaller refinance loan than they thought they had a right to. A
buyer seeking a first mortgage could be denied a loan if the property
appraises for less than the agreed-upon purchase price.

Homes in black neighborhoods sell for less than similar homes in
white neighborhoods, partly because many whites are unwilling to
pay as much for them. Also, African Americans have lower average
incomes and savings, so have less to bid than whites for similar properties. A proper appraisal can't ignore these influences in its estimate
of a house's value.

But sales prices can also be affected by appraisers who undervalue
homes in black neighborhoods without justification. Banks then lend
less to home buyers in these areas because they will not issue a mortgage for more than the home's appraised value, minus a required down
payment. Purchasers will not be able to offer as high a price as they
would if the appraisal was higher and a bigger mortgage were available
(unless they agree to pay more than the appraised value and assume a
higher cost burden). So it is possible that while appraisals are designed
to predict a true value (or resale price), that true value might reflect the
bias of appraisers. It is a chicken-and-egg conundrum—which came
first, the appraised value or the market value? Do lower sale prices in
black neighborhoods reflect buyers' unwillingness to pay more or is
that unwillingness the result of lower appraisals?

Black homeowners often allege that their properties were underappraised on account of race. African American realtors and advocacy
groups in black neighborhoods make similar charges, noting that a pattern of underappraisals undermines the health and resources of their
communities. Systematic undervaluing of black-owned homes limits
African Americans' wealth-building potential from homeownership.

In some highly publicized cases, black homeowners requested reappraisals and got higher values after they removed family pictures and had a white friend or relative pretend to be the owner when the new appraiser arrived. This ruse apparently tricked appraisers into believing the property was white-owned and thus worth more. All appraisals reflect judgment. Whenever a lender commissions more than one appraisal, results will likely vary. But variations should never be as large as those that the publicized homeowners reported: in a Chicago case, a second, race-changed appraisal came in 22 percent higher; in Denver, it was 35 percent; in Jacksonville, Florida, it was 40 percent; in Marin County, California, it was 50 percent; in Baltimore, it was 59 percent.

These cases are anecdotal; we can't know how frequently they occur. Homeowners whose reappraisals remain disappointing with white stand-ins don't report their experiences to journalists. But the evidence of systematic racial discrimination in appraisals is strong. On average, when African Americans buy homes, appraised values are further below purchase prices than when whites buy homes. The same is true of all home sales in majority-black neighborhoods: appraised values are further below sales prices than in majority-white neighborhoods.

This must reveal racial bias not far beneath the surface. Banks commission appraisals after properties are under contract and buyers seek mortgages. The appraiser, therefore, knows the agreed-upon sales price when determining the home value. At the very least, that appraisals typically come in further below sales prices in black and Hispanic neighborhoods indicates that appraisers have less respect for market values in these neighborhoods than in white ones.

This has severe consequences for black and Hispanic homeowners' economic well-being. Because banks will not offer mortgages for more than a home's appraised value, black and Hispanic home buyers need more cash to cover the difference. Whites, whose homes appraise higher, can qualify for mortgages that are a larger share of the purchase price.

But knowing that this is generally true does not tell us whether it is true in any particular case: whether a particular appraisal is too low because of the race of the home buyer or the neighborhood's racial composition. In the case of assessments, estimating the overall harm to black neighborhoods is necessary to calculate the amount of refunds due to homeowners for excessive tax payments. But for appraisals, there is no equally obvious way to remedy past values that were too low.

Create a System for Vetting Appraisers

Appraisers are state certified, with standards set by a national board, which itself is overseen by the federal government. Qualified appraisers should examine recent sale prices of three nearby homes (known as *comparables*) that seem as similar as possible to the house they are evaluating and then, if necessary, take into account any unique features of the property they evaluate: a remodeled kitchen, a well-tended garden, and so on. This is tricky; if sales prices of nearby homes were low because appraisals were low due to appraiser racial bias, then an uncritical use of comparables will likely reproduce the previous racial biases, even if the appraiser of the home in question has no bias. Picking the right comparable houses and making appropriate adjustments is not a science but requires educated judgment. Certification of appraisers should ensure that when making such judgments, they are well trained in their obligations not to discriminate.

But old habits die hard: into the 1970s, the American Institute of Appraisers instructed its members to take into account that African Americans in a neighborhood had an "adverse effect" on home values. Still today, even without such an instruction, appraisers who think of themselves as unbiased may hold unexamined beliefs that African American homes or African American neighborhoods are less desirable than white ones.

Appraisers' livelihoods should depend on making accurate judgments; if they don't, banks will lose money on foreclosures if appraisals are too high or suffer from lost loan business if appraisals are too low. Appraisers who frequently misestimate value may cease to get assignments. But if bankers with racial biases are more fearful of appraisals in black neighborhoods that are too high than of those that are too low, appraisers who are dependent on banks' repeat business may err more often in making estimates on the low side for African American buyers, owners, or neighborhoods.

We know that even in recent times, banks have insisted on inaccurate appraisals that were too high, so it is conceivable that appraisers are now feeling pressure to make judgments that are too low. During the housing bubble prior to the 2008 collapse, mortgage brokers and banks pressed appraisers to inflate their evaluations of resale values in black and Hispanic neighborhoods. Bankers knew they could use these excessive estimates as justification for the inflated mortgages that they would then sell to Fannie Mae—which in turn passed them on to unscrupulous speculators—and so didn't care that they were setting minority borrowers up for default.

Appraisers are required to take ongoing education programs but the mandatory nondiscrimination training is too often inadequate. Appraising remains a mostly white and male profession. Recruiting, educating, and certifying African Americans, Hispanics, and women of all ethnicities is needed; racial justice activists can monitor appraisal recruitment and training programs and press local banks to contract in their home mortgage business with a diverse group of appraisers, especially those who are comfortable in and not afraid of neighborhoods they visit.

In 2022, Fannie Mae announced that in some cases it would substitute electronic appraisals for human ones. Computerized systems could assemble data from sources like Google Map street views and photos of home interiors posted on real estate websites. But important data will still be missing—homes that haven't recently been put up for sale are likely to be missing such photos—and the difficulty of selecting the right comparables will persist, including the likelihood that if past appraisals in a neighborhood were influenced by racial bias, Fannie Mae's software will perpetuate it.

The only way to know whether this or any change has succeeded in eliminating racial bias is to see how close appraisals are to sale prices in black and white neighborhoods. Fannie Mae has the only database that includes these data by race and by neighborhood, but it's not public. If it were, civil rights groups could judge whether homes in black neighborhoods were discriminatorily underappraised. Activist groups, states, and localities can insist that Fannie Mae release this information.

Especially for loans in African American and Hispanic communities, mortgage brokers and banks should be required to agree to a reappraisal whenever a homeowner or buyer is dissatisfied with the first one. In most cases, firms are unwilling to commission reappraisals; when they do, the second one usually (but not always) has a value not much different from the first. The reappraiser, however, is usually aware of the first result and may be influenced by it.

Community groups could press mortgage originators to use only appraisers without records of racial bias. Banks are familiar with such restrictions—they already must draw from approved lists when they make government-insured loans—but eligibility qualifications are minimal and don't require demonstration of nondiscriminatory behavior. To certify trustworthy appraisers, racial justice advocates should enlist banks and mortgage brokers to commission random second appraisals for an initial period. If the evaluations significantly differ, civil rights groups (usually, fair housing centers) should have the right to examine the evidence each appraiser used, in order to determine why disparities occurred and whether the initial judgment was justified. Banks and mortgage brokers can then develop a list of vetted appraisers, share the information with fair housing centers, and draw from it when appraisals are disputed. Appraisals are expensive, and banks will resist such a program for this reason alone. Local activists should insist that banks consider these costs as part of their touted diversity, equity, and inclusion efforts.

Like most fair housing violations, victims of biased appraisals rarely know they have experienced discrimination. White members of activist groups could volunteer as pretend owners when an African American who is dissatisfied with an appraisal requests a second one. Banks should also commission ongoing and random second opinions, even when a home buyer or owner makes no complaint. In this way, not only will the list of vetted appraisers grow, but African American homeowners will gain faith that the process is, finally, fair.

Unfair Property Assessments Can Lead to Foreclosures

Before the state of Michigan ordered Detroit to conduct a property reassessment in 2017, it had overvalued houses in black neighborhoods for decades. Home prices had fallen with the decline of the auto industry; still, assessed amounts upon which the city calculated property taxes often increased. When owners could not pay these discriminatorily inflated taxes, the county foreclosed and resold their homes to investors to recoup the unpaid taxes. Between 2011 and 2015, Wayne County foreclosed on 100,000 Detroit homes, one in four in the city, for overdue taxes. Ten percent of the foreclosures were due to improperly inflated tax assessments. Most victims were black.

Di Leshea Scott, an African American single mother, bought her home in Detroit for $64,000 in 2005. Six months later, the city valued it at $72,000 and while house prices in Detroit fell 25 percent over the next several years, the city's valuation of Ms. Scott's property increased by 20 percent. By 2011, she had paid the city $6,000 more than a proper assessment would have required. Ms. Scott then lost her job and missed a $3,100 tax payment. Two years later, the debt had grown to almost $10,000. The city foreclosed and auctioned her home to a Utah-based rental firm for $5,000. In 2018, that company resold the property to another firm for $32,500, which resold it two years later for $84,000. Ms. Scott and her children now rent the house, whose value has increased partly because her rent keeps rising. The city's reassessment now values the home at $25,000.

Tax Liens—Investors Win While Homeowners, Often African American, Lose

When owners like Ms. Scott fall behind on property tax payments, local governments can place liens on their homes. If the back taxes remain unpaid, cities can foreclose and sell the properties to recoup the outstanding obligations. Some localities get their money sooner by auctioning off the tax debt to investors instead of going through the foreclosure process themselves. The bidders then pay the taxes owed to the city right away, in exchange for a right to collect it from the homeowners, along with interest and fees. If investors cannot collect, they can foreclose on properties and later sell them, often for far more than they paid. Foreclosed homes that do not sell may remain vacant for years, leading to neighborhood destabilization. Bidders may collude in auctions to reduce what they pay to cities—some investors have been convicted of antitrust violations for doing so.

Every jurisdiction has a tax lien process, whether it auctions off the home itself or the right to collect back taxes. Either way, homeowners can lose their properties, sometimes for unpaid taxes as little as $100. An internet search will reveal a county's list of tax lien properties and their auction dates.

While the process allows municipalities to collect unpaid taxes, the investors are the winners. Most states set maximum interest rates that those who purchase tax collection rights can charge homeowners. It's usually much higher than typical returns—often over 18 percent and sometimes as high as 50 percent. Investors can also add thousands of dollars in fees. An original tax bill of a few hundred dollars can become a debt of several thousand. Afraid of losing homes, owners will pay these exorbitant amounts if they can, and many do.

Middle-class owners of high-value properties with long-term mortgages may find this process puzzling. Their banks require them to buy a policy that insures against damage from fire, floods, or other disasters. Monthly payments include not only actual principal and interest charges but also tax and these insurance costs. Their banks take responsibility for passing these on to city tax collectors and insurance companies. The lenders make sure to do so to avoid being faced with their borrowers having tax liens that allow cities to foreclose on properties without taking the banks' interests into account—tax obligations have legal priority over mortgage payments.

Tax liens are more likely in cities like Baltimore, Philadelphia,

A 2013 tax lien auction in Washington, D.C. Three purchasers had previously pleaded guilty to felony conspiracy for bid rigging in Maryland's auctions. One of them subsequently spent $1.2 million to purchase 326 liens in the District. He charged homeowners exorbitant fees and then foreclosed on 144 of them.

Detroit, and Cleveland, where low- and moderate-income African Americans have inherited homes or have owned them for long enough to pay off mortgages, so no bank is collecting and forwarding their tax payments. If they bought their home on contract, they may be unaware that the "seller" who kept title failed to pay taxes. Most predatory subprime loans made before 2008 that targeted black and Hispanic homeowners did not include taxes and insurance in monthly bills. That way, the lenders could make mortgages seem unrealistically affordable to borrowers who would too frequently default.

Homeowners with responsibility for monitoring their own tax payments may not realize they have an outstanding bill until their home is delinquent (and interest and fees have started accruing) or until the tax lien has been sold. They may consider their bills only one of many burdens that pile up, especially if the taxes are unexpectedly high because of inflated assessments or because property values are in fact increasing. Residents of gentrifying areas, disproportionately African American, are especially likely to face such crises. However, in recent years, home values have been increasing everywhere. Working- and lower-middle-class households that live from paycheck to paycheck are vulnerable to suddenly unaffordable property taxes. They can sell their homes at a profit, but if they try to remain without making timely tax payments, they are at risk of tax liens.

In the decade ending in 2013, investors foreclosed on two hundred homes in Washington, D.C., for failure to pay taxes—in some cases, for debts of less than $500 that had ballooned to several thousand dollars with interest and fees. Not all errors were those of homeowners, though. In five of those years, the city sold nearly two thousand tax liens to investors by mistake, the result of inaccurate office payment records or bills sent to incorrect addresses. The blunders occurred in one-fifth of all tax lien sales. If the District of Columbia itself discovered an error, it reversed the sale and refunded what the investor paid. If the homeowner didn't know of the error or did not have legal assistance to challenge it, the lien sale remained valid, and the investor could foreclose. Many homeowners were never compensated.

The state of Illinois requires counties to conduct tax lien sales annually for the previous year's unpaid taxes. Cook County put thirty-six thousand homes in its 2021 tax lien sale. Three-quarters were in majority-black or Hispanic communities in or near Chicago, and half owed less than $1,000. Homeowners then had thirty months to pay off the outstanding debt, interest, and fees before the tax purchaser could foreclose on the properties. The county has a fund to compensate owners for loss of equity in tax lien foreclosures. Speculators are supposed to contribute to it but it is underfunded and covers the loss only partially; in addition, homeowners must know how to petition for payment.

Most states also allow localities to convert unpaid water and sewer bills into tax liens. Bills for water have increased rapidly in recent decades, making them less affordable for low-income households whose incomes have been more stagnant. Cuyahoga County, which includes the city of Cleveland, placed eleven thousand water bill liens between 2014 and 2018, disproportionately in African American communities, for overdue payments as low as $300. Home foreclosures resulted.

Reform the Tax Lien Process

Local governments' ability to support schools, police, libraries, and other public services depends on residents paying what they owe. When homeowners fall behind, public authorities have an obligation to recover the debts while causing the least possible harm. Families should not have to lose homes and communities be destabilized while investors profit.

Municipalities should reform their tax lien processes to minimize the damage that results. The tax lien sales in Washington, D.C., were the subject of an exposé in 2013. As a result, the city capped investors' attorney fees charged to homeowners, ended its practice of selling tax liens for properties that owed less than $2,500, and required that homeowners receive proceeds from sales of foreclosed properties after taxes, interest, and fees were paid. A lawsuit followed that won compensation for homeowners who owed small amounts of taxes and to whom the new rule would have applied but who lost all their home equity before the reforms took effect.

Officials should do more to inform householders about overdue bills, long before they initiate a lien. Municipalities should partner with local community groups to contact residents with outstanding bills and allow them to authorize sending copies of their bills to activist organizations or relatives to ensure they are not overlooked. Procedures can include notices delivered in person to homeowners and longer times for them to bring accounts up to date. Community groups can also press philanthropies to pay outstanding debts that have grown to unaffordable amounts.

Some states have banned tax lien sales altogether, and civil rights groups should press their own states to do the same. When governments collect back taxes in-house rather than selling the right to investors, flexibility is possible that doesn't exist with private firms, which lack public accountability.

Local governments should offer more options for delinquent homeowners, such as payment plans, emergency loans, debt reductions, and exemptions for property owners with limited means. Deferment programs can allow owners to pay tax debts when they later sell their properties. Jurisdictions can sell bonds, secured by these later tax payments, to raise the money immediately. Many counties already borrow money to anticipate on-time tax payments and could use a similar procedure to assist homeowners in arrears. Every state offers property tax relief for residents in need due to age, disability, or income, but African American homeowners are less likely to get this relief than whites, in part because inherited properties are often excluded from the exemption and because homeowners usually must apply and few know how.

In Minneapolis, the City of Lakes Community Land Trust helps homeowners struggling with tax debt by paying off the debt along with needed deferred maintenance. In exchange, the trust takes ownership of the land under the house and then leases it to the homeowner for a few dollars a year. The city gets its taxes paid, the family remains in its home, and the home's resale price is restricted so it remains affordable for future buyers.

April 25, 2018. San Francisco Bay Area renter groups protested First Republic Bank's restriction of housing opportunities for lower-income households, a violation of the Community Reinvestment Act. After the coalition's campaign in 2015, First Republic agreed to cease lending to borrowers who intended to remove rent-controlled tenants. The organizations then conducted a second campaign in 2018 to press the bank to sign an anti-displacement code of conduct.

Chapter 9

Where the Money Flows

*Monitoring Bank Practices to Ensure Equitable
Investment in All Communities*

T he Fair Housing Act outlawed redlining in 1968 but the practice continues: many banks provide fewer services and make fewer loans to residents of black and Hispanic neighborhoods than to similar borrowers in white neighborhoods.

Potential borrowers may not know when a bank underinvests in their community. Home buyers denied loans don't know if the bank is more prone to issue them elsewhere. Yet when few of their neighbors can get mortgages and they must travel to whiter areas to find a bank branch or a loan officer, they understand they are not being served well; still, they may not know what to do about it.

Use the Community Reinvestment Act to Boost Investment in Neglected Communities

The Home Mortgage Disclosure Act requires banks to report annually on loan requests and the mortgages they originate, including applicants' and borrowers' race, ethnicity, and location. Fair housing centers use these data to analyze lender performance and identify possible discrimination in their regions.

In 2019 the Fair Housing Center of Central Indiana concluded that its largest local bank, Old National Bank, made far fewer loans in African American neighborhoods than its competitors. The bank had closed many branches in black communities in the previous decade; by 2021, only four of its twenty-one area branches were in locales where more than 10 percent of the population is black; no loan officers were located in these places.

Center leaders met with Old National officers in 2019. The bank's chief executive acknowledged it needed to improve and said he was working to do so but declined to communicate further with the fair housing group.

The center then conducted "paired testing" of Old National's lending practices. It sent black and white potential home buyers with similar credit worthiness to contact the bank by phone and in person in search of loans. Mortgage officers provided inferior service and less detailed information to black than white testers; in one case, for example, a branch offered a black tester a high-interest loan although she qualified for a less expensive one.

By 2021, the bank's lending patterns hadn't changed but a new development gave the fair housing center added leverage. Old National announced plans to acquire First Midwest Bancorp and requested a meeting with the housing center. Banks proposing to merge must apply for federal approval and regulators are supposed to consider the effect on low-income communities. Opponents of an application can slow the process or even achieve a denial. This threat can motivate banks to negotiate.

The Community Reinvestment Act of 1977 requires banks to invest in neighborhoods that have been underserved by the financial industry. Regulators periodically evaluate whether banks adequately make mortgages and small business loans to low- and moderate-income individuals, and whether they invest in economic development and affordable housing projects in low- and moderate-income communities in their service areas. The government makes its ratings of bank performance public, and while this seems to prod some financial institutions to do better, regulators rarely give poor ratings and they have little power to force banks that get low scores to improve.

Except: when federal officials review merger and acquisition proposals, they can take the scores into account and ask for public comment. Whether they approve a merger may be influenced by challenges from local and national advocacy groups. Organizations like the Fair Housing Center of Central Indiana can submit public comments opposing a merger, and federal regulators may then feel compelled to call public hearings at which the comments of activists can have an impact.

Financial institutions want their merger applications approved quickly and without negative public attention. Delays can damage investor confidence and drive down banks' stock values. Civil rights activists can use this to their advantage by demanding public hearings that will slow the process. Advocates can attempt to persuade a bank to increase investments in low-income areas in exchange for an agreement to withdraw opposition to a merger. Using this power, groups have negotiated bank commitments to fund mortgages, small business loans, financial literacy courses, and to make donations to local nonprofits, down payment assistance programs, and local development and affordable-housing projects, as well as to provide banking and mortgage services to low-income, African American, and Hispanic residents.

The National Community Reinvestment Coalition supports the efforts of fair housing centers like Indiana's. It monitors merger applications and helps organize opposition when banks have not properly served low-income neighborhoods. Coalition leaders met with Old National Bank executives after it announced its proposed First Midwest acquisition and submitted a letter to federal regulators signed by twenty-four organizations throughout the First Midwest service area, requesting public hearings to demonstrate the need for Old National to commit to a community benefits agreement. Old National refused to negotiate.

With the merger still pending, and no prospect for an agreement, the Indiana fair housing center sued, alleging that Old National's lending practices violated the Fair Housing Act. Two months later, the bank consented to a settlement in exchange for the organization's support for its merger. In majority-black neighborhoods in and around Indianapolis, the bank agreed to open two new branches with mortgage officers, originate at least $20 million in mortgages, and provide $1.1 million in loan subsidies and down payment assistance. It also promised to lend at least $7.5 million to low-income housing developers and grant $1.3 million to community organizations that serve the area's black neighborhoods. Old National also committed to conduct a redlining assessment of its operations, train its staff on fair lending, and market its loan products more aggressively to African Americans.

A year later, the national coalition and Old National announced another agreement, this one covering First Midwest's service area, which the bank was about to take over. Old National agreed to provide $2 billion in mortgage lending, $3 billion in small business loans, $3 billion for economic development and affordable housing, a $2.5 million loan subsidy fund, and $24 million in philanthropic support, all to low- and moderate-income black and Hispanic borrowers and communities. In exchange, the twenty-four organizations that initially opposed the merger supported it; the Federal Reserve approved Old National's acquisition of First Midwest.

Aggressive Advocacy Can Change Bank Behavior

The Greenlining Institute in Oakland, California, was founded in the 1970s to press for greater investment and access to capital in black and Hispanic neighborhoods. In the 1990s, it took aim at banks applying for mergers and acquisitions, demanding comprehensive benefit packages in exchange for ending opposition to merger approvals. It held rallies, took out newspaper ads, held protests at bank executives' homes, and turned out as many as a thousand supporters for public hearings to oppose mergers and acquisitions.

The organization's tactics were creative and attention-getting. For one protest against Bank of America, it purchased fortune cookies with messages about the institution's failure to serve the Hispanic community. Greenlining supporters walked through bank headquarters to distribute cookies to office workers—while a mariachi band played outside.

During a national bank merger wave from 1995 through 1998, Greenlining's pressure succeeded in winning pledges during merger approval negotiations for more than $400 billion in low-income neighborhood investments from Wells Fargo, Washington Mutual, and NationsBank. After its takeover of Home Savings of America, Washington Mutual negotiated a $120 billion program to prevent Greenlining from opposing its future mergers.

Civil rights activists can assert influence over bank practices by studying local banks' lending and investment activities and monitoring when any such institution seeks federal regulatory approval. They can use the National Community Reinvestment Coalition's reports about pending mergers, access local banks' ratings, and investigate their mortgage lending with accessible federal data. A new federal law will also make race information public on banks' small business lending. African American and Hispanic residents of low-income communities, as well as fair housing agencies serving them, likely know which banks routinely deny them loans and which area banks have inadequate local presence. These should be the focus of more intensive investigation.

PART FOUR

OPENING UP WHITE COMMUNITIES

How we can make exclusive suburbs accessible to African Americans who wish to live in them and maintain those neighborhoods and their schools as diversified areas of opportunity by preventing white flight and disinvestment.

Minneapolis, 2018. As the planning commission debated the end of single-family zoning, supporters ("Neighbors for More Neighbors") said smaller lots would allow more lower- and moderate-income housing. Opponents ("Stop the 2040 Plan") predicted that developers would replace single-family homes with costly condominiums.

Chapter 10

Make the Exclusive Inclusive

Zoning Codes, Developer Subsidies, and Housing Vouchers
Conspire to Keep Some Areas All-White; Let's Reform Them

Zoning codes dictate the housing types that cities and suburbs allow. In mostly middle-class white areas, they often permit only single-family homes on large lots and forbid less-expensive duplexes, triplexes, town homes, and apartments. These exclusionary rules are not on their face racially discriminatory but are so in effect because they ban the only dwellings that many African Americans can afford.

Beginning in the 1930s, the federal government imposed segregation on metropolitan areas. It built separate public housing projects for blacks and whites, sometimes even in neighborhoods that had previously been integrated. It financed the suburbanization of the nation, but insisted that developers exclude African Americans from the new communities. Then in 1962, President John F. Kennedy ordered federal agencies to end their discriminatory practices; in 1968, the Fair Housing Act extended the ban to private discrimination. The courts, however, still consider it legal to maintain residential segregation with zoning, provided racial discrimination is not too explicit.

When zoning makes suburban housing scarce, competition for existing homes intensifies, so prices increase. With the number of houses limited and lower-income families kept out, the combination of a high tax base, because of the inflated property values, and fewer people needing services results in more and better public goods. Those lucky enough to outbid other buyers and live in such places have better parks, libraries, and especially schools. Residents conclude they have a right to these benefits as their neighborhoods become more resource rich over time. They fight (and vote) to maintain their advantages by opposing any changes that threaten to lower their property values or that require them to share their community's resources with others. This all comes at the expense of middle- and lower-income households, who are limited to communities with less adequate public services.

Reform Suburban Single-Family Zoning That Perpetuates Segregation

Elimination of restrictive land-use rules is a necessary first step to undo residential segregation. Single-family zoning may be the most powerful policy that perpetuates racial inequality. Its end will not in itself fix things—much more is needed—but its persistence guarantees permanent apartheid for America.

Zoning reform should be a no-brainer, because conservatives and liberals all say they agree. It's a strategy that liberals who attempt to implement the Affirmatively Furthering Fair Housing process can employ. Conservatives say they oppose restrictive regulation like exclusionary zoning because it interferes with a free market. When Donald Trump assumed the presidency in 2017, his secretary of housing and urban development, Ben Carson, vowed to punish suburbs that didn't repeal their exclusionary zoning rules. The promise was never heard from again, and by the end of his term, the president had flipped and charged that Democratic support for lower-cost housing in areas where it is currently prohibited "would mean abolishing, ruining the suburbs."

Yet both Democrats and Republicans depend on suburban voters, and most in both parties, regardless of professed commitments to the abolition of needlessly restrictive zoning, rise in opposition whenever they confront actual proposals for reform. A commonplace description of these voters is NIMBY, "not in my backyard"; the term describes their conviction that exclusionary rules should be banned everywhere except in their own neighborhoods.

Connecticut Zoning Ensures That the State Remains Segregated

Like every state, Connecticut is segregated by race, with most African Americans concentrated in a few cities that allow multifamily and small-lot housing. Elsewhere, almost all residential land is zoned for single-family homes only, preserving suburbs as primarily white.

Connecticut requires that local zoning commissions permit denser development to promote housing choice—most defy the law, though. Today, multifamily housing is allowed on less than 2 percent of residential land in the state without requiring special permission. In towns where this permission is possible, planning boards have responded by blocking such development for decades. Some go ahead and hold hearings, but then retreat in the face of vehement NIMBY opposition to changing the area's "character." As one homeowner in an exclusive area of West Hartford put it, only single-family homes on large lot sizes would "fit the complexion of the community."

Robert Whitten, a nationally recognized planning consultant, ensured that complexion in 1924 when he guided the development of West Hartford's first zoning code. Two years earlier, Whitten had written a racially explicit zoning ordinance for Atlanta that divided its residential zones into white and colored districts, stating that "race zoning is essential in the interest of public peace, order and security." Whitten later served on the subdivision committee of President Herbert Hoover's 1931 Home Building and Home Ownership conference. It was packed with fellow segregationists who promoted single-family zoning as a tool to maintain segregation and recommended that all new subdivisions have deeds that prohibited sale or resale of homes to African Americans. West Hartford leaders certainly considered Whitten's racial planning principles before they hired him to craft rules that banned anything but single-family homes.

Today, the town permits higher-density development in a few areas, and so almost one-third of residents live in duplexes, triplexes, and apartments. This makes West Hartford more racially and economically diverse than other suburbs in Connecticut that have maintained single-family zoning of almost all residential property for decades. Yet most of West Hartford is still zoned exclusively for single-family homes.

Whitten's work in West Hartford was not unusual. His legacy becomes clear when we compare West Hartford with its neighbor, the city of Hartford. Five percent of West Hartford's residents are black while 80 percent are white or Asian, and most own their homes. In adjoining Hartford, only 18 percent are white or Asian, with the rest either black or Hispanic, and most are renters. The few who own homes have properties with values that average only half of those in the Hartford suburbs. In Hartford, 40 percent of all housing is reserved for the poor, financed with federal subsidies. In some neighborhoods, it's as much as 70 percent.

After Hartford, New Haven is the Connecticut city where the black population share is largest. It is about one-third white and Asian, with the rest either black or Hispanic and most residents are renters. Only one-fourth of New Haven families own their own homes; the median value of houses in the city is half that of properties in the adjoining almost all-white suburb of Woodbridge. That community zones 98 percent of its residential land for single-family houses on lot sizes of at least one acre. They have wells and septic systems, and the town cites its lack of sewers as a reason it can't comply with the law requiring it to authorize multifamily buildings. Connecticut courts accept this excuse. Yet Woodbridge has a sewer system—for its downtown commercial area. As an initial step toward desegregation, multifamily housing could be placed close by. Current proposals in Woodbridge to modify the town's zoning code to permit affordable housing abolish single-family zoning but do not change allowable height limits or lot sizes, so large multifamily projects would still not be permitted. The town could approve many projects of a few units each that would not burden septic or well capacities.

On many occasions, officials have acknowledged that the town needs housing affordable to lower- and moderate-income families and that state law requires the town to authorize it, but each proposal has been withdrawn after public protests that it would "degrad[e]," "deteriorate," and "destroy" Woodbridge. Some objected that a zoning change would permit families to move in who weren't already town residents. But a proposal to house the town's firefighters, police, teachers, and other employees was also rejected after citizen testimony that it "would set a bad precedent." One transparently racial complaint was that multifamily development would attract families from nearby black cities who would then send their children to Woodbridge schools. Another was that multifamily construction would necessarily increase police expenditures, although the project under consideration would bring in a small number of new residents. Yet another was that if Woodbridge accepted apartment renters, they would climb over a fence and steal cars or hurt local children.

When the Country Club of Woodridge went bankrupt, the town bought the property after the town attorney warned voters that if they did not take control of the site, affordable housing might result. Residents opposed an attempt to build senior citizen apartments on the site because it might open the door to apartment construction that wasn't age-restricted. The Woodbridge zoning commission then withdrew its proposal, citing community opposition as the reason.

Woodbridge is a liberal Democratic town. In a recent four-year period, residents made financial contributions to Democratic candidates and liberal political campaigns at nearly twenty times the rate of those to Republican candidates and conservative political campaigns. But the town's liberal leanings do not extend to support for creating housing that might expand the presence of African Americans.

Ned Lamont, Connecticut's Democratic governor, says that his state's suburbanites are "nuts . . . not to have more multifamily housing, not to have more affordable housing, not to allow more of their community to live where they work." Nonetheless, he supports leaving these decisions to local officials. Instead, he says, he will be "arguing to them loud and clear" about the importance of affordable housing. It is unlikely that loud and clear arguments will intimidate elected zoning commissioners who owe their positions to residents who seek to keep their neighborhoods white and rich.

Some residents feel differently, though, and can organize to open their communities. In 2022, a civil rights group sued Woodbridge, insisting that, in order to meet the state mandate for affordable housing, the town abolish single-family zoning and approve multifamily projects. When the zoning commission convened to consider the proposal, a group of about thirty people showed up to testify in favor of zoning reform. Outnumbered three to one by opponents, they, too, were typical taxpayers and voters—except for their greater commitment to racial justice. One was a math teacher at a local school; another the managing attorney at the Connecticut law firm that won a wrongful death settlement from the Remington gun company for the families of schoolchildren killed in the Sandy Hook massacre; another an epidemiology research manager at the Yale School of Public Health; another an organizer for a coalition of churches and synagogues in the greater New Haven area. Also testifying were a group of high school students and recent graduates who spoke of the harm experienced when they moved on to college and work with no preparation for collaborating with fellow students or colleagues who were not from affluent white suburban families. One complained that his advanced placement history course covered redlining and segregation as an abstract topic, but never related these to the contrast between his wealthy white Woodbridge and low-income black New Haven close by.

The epidemiology researcher, Alana Rosenberg, has taken informal leadership of the affordable housing advocates, calling them the "Welcoming Woodbridge" residents. They write letters to the local newspaper and are preparing a video to educate townspeople. The organizer of the regional faith-based coalition, Matt McDermott, says his organization was too involved in other campaigns to undertake a challenge to exclusive zoning, but he might consider it in the future. He thinks that some, though not all, church and synagogue leaders in Woodbridge might join the effort. He would begin with house meetings of supporters who would then recruit others. As they gained support, they might urge elected officials to change their stance on zoning reform and build toward challenges to zoning commission members who had caved to opponents of multifamily units and racial diversity.

Challenging Suburbanites' Racially Motivated Opposition to Affordable Housing

NIMBY obstruction is sometimes, but not always, undisguised in its racial motivations: opponents have sometimes warned that affordable housing will "bring the ghetto" to their communities. More often, though, opponents use language similar to those in Woodbridge that thinly veils their underlying prejudice.

It is true that diversifying elite white neighborhoods and allowing more density will bring change. There may be more students in the local public schools and an increase in traffic and demand for public services. However, NIMBY fears are often unfounded or exaggerated. New affordable-housing developments in higher-income neighborhoods usually have no effect on surrounding property values and neighbors may even be unaware of their presence. But if values do decline, racial justice advocates should be prepared to defend this as a necessary cost of desegregation.

Too often, opponents of affordable housing and desegregation dominate the debate, and even when they don't succeed in blocking development entirely, they delay and extend its timeline. A long public process debating project approval creates an uncertain landscape for developers. This discourages some from proposing any projects and makes those that they do propose more expensive. Planners and local officials should solicit community input into development proposals but should not allow residents' opposition to block or unreasonably delay their ability to expand housing opportunity. Local civil rights advocates should participate in these processes as consistently and vocally as NIMBYs.

Some States Require Local Zoning Reform

Allowing large, multifamily housing developments in affluent communities is not the only way to make them less exclusive. A more modest approach allows two, three, or four units per lot and can create communities that are affordable to low-, middle-, and upper-income households. Some jurisdictions have recently begun to make these changes.

Two states faced with housing shortages and affordability crises have used the authority that Connecticut won't to require municipalities to change their exclusionary zoning rules. A 2019 Oregon law requires all cities with populations of more than 10,000 to allow duplexes on any residential lot zoned for single-family use and cities with populations more than 25,000 to allow duplexes, triplexes, quadplexes, cottage clusters, and town houses on those same lots.

After years of defeat for zoning reform, in 2016 and 2017 California adopted requirements that city codes allow single-family homeowners to add small homes to their lots. Called accessory dwelling units, in-law units, or granny flats, they are usually backyard dwellings—studio or one-bedroom stand-alone structures, for example—or conversions of garages or basements to living spaces. Such units can add new residences without removing existing houses or altering the single-family aesthetic of a neighborhood. The legislature required cities to streamline the permitting process and modify building code rules that had made these structures hard to create. A marked increase in their number followed.

But homes of this size could not put a dent in the inability of working-, lower- and moderate-income families to find housing. In 2021, as its homeless population swelled and forced many opponents of zoning flexibility to reconsider, or at least temper, their obstruction, California took a bigger step, becoming the first state to prohibit single-family zoning altogether. It authorized homeowners to split single-family lots and build up to two units on each half, allowing four homes on properties that previously permitted only one. It is not yet clear whether the state will effectively enforce the requirement or significantly more housing units will result.

Massachusetts and New Jersey now require every community to provide housing for low-income families without regard to zoning ordinances that would otherwise block it. If these rules are not met, a jurisdiction's ability to block affordable-housing developments is diminished, which gives advocates and developers significant leverage. But many communities still resist, so although implementation of the policy has been steady, it's been slow. Neither state, however, imposes an obligation to provide housing for moderate-income families whom zoning provisions also effectively exclude.

Zoning Changes Alone Will Not Desegregate Exclusive Neighborhoods

In the early twentieth century, Minneapolis was somewhat integrated. This changed in 1909, when a white mob tried to drive a black household out of a white neighborhood. The family refused to budge; soon, restrictive deeds became the favored way to create racial boundaries. Then, in the 1970s the city zoned white areas exclusively for single-family homes. Today, Minneapolis is highly segregated, with large black-white disparities in education, employment, poverty rates, and homeownership.

In 2018, it adopted a plan for future development, including new zoning rules to reform discriminatory land-use policies. In 2022, environmentalists persuaded a judge to block the plan on the grounds that more density would cause greater pollution. The judge stayed his order, pending appeal.

The change allows duplexes and triplexes on any lot, making Minneapolis the first major city to pass such a reform. With 70 percent of its residential land previously restricted to single-family dwellings, the reform has the potential for a large impact on housing supply. If only 5 percent of its large single-family lots were redeveloped with triplexes, the city would gain six thousand housing units.

Proponents of the zoning change said it would increase housing supply, reduce costs and segregation, and combat climate change by shortening commute times. Opponents argued that developers would use the new rules to replace moderate-income residences with higher-end ones. Each side claimed support for affordable housing and inclusive neighborhoods and accused the other of "racism."

In the first two years of the new rules, the city added eighty-one units in duplexes and triplexes, hardly noticeable in a city with 180,000 households. But zoning changes take time to affect home building, so it's difficult to gauge the reform's long-term impact. It is likely that without additional measures, it will not achieve its racial justice objectives. As in many American cities today, working- and middle-class families in Minneapolis, both black and white, can't find affordable housing. Without an affirmative action plan, whites are likely to outbid African American home seekers for the new units, so the zoning change may do little to fulfill its proponents' promise to reduce segregation.

In Minneapolis, single-family lots are five thousand square feet. Zoning reform did not increase allowable height or building size, so new triplexes must squeeze into the same building area as a single-family home. It may not be profitable or feasible for developers to build small duplexes or triplexes in that space. The city has made modest, and less publicized, changes to its building rules that have been more effective at increasing housing production. Before the zoning change, Minneapolis dropped its parking requirements for multifamily units and allowed accessory dwelling units. These changes led to a doubling of housing permits issued, mostly for large apartment buildings.

Neighboring suburbs may offer more opportunities for zoning changes that increase housing production and reduce segregation, because they usually have more available residential land. For example, Maple Grove, a nearby Minneapolis suburb, requires at least ten-thousand-square-foot lots in its most dense residential zone and allows only single-family homes there. Like Woodbridge in Connecticut, Maple Grove might be a productive place for activists to pursue zoning reform that can lead to desegregation. What's required is a community-wide ban on single-family zoning, as Minneapolis implemented and the Woodbridge lawsuit attempts. Also required are proposals for specific projects that increase density, such as the redevelopment of Modesto's abandoned golf course or Woodbridge's bankrupt country club. But, without the work of racial justice activists, none of this will overcome residents' likely opposition.

This question remains: If cities and suburbs change zoning rules that they implemented to ensure racial segregation, will this change reverse that segregation? It should lead to increased housing supply, but so far there is no answer to this important question. The few places that have abolished exclusionary zoning have done so only recently. What's clear, however, is that without zoning reform, other actions to desegregate white areas will be less effective. An end to requirements for large-lot single-family neighborhoods is an essential, but not sufficient step to diminish residential segregation and increase housing affordability.

Inclusionary Zoning

Reforming a suburb's zoning to allow multifamily housing will not guarantee that new housing built is affordable to lower-income households. But combining this zoning reform with an inclusionary requirement will.

Like inclusionary zoning in gentrifying communities, set-aside rules in suburbs require new market-rate developments to include units for moderate- and low-income households. This can diversify exclusive communities and ensure that lower-cost units are deconcentrated and in the same neighborhoods and even in the same buildings as more expensive units. In designing these ordinances, jurisdictions must balance their policy goals around unit affordability with the cost of compliance to the developer. If the costs are too great, developers will stop building housing. If the affordability requirements are too lenient, the jurisdiction misses out on opportunities for low- and moderate-income households to live in higher-opportunity neighborhoods.

Inclusionary zoning reduces what developers can earn from selling or renting the set-aside units. However, if the requirements are well crafted to local market conditions, development will remain profitable and will continue. The community will gain affordable housing produced without public subsidy and integrated with market-rate units. If some public subsidy is needed, it's a cost we should expect high-property-value communities to assume for the redress of their segregation.

When suburbs establish the required sizes of set-aside units, activists should make certain that the needs of their metropolitan area's black households are addressed. If a market-rate development includes mostly studios and one-bedrooms, but the area lacks affordable housing for African American families, the zoning law should require appropriately sized affordable houses or apartments, or allow developers to build larger ones, but fewer of them. Or the community can permit single-family developments to comply by building affordable town homes to produce more units. Zoning reform discussions should include black leaders whose constituencies don't presently live in the suburb but who will be most affected by decisions about affordability, placement, sizes, and finishes.

A suburb may transfer the set-aside sale and rental properties to a land trust to ensure long-term affordability. If it doesn't already have one, a community may create such a trust for this purpose. Alternatively, the inclusionary zoning ordinance itself should restrict resale prices of for-sale homes, limiting the equity that sellers can gain. Any such effort has to balance wealth-building for low- and moderate-income households through homeownership with preservation of long-term access for future home buyers.

Bluffton, South Carolina, a mostly white, middle-class town of 27,000 located between Hilton Head and Savannah, requires new ownership and rental projects to set aside at least 20 percent of their units as affordable in exchange for a density bonus (an increase in the number of allowed dwellings) and reduced building fees. The ownership units must be affordable to households making up to $55,000, while rental units are for those making up to $37,000—moderate income in that area—and all must remain so for thirty years. The affordable and market-rate units must be mixed throughout the developments, be built at the same time, and have similar external appearance.

An inclusionary zoning ordinance should require that set-aside units be especially marketed to African Americans, or even reserved for black households, or it can establish a priority for residents of surrounding lower-income communities. The ordinance should also expect developers to accept Section 8 voucher holders as tenants and limit apartment managers' use of criminal history to determine tenant eligibility. The proposal of the Woodbridge advocates includes inclusionary zoning and a requirement that some of the set-aside rental units be reserved for Section 8 tenants.

Charlotte, North Carolina, promotes mixed-income housing by providing a density bonus to developments where half of the added units are affordable to lower-income households. Set-aside units cannot be more than 25 percent of the project, must be dispersed throughout, and have the same finishes as the market-rate homes. The inclusionary rule applies to areas with home values at or above the city's median, ensuring that it increases housing opportunities in higher-cost areas.

An inclusionary ordinance should require developers to collect information about the race and ethnicity of residents in the set-aside units. Local activists should monitor this to ensure that black households are being served. Inclusionary zoning can be useful for desegregating white, affluent neighborhoods, but only if it is designed with this goal in mind. Local racial justice activists should make certain that their community's inclusionary requirements serve this purpose.

The Low-Income Housing Tax Credit

The Low-Income Housing Tax Credit is the largest national housing subsidy for building rental housing. However, the country's homelessness crisis is so severe that, although the rules allow the program to provide apartments for working-class households, in practice it mostly serves the very poor. When developers and housing experts refer to "affordable housing," they usually mean tax-credit housing only for this most needy group.

Tax-credit apartments now house more than two million households. At that scale, the program has a large impact on where poor families live—and it often limits their choice to low-income, racially segregated areas. While tax-credit projects can be mixed-income, most are not. To maximize the available subsidy, most tax-credit projects contain only units for low-income households, which isolates residents and perpetuates racial segregation.

The U.S. Treasury Department gives the credits to states in proportion to their populations. Housing developers, often nonprofits, compete for them; state agencies establish point systems to determine the awards. The winners then sell their tax credits to investors and use the proceeds to cover project construction costs. The investors, frequently banks that hope to satisfy their Community Reinvestment Act requirements, become limited partners in the undertaking; they receive reduced taxes for ten years, provided the project remains affordable to low-income households for thirty years. Even with these restrictions, rents in these projects are still out of reach for many households, so residents often use Section 8 vouchers as well.

Federal guidelines require states to give tax-credit preferences to projects in high-poverty areas if they will contribute to overall community development by attracting jobs, better retail, and improved infrastructure. In practice, states routinely ignore this mandate and support projects that contribute instead to dense pockets of poverty. The federal government also instructs states to give added support to projects in high-cost areas. These developments tend to have tenants who are less poor and more often white than those located in low-income areas.

With a limited supply of tax credits, many states give extra points to projects that demonstrate local support. This almost guarantees that few will be built for families with children in middle-class white suburbs, because NIMBYs will aggressively oppose them. The allocation process gives a voice to residents who want to keep African Americans and Hispanics out and no voice to these groups who want to move in.

The government can take back investors' tax credits within the first fifteen years if their projects do not maintain the low rents they promised, but this is uncommon. Most often, at the end of that period, the nonprofit developers who initially won the tax credits buy out their for-profit partners for low prices and then maintain the units' affordability in perpetuity. By whatever means it is accomplished, the government specifies that the rules must remain in place for a second fifteen-year-period.

But sometimes, tax-credit investors (usually banks) evade this requirement. Especially in areas with rising rents, they end the rent restriction after the first fifteen years and then sell their interests to giant investment firms, who raise rents to maximize profits. The federal government can revise its program guidelines to prevent this. Until it does so, community groups can insist that their states guarantee nonprofit developers' rights to purchase tax-credit properties at year fifteen for a specified low price. If this is not made explicit, higher-cost and gentrifying communities may be at risk of losing their low-rent units.

State finance agencies must hold public hearings and update their point systems annually. Local activists can speak and comment on the final plans to press for promotion of choice and desegregation.

At these public events, advocates should attempt to ensure that their state's plan balances support for projects in middle-class high-opportunity areas with those in distressed and gentrifying communities. State plans should award points to developers who propose to build in low-income areas only if they will construct projects that do not contribute to segregation and poverty concentration and that include investments in community revitalization and infrastructure. Projects with family-sized units should get more points if they are located near well-resourced schools and public transportation. Most important, advocates should stress that state plans insist on mixed-income developments that combine tax credit with missing-middle and market-rate apartments.

Local activists should lobby their states to remove priorities for projects that demonstrate local support, so developments in high-income and suburban areas become more likely. Advocates should try to ensure a requirement that such projects have affirmative marketing plans to reach African American and Hispanic tenants who do not yet live in those areas.

Housing Choice Vouchers—Section 8

Improving conditions for low-income families requires investments in poorer segregated communities *and* providing them with opportunities to move to better resourced places if they desire. Desegregating white neighborhoods requires not only ensuring that middle- and upper-income African American households can have access but that low-income households can as well.

The federal government says that low-income households shouldn't pay more than 30 percent of their income on rent. In today's tight housing market, this is often impossible even for moderate-income families. The government program known as Section 8 subsidizes some renters with vouchers that cover the difference between that 30 percent income share and a maximum amount based on typical apartment rents in their region. If a household's income changes, so does its subsidy amount and rent share. This allows low-income families to weather income fluctuations while remaining housed and offers landlords a guarantee of consistent rental payments.

Families are eligible if they earn less than about 80 percent of their area's median, but the government requires local housing agencies to assign most vouchers to households with incomes far below that. More than two million families, almost half of whom are African American, receive vouchers but the program is underfunded and four times that many qualify but get nothing.

The voucher program is designed to give eligible families a choice of where to live. Most want well-maintained neighborhoods with low crime, well-resourced schools, open space and parks, and access to jobs and transportation. Children who live in such places have better educational results, better health, and, as adults, better incomes. Adults have less stress and depression than residents of more disadvantaged communities.

Yet only 5 percent of voucher households manage to move to high-opportunity areas, and African Americans are less likely to do so than whites. This is because of the often insurmountable obstacles faced by those hoping to make such a move. One is lack of information about healthier communities. Housing authorities are supposed to provide lists of willing landlords in wealthier areas, but the requirement is not enforced. Many recipients also do not have transportation to investigate these places. With few vouchers to award, some housing authorities in highly resourced areas give a priority to current residents, making it harder for eligible families elsewhere to relocate to those communities. Federal regulations ban this practice if it results in racial discrimination but the prohibition is difficult to enforce.

Voucher-Holding Families Face Discrimination

Many landlords, especially in middle-class neighborhoods, are unfamiliar with the program and those who know about it frequently refuse Section 8 renters. The federal government permits this discrimination, but local laws can ban it. Twenty states and more than one hundred localities have done so, covering about half of all voucher holders nationwide. Passing such laws and ensuring they are effective requires educating apartment owners and the public about Section 8, to counter stereotypes that voucher families are bad tenants and reduce the bias they face in the rental market.

Once adopted, monitoring and enforcement of nondiscrimination laws is essential. Victims should be able to recover damages. In Washington State, landlords who discriminate against voucher holders can be liable for more than four times the monthly rent, court costs, and attorney fees. The law is a rare exception to the usually toothless antidiscrimination ordinances elsewhere.

Families are usually given only sixty days to find a unit, after which they lose the voucher, which is then given to the next household on the waiting list. In places that outlaw Section 8 discrimination, recipients

Alecia Mackey (left) owns three single-family homes in Providence Village, a mostly white Dallas suburb. She can modestly profit from Section 8 rentals because vouchers have greater value when used in more expensive neighborhoods; she prefers such tenants because they take better care of properties and are less transient. Tashiana Jackson (right), a nursing assistant, sought the rental as a safer place to raise her two children. In 2022, the village's homeowners association ordered all Section 8 tenants evicted. HUD blocked the action while investigating its racial motivation.

are more likely to find an apartment within the time limit and avoid forfeiting their eligibility. Nondiscrimination rules can also result in more Section 8 families able to locate in more racially diverse neighborhoods with lower poverty rates. Fewer landlords in areas with nondiscrimination laws refuse to accept voucher tenants, although weak enforcement means that many still do.

Enforcement is especially difficult because of the sixty-day rule. Few rental applicants will file a complaint after being told that Section 8 tenants are not accepted. It is the rare complaint that is settled or adjudicated within that time limit, so filing one will do little good for the victim of the discrimination.

The Voucher Subsidy Limits Recipients to High-Poverty Neighborhoods

The Section 8 subsidy is designed to allow rentals at a price slightly below the median rent in a metropolitan area, called the *fair market rent*. Voucher holders are therefore unable to afford more than half their area's units, often those in higher-opportunity neighborhoods. The calculation also means that vouchers go further in less expensive, more disadvantaged, and more segregated communities, allowing rental of larger units in those areas. This option can outweigh preferences for higher-opportunity neighborhoods.

In 2007, a Dallas civil rights group sued the federal government, claiming that the payment standard denied black and Hispanic Section 8 households the ability to live in lower-poverty, predominantly white neighborhoods, concentrating them in segregated areas. Regional housing authorities then agreed to change their system to make vouchers worth more in higher-cost neighborhoods and less in low-cost ones. This allowed more voucher holders to live in areas with less crime and lower poverty rates. The settlement was a model for a federal rule that now requires 180 housing authorities in twenty-four metropolitan areas to use neighborhood-based rents, covering four hundred thousand households. Voucher holders in these communities are now more able to live in high-opportunity neighborhoods.

Other housing authorities (with a total of two million Section 8 families) are not required to use the new standard but can voluntarily adopt it. They mostly resist doing so because they worry it will increase the program's cost and alienate landlords in poorer areas by reducing their allowable rents. In fact, agencies' administrative expenses are modest, and the federal government covers them. When families move to wealthier areas, agencies must cover their increased voucher amounts for the first year; they then receive increased federal funding for subsequent years. Landlords in lower-income areas will see their incomes decrease, but this concern should not outweigh agencies' interest in helping families leave high-poverty neighborhoods.

Local activists should press agencies in their areas to adopt neighborhood-based payment systems so that families can afford to move throughout their region if they wish.

Make Section 8 a Tool for Desegregation

A few court orders have required local housing authorities to create mobility programs to address obstacles that voucher holders face in moving to higher-opportunity areas. Some agencies are now in a government-sponsored study to evaluate how to promote mobility. Others have joined with local fair housing centers, nonprofit groups, researchers, and philanthropies to offer a choice of better resourced neighborhoods.

Milwaukee, where only 5 percent of vouchers are used in low-poverty areas, has one such partnership. There, the nonprofit metropolitan fair housing council is collaborating with the area's three public housing authorities, which serve the region's city and suburbs. They are conducting an experiment in which Section 8 households can enroll. The program randomly assigns the volunteers to two groups. To support moving to high-opportunity areas, one group gets counseling, landlord recruitment, and short-term financial assistance, including up to $1,200 for security deposits or rental application fees. Counselors continue support after the move, to help participants, almost all African American, navigate life in white neighborhoods. The other group does not get these special services. Results are not yet in from Milwaukee or the new federal study, but previous investigations have shown great success for initiatives like Milwaukee's.

The first such analysis described a program in Chicago, where a 1966 lawsuit alleged that the Chicago Housing Authority violated the Constitution by building public housing only in poor, segregated areas. The Supreme Court endorsed an order that the agency give vouchers to seven thousand low-income black families who were randomly placed, half in predominantly black urban areas and half in the white suburbs. Ten years later, the suburban families had better employment, income, education, and health. Impressed with those results, the federal government then sponsored a similar five-city experiment. There were substantial improvements in income and education for children who made these moves before age thirteen. In 2019, another Section 8 mobility experiment in Seattle showed that counseling and help with landlord negotiations increased moves to high-opportunity neighborhoods. These studies all establish that housing mobility is a successful way to break the cycle of poverty by challenging racial segregation.

Still, families in the Milwaukee study face enormous obstacles as they attempt to take advantage of mobility choices. Almost three hundred families, nearly all headed by African American women, have enrolled in the program, but only twenty-six have successfully moved to a high-opportunity area. The reasons, it appears, are several:

- While participants are given more than the normal sixty days to secure units, they still struggle to find landlords in high-opportunity areas who will rent to them. Rather than giving notice on a current lease and risk ending up homeless, many opt to stay where they are and forgo their mobility option. This is even more frequent for voucher families across the country who want to move to better neighborhoods but do not get the experimental time-limit extension.
- The city of Milwaukee's housing authority has agreed to use the neighborhood-based subsidy adjustment in only a few select areas. Participants in the mobility experiment can get extra assistance for security deposits or rental application fees. But with most voucher amounts based on metropolitan-wide median rents, families still can't find apartments they can afford in most higher-cost communities, especially in the suburbs. If the small area payment standard had been adopted throughout the metropolitan area, more than thirty thousand voucher-affordable units could be available in the region's high-opportunity neighborhoods, certainly enough to house the area's four thousand voucher families with children, even if all chose a mobility option.
- Milwaukee County has a Section 8 antidiscrimination ordi-

nance, while neighboring Waukesha County does not. The law seems to make little difference, though. It's been difficult to recruit landlords to participate in high-opportunity areas of both counties.

Make Section 8 a Tool for Wealth Building

Section 8 can also be used for home purchases. Participants must complete ownership counseling and a program to help them save toward a down payment. As in rentals, voucher holders contribute a share of their income, and Section 8 covers remaining expenses, including mortgage principal and interest, taxes, insurance, and sometimes an allowance for utility and maintenance expenses, up to the maximum voucher amount. By adjusting to any changes in the homeowner's income, the voucher can provide a safety net that other homeowners do not have. Participants build wealth, gain stability, and no longer face discrimination from landlords.

In metropolitan areas where home prices are moderate, home purchase vouchers can work. Housing authorities that offer higher voucher amounts for rentals in higher-cost areas must give similar increases to support home buying. This can help low-income families permanently move out of low-income neighborhoods. Community groups should educate voucher holders about this option and work with lenders to offer them favorable mortgages and down payment assistance.

Yet few housing agencies permit vouchers for homeownership. As with the option to adjust vouchers for typical rents by neighborhood, officials are reluctant to take part in this program because doing so reduces how many rental vouchers they can issue, and their waiting lists are long.

Section 8 Remedies Should Not Be Left to Government Alone

The federal government should make mobility programs easier to adopt, but even without nationwide changes, localities can implement such initiatives. Some states have offered incentives that help ease landlords' worries and make Section 8 rentals more appealing. Oregon compensates landlords for property damage or unpaid rent of up to $5,000 from voucher-holding tenants. As it turns out, compensation payments have rarely been made, demonstrating that the characterization of voucher families as irresponsible is unfounded. Illinois and Virginia offer tax credits to landlords in low poverty areas that rent to voucher holders.

A private real estate company based in Dallas purchases single-family homes in high-opportunity neighborhoods to lease to voucher holders. The firm operates only in areas that use higher rent standards for more expensive communities, ensuring that it can charge enough for the units to make a small profit. It offers its tenants transportation, financial literacy, and job training.

White suburban racial justice supporters should work with landlords, foundations, and private firms to create mobility opportunities and fund support services in their communities. They should ensure that Section 8 apartment listings include units in high-opportunity areas. Activists should press for adequately enforced antidiscrimination ordinances where they don't now exist, for neighborhood-based rent standards so that voucher holders can afford to move to places that lack concentrated poverty, and for allowing a homeownership option if voucher holders wish to pursue it.

Since 1979, Fred Freiberg has trained fair housing centers to undertake paired testing programs that can uncover landlord and realtor discrimination. He has coordinated more than 12,000 tests in over 20 states, personally used hidden recorders as a tester in 1,500 investigations, and been a witness in 500 cases.

Chapter 11

Hold Them Accountable!

*Bankers, Developers, Builders, and Realtors Created
Segregation and Should Contribute to Remedies*

Francis Newlands was born in Mississippi in 1846 and settled in Nevada as an adult. At the age of thirty-three, he inherited a family fortune. Elected to the Senate, he served until his death in 1917. The other Nevada senator, William Stewart, also had family wealth; he joined Newlands in a real estate scheme, building a streetcar line to the northern border of Washington, D.C., and then organizing the Chevy Chase Land Company to build a whites-only subdivision there. Some houses were for the affluent, but others were more modest. Washington's growing black middle class (federal civil servants, for example) could have afforded to live in the suburb but were banned.

The company sold some acreage to another white developer who was a front for four African American businessmen who knew that the company would never sell to them. In 1906, they laid out a subdivision and planned to sell lots to both blacks and whites and succeeded in doing so—black professionals purchased twenty-eight of the lots. But when Senator Newlands discovered this, he claimed the original purchaser had committed fraud by selling to Negroes and sued. The Chevy Chase Land Company foreclosed on the land and rescinded the sales.

Lots that the land company sold through the mid-twentieth century have racial deed restrictions. In 1942, the company sold a lot to the Christian Science Society for a church that stands there today. The society's deed demands that if it ever built housing on its property, it would exclude African Americans.

Senator Newlands's racial views were extreme but still acceptable in the Democratic Party. He tried to deny African Americans the vote, writing in 1909 that it was "perhaps, mistakenly granted to them" because they were a "a race of children" and a "danger . . . to our institutions and our civilization." He proposed a plank in the 1912 Democratic platform calling for repeal of the Fifteenth Amendment, which, he wrote, committed "the folly of investing an inferior race with which amalgamation is undesirable with the right of suffrage." The convention rejected his plan only because delegates thought it superfluous, since Southern states already terrorized African Americans who attempted to vote. The Democratic Party's candidate, Woodrow Wilson, was elected president. When he nominated Louis Brandeis, a Jew, to the Supreme Court, Republican senators' antisemitic opposition was fierce; Newlands was the only Democrat to join them and vote against confirmation.

The Chevy Chase Land Company continues as a regional housing developer. It contributes to charitable causes—a bike share program, scholarships for students, a social service agency, historical societies, Special Olympics, and a nonprofit affordable-housing development firm, none of whose affordable housing is in Chevy Chase. Today African Americans are only 6 percent of Chevy Chase, in a metropolitan area where they constitute 25 percent of the population. Median household income is nearly $200,000, and typical property values are about $1 million. The Washington area's large black middle class should be better represented, but even middle-class families can't afford homes costing $1 million, without substantial wealth bequeathed by parents who accumulated it when housing policies denied blacks that opportunity.

Should the Chevy Chase Land Company use its charitable funds to subsidize African Americans to desegregate Chevy Chase? Should the Christian Science Society raise funds to do the same? Should activists in Chevy Chase and Washington organize to persuade them to do so?

Black Lives Matter demonstrations in 2020 inspired some residents to campaign for renaming a Chevy Chase fountain that honored Francis Newlands. Prominent Democratic senators and representatives joined in and passed a congressional resolution supporting the move. The company reacted with a statement that its founder's "views on race contradict the ideals of our company fabric [and] should the community vote to rename the fountain, we wholeheartedly support their decision."

But changing a fountain's name does not create opportunities for African Americans to live in neighborhoods from which they were excluded when they were affordable. Politicians should instead lead an effort to reform Chevy Chase's zoning rules, which prohibit construction of housing that is accessible to middle-class black households. To remind the community of its obligation, perhaps the fountain should be renamed after one of those twenty-eight black families who were evicted from Chevy Chase years ago.

Many Chevy Chase homeowners displayed Black Lives Matter window and lawn signs. A campaign to desegregate Chevy Chase so its racial composition more closely reflects that of its broader community could make this concern more real.

Companies That Created Segregation Now Do Little to Reverse It

In many other white suburbs, local researchers can identify developers, banks, and realtors that excluded African Americans when homes were affordable. These firms continue in business, perhaps no longer in their earlier form as they were absorbed by successor firms that assumed their assets and liabilities. These also include moral liabilities that carry an obligation to remedy.

Many black Americans flocked to the San Francisco Bay Area for war production jobs during World War II. There, David Bohannon was the biggest mid-twentieth-century developer of whites-only housing. One project was Hillsdale, a neighborhood south of San Francisco that was affordable in the 1940s to white and black working- and middle-class families. The American Trust Company financed some of the projects; it insisted on deed clauses stating that "[no] persons other than members of the Caucasian or White race shall be permitted to occupy any portion of said property, other than as domestics in the employ of the occupants of the premises." A real estate firm, Fox & Carskadon, marketed Hillsdale homes with newspaper ads boasting of the restriction.

In 1960, the mega-bank Wells Fargo absorbed American Trust. In

1995, the mega-realtor Coldwell Banker acquired Fox & Carskadon. The Bohannon company continues, owning the Hillsdale Mall, which remains profitable unlike many shopping centers in the 2020s. Hillsdale remains all-white to this day, and the firms that created its segregation have done little to challenge that.

Coldwell Banker's website celebrates the company's "more than 100 years of excellence" and boasts of its early adherence to a National Association of Realtors' Code of Ethics. In 1924, the code added a warning that "a realtor should never be instrumental in introducing into a neighborhood . . . members of any race or nationality, or any individuals whose presence will clearly be detrimental to property values in that neighborhood." The requirement was in force when Fox & Carskadon handled Hillsdale sales for Bohannon.

The Bohannon company has claimed that one of its hallmarks is "our commitment to community. We look for opportunities to serve organizations and help causes that benefit the communities where we develop properties."

Wells Fargo has a foundation that says it's "committed to addressing the full spectrum of housing issues . . . ranging from homelessness to rental housing to homeownership—all with a goal of unlocking more housing options for those in need." One program provides down payment assistance to low- and moderate-income home buyers. In the San Francisco region, it has provided up to $25,000 apiece to families whose incomes are at or below the area median. Even when households could add their savings, in a region where median home prices exceed $1 million, down payments like that permit home purchases only in a few low-income neighborhoods that have not yet gentrified. No grants have been made for purchases in cities like San Mateo, where Hillsdale is located, and it is unlikely that such a program could ever be adequate to give black families access to neighborhoods that Wells Fargo's American Trust Company created as white-only. Facing up to this is what "addressing the full spectrum of housing issues" requires.

In suburban Chicago, a curious resident found a racial restriction for her childhood home in the affluent Deere Park neighborhood. She shared it with a leader of the Montgomery Travelers, who sent it to us. The deed revealed that the real estate firm Baird & Warner created the segregated subdivision in 1927. The racial exclusion clause was written by the Chicago Title and Trust Company, the same firm that shielded contract sellers from public scrutiny in the 1960s.

Baird & Warner continued to enforce segregation in Chicago suburbs for much longer. In 1992 it settled an antidiscrimination lawsuit filed by the city of Evanston with a payment of $450,000 ($938,000). The city filed its complaint after paired testers for a local fair housing center found that the company's agents steered white and black home seekers only to same-race neighborhoods. Settlement funds were divided between the city and the fair housing center to support its ongoing testing program.

Baird & Warner and the title company remain active in the Chicago area. They should do more to redress the segregation they created.

Student Questions Inspired a Teacher to Examine Rochester's Racial History

In suburban Rochester, New York, Shane Wiegand taught fourth grade in the early 2000s. As he recalls, "I was challenged by a student who wanted to know if there was a civil rights struggle here. I was embarrassed that I had no answer. My colleagues didn't know either. If I was going to answer my students' questions, I had to begin researching it myself."

He created an elementary school curriculum to explain why his students' community was so white in a diverse metropolitan area and how discrimination by government, banks, and realtors bear responsibility for the poverty of the city's black neighborhoods. Mr. Wiegand also developed a lecture that he delivered throughout the region, and he recruited university researchers to detail Rochester's segregation history.

Mr. Wiegand's work inspired Kesha James, an eighth-grade teacher, to join his efforts. A third-generation African American Rochester resident, she was an experienced trainer of other faculty but had never before considered why her family seemed stuck in a lower-income black neighborhood. Together, Mr. Wiegand and Ms. James delivered public lectures and developed units for middle and high school classes. These were added to the school district's curricula.

One neighborhood they profiled was Meadowbrook, which consists of nearly four hundred homes that the Eastman Kodak Company built for its white employees in the 1920s and '30s. Each property's deed stated that "[n]o lot or dwelling shall be sold or occupied by a colored person." The restriction was superfluous. Kodak, the city's largest employer, had a workforce of sixteen thousand in the late 1930s, only one of whom was African American—a porter.

To finance employee mortgages, Kodak created the Eastman Savings and Loan Association, now called the ESL Federal Credit Union, which today has a striking charitable presence, with $26 million in grants in 2021. It supports scholarships, job training, parent education, afterschool and summer programs, and other good causes, including promotion of Shane Wiegand's curriculum in schools throughout Rochester and its suburbs.

With the authority financial institutions have to offer race-based assistance to disadvantaged groups, the credit union provides black and Hispanic home buyers a ten-to-one matched savings program in which they can receive up to $10,500 toward a down payment. The effort launched in late 2021, and in its first fifteen months enrolled 138 participants, 96 of whom had graduated, all with the maximum grant. Of the first nineteen households to find and buy houses, thirteen were African American and six were Hispanic.

The grants are intended to enable recipients to purchase properties not only in Rochester but also in its white suburbs, and some have been able to do so. This is encouraging, but the program is still in its infancy. If recipients can continue to access all neighborhoods, not only segregated ones, the initiative will create housing opportunities for African Americans in Meadowbrook and other communities Kodak helped to segregate. If they face serious restrictions in their choice of neighborhoods, the ESL program will have less success in breaking down the segregation that its Kodak parent promoted.

Kodak was not the only institution that segregated Rochester. The Wiegand research team learned how the county legislature sold unused lots to a developer in 1939 on condition that the lots "be occupied by persons of the Caucasian race only." The local government also gave white property owners the right to sue anyone who sold to an African American, a right that was enforceable until 1953.

Developers and realtors collaborated. In 1940, Frank Drumm and

Norman Huyck created the Brooklea Heights subdivision—250 homes with deeds stating that "[n]o lot shall ever be occupied by a colored person," except, of course, domestic servants. These were less expensive than Meadowbrook houses and would have been easily affordable to many working- or lower-middle-class black families. Drumm had served as president of the local realtors association and Huyck as president of the local builders association. We can assume they were selected to lead their associations because their practices reflected those of their industries generally. Those practices made Rochester the segregated metropolitan region we know today.

The Rochester realtors association donates to several organizations that support housing affordability, but none to groups that are tackling the racial exclusivity of places like Brooklea Heights and similar suburban neighborhoods. The builders association makes no boasts of good citizenship, although some of its member firms do. But like the realtors, none makes the serious investments needed to undo Rochester's segregation.

Crowdsourcing a City's History

Jordy Yager grew up in Charlottesville, Virginia, not terribly aware of the black side of town. He went to college in the north, getting a graduate journalism degree from Boston University, and then worked as a reporter in Washington, D.C. In 2013 at the age of thirty-two, he returned to his hometown to do freelance reporting for public radio stations and an online newspaper, supporting himself with odd construction jobs.

In 2017 the city created a commission to examine excessive police interaction with black youth. Mr. Yager was concerned that nobody was reporting on its findings, so he spent eighteen months independently interviewing African Americans who'd had interactions with the police; they told him stories that the official commission barely uncovered. Many were afraid to talk for fear of being fired from a job or other retaliation, but a few mentioned that their homes, in previously white neighborhoods, had deeds prohibiting occupancy by nonwhites. A Charlottesville weekly newspaper published his report and Mr. Yager, intrigued, went on to spend lunch hours at courthouses looking at deeds. He concluded that black residents had been banned from most white neighborhoods of Charlottesville.

Charlottesville, Virginia. Jordy Yager researched how realtors, contractors, and government segregated the city; he then gave public tours to educate fellow citizens. In front of a downtown mall, he recounted how African Americans once lived in this very place but were removed.

That August, a self-styled Nazi murdered a young white woman by driving his car into a crowd of demonstrators. They had gathered to counter white supremacists who opposed removal of a statue honoring the Confederate general Robert E. Lee. A year later, a local foundation announced grants to forty-two applicants who could help to "heal Charlottesville." One went to the African American Heritage Center for support of Jordy Yager's investigation.

Sympathetic city officials turned over their entire collections of three hundred thousand deeds, executed from 1903 to 1968, freeing Mr. Yager from having to request and pay for them one by one. Even so, identifying racial exclusion clauses was impossible for a single researcher with a modest foundation grant. He digitized the collection and developed word recognition software to spot key words like "Caucasian" and "negro" and then set up a crowdsourcing website; anyone seeking to help could go online and get a deed to evaluate. He gave talks to recruit volunteers at churches, nonprofit organizations, and afterschool programs. Eleventh-graders at Charlottesville High School were studying Lorraine Hansberry's play *A Raisin in the Sun*, which revolves around a racial deed in Chicago. Mr. Yager invited students to participate in the project and connect the drama they studied with the history of their own community.

Volunteers filed forms for the deeds they examined, describing racial language, if any, and identifying the builders who imposed racial restrictions, banks that financed them, and realtors who marketed them. Five volunteers had to agree on a property's racial exclusion before Mr. Yager deemed it established.

Some examples of what he found:

- The Roy Wheeler Realty Company, founded in 1927, marketed many homes for whites only. In 2020, it merged with one of the nation's largest independent real estate agencies, Howard Hanna, and continues to do business in Charlottesville.
- The People's National Bank of Charlottesville financed many home mortgages on whites-only properties. It's now part of Virginia National Bank.
- The R. E. Lee and Son construction company executed racial deeds for houses it built in many neighborhoods. Successive generations of this family business had leaders named "Robert E. Lee" (each with a different middle name beginning with "E"). In 2020, the firm ceased honoring its alleged ancestry and became the Lee Building Company; it continues to operate in Charlottesville.

A 1946 subdivision that R. E. Lee and Son built has a deed disclosing that a federal program for returning World War II veterans provided financing. Selling for $7,500 ($113,000), the properties were affordable to middle-class families. A white veteran who attended law school at the University of Virginia, supported by the G.I. Bill, bought one of the houses. The wealth his family accumulated by owning the house became an intergenerational benefit, as his son became a lawyer and his daughter a Ph.D. research psychologist.

States administered veterans' benefits; Virginia did not permit African Americans to use the G.I. Bill to attend law school. Instead, they could use it, if at all, for trade schools. Black veterans could not purchase homes in the Lee company's subdivision, both because of the deed exclusion and the denial of benefits to support families while continuing their educations. Today, the homes sell for about $370,000, about five times median family income, unaffordable even to young white middle-class families without substantial parental gifts for down payments.

Firms like Howard Hanna Real Estate, the Virginia National Bank, and the Lee Building Company could take responsibility for remedying the segregation of Charlottesville that they or their predecessor companies imposed. They could create funds substantial enough to subsidize middle-class black families to purchase homes from which these firms, or their antecedents, excluded African Americans.

During Black History Month of 2021, the Howard Hanna firm posted a remarkable acknowledgment that is rare in the real estate industry today:

> [I]t is clear to us that the practices implemented in real estate in the last 53 years [since the passage of the Fair Housing Act] have not worked, meaning they have not addressed every barricade created throughout the history of our industry. It is our goal to continue to reflect on what has not worked. And ultimately, through reflection and dialogue, we hope to create new efforts and policies that do make a difference.

Yet reflection and dialogue have not yet produced efforts and policies that reverse the segregation in which the industry participated. Howard Hanna's philanthropy consists of fund-raising to provide medical care for children without insurance, collecting coats to distribute to children in Ohio (a state where it does business), and college scholarships for children of employees to attend the University of Pittsburgh or John Carroll University, colleges that Hanna family members attended.

Virginia National Bank states its embrace of diversity, equity, and inclusion and a commitment to charitable organizations (it supports the United Way) but says nothing about how it might expand its commitment to remedy the inequality of its city.

The Lee Building Company's website announces a "commitment to excellence," and its motto is "Pioneering, Honorable, Professional." Being "honorable" should include contributing to the reversal of harm that Charlottesville's segregation caused its black citizens. But it does not.

In 2020, Jordy Yager asked his Twitter followers if they thought responsible companies in Charlottesville should establish remedial funds: sixty-nine people answered yes. Mr. Yager is a journalist, not a community organizer, and no one has yet come forward to take advan-

HOUSES SALE—SUBURBAN (35)

TOWSON
CHESTNUT HILL
WEST OF CHARLES ST.
ALLEGHANY AVE.

In this restricted development, just 3 yrs. old and where over 100 lots have been sold, we are now offering a complete service of home construction as follows: We can sell you a lot as low as $1,650 (average $2,000), render architectural service, give a contract price on your house through reputable builders, who can show houses under construction and completed, occupied homes, assist in financing, and in other words "take the headache out of building."

All lots are on wide paved streets, have sewer, water & gas.

See for yourself by coming out to "Chestnut Hill" how this development is shaping up through originality of design into the most desirable place in the Towson area to live.

Appointments made any time day or evening.

TOWSON

New One-Story Ranch Type. Located in the Restricted Development of "Chestnut Hill." This house is startlingly different with its long, low-lying L-shaped appearance. There are 6 very good-sized rooms, all on the first floor, 2 baths, ultra modern kitchen, large plate glass windows, tremendous flagstone recreation terrace; garage.

This is truly a "magazine" house and is outstanding in value, livability and charm.

Open Today, 3.30 to 6.30 P.M.

Location: 2 squares W. of Charles St., 1 square S. of W. Joppa Road on Trafalgar road.

Before the internet, buyers learned of homes for sale from the "classified" section of newspapers. The July 31, 1949, edition of The Baltimore Sun included this advertisement for lots in a "restricted development." Race restrictions were spelled out in the subdivision deed. The newspaper has never acknowledged its direct role in segregating Baltimore, or taken steps to make amends.

tage of that interest and create campaigns to make such compensation happen.

Help Wanted, Houses for Sale—but Whites Only

In 2022, *The Baltimore Sun* apologized for its nearly two centuries of promotion of black racial subjugation, beginning with its publication in 1837 of a reward for the capture of a fugitive slave, and continuing

through coverage well into present times that consistently characterized African Americans as less than human and having a criminal bent.
But what its apology neglected to mention was the direct role that the
newspaper itself played in the impoverishment of its city's black population and in the segregation of its neighborhoods.

Before the internet, newspapers' profitability depended on classified advertisements, usually just a few lines that described a job opening ("help wanted"), a home for sale, or an apartment for rent. Also
lucrative for the papers were larger display ads of real estate agencies.

In Baltimore, the *Sun* routinely published whites-only employment
and real estate ads throughout much of the twentieth century, so it
bears complicity in black unemployment, underemployment, and residential segregation in that city. Numerous other newspapers employed
the same language in their ads.

As newspapers grapple with their pasts, enterprising reporters can
conduct investigations of these ads. They would disclose firms that
excluded African Americans from employment, as well as realtors
whose race-specific advertisements helped create the inequality their
communities know today. Civil rights groups can use the information
to pressure these companies to contribute to remedies.

We Shouldn't Allow Firms to Be Satisfied with Diversifying Their Staffs

After police killings of Michael Brown (Ferguson, Missouri, 2014) and
George Floyd (Minneapolis, 2020) many corporate leaders awoke to
racial injustice and to their own firms' culpability. Banks, realty firms,
insurance companies, and housing developers have hired officials
(usually African Americans) whom executives charged with responsibility for the corporations' DEI—diversity, equity, and inclusion.

These managers organize employee educational seminars (attendance frequently voluntary), urge recruitment and promotion of
African Americans or other "people of color," and press for change in
ongoing corporate practices that unintentionally discriminate. Sometimes (but rarely) they persuade their companies to finance small programs to enhance equality, like provision of down payment assistance
to first-time home buyers.

Efforts like these do little to compensate for segregation and inequality that the firms themselves helped create. Cleaning up behavior going forward can, at best, prevent segregation from deepening further, but past practices were racially explicit and generated huge profits. No corporations have acknowledged the need for equally explicit action of comparable size to remedy harms for which they bear responsibility.

Certainly, government at all levels has a duty to lead. If public agencies had not violated their sworn constitutional obligations by enforcing segregation, the private sector could not have implemented it independently. Still, corporate America was a powerful pressure group that demanded discriminatory public policy. It should not now sit back and wait for government to lead.

Corporate culprits existed in almost every city, although in some it will be hard to identify successors. But the segregation of our metropolitan areas resulted from actions of the entire real estate, banking, and development industries. All contributed, and all should participate in remedies.

Realtors Claimed a Constitutional Right to Discriminate

The real estate industry mostly caused today's neighborhood segregation and the racial inequality that ensues. In the twentieth century, realtors openly collaborated with and usually *led* banks, developers, and public officials to create whites-only suburbs, which gained in value, while denying similar opportunity to blacks. Government was ultimately responsible; it failed to reject the realtors' stance. Agency administrators were recruited from the real estate profession. Bringing their bigoted attitudes with them, they developed and carried out policies to require segregation of white subdivisions and to deny support for housing in black neighborhoods.

In 1924, the national realtors association adopted a code of ethics that required the imposition of segregation. In 1950, it amended its code to prohibit sales that would reduce property values, language that the industry understood to continue exclusion of African Americans from most homeownership.

This veiled language was probably adopted because of the 1948 Supreme Court ruling that forbade enforcement of racially exclusive deeds. The Los Angeles Realty Board then launched a national campaign for a constitutional amendment to authorize race discrimination. In support, the California Real Estate Association explained that the amendment was necessary because "prices of homes in [white] areas are well within the purchasing power of vast numbers of Negroes." This "greatly aggravates the hazard to which [white] homeowners are exposed [and] the insistence of some Negroes" to move to affordable neighborhoods will "do much harm to our national social structure." Many whites today think that few African Americans live in middle-class, mostly white, suburbs because they have lower incomes, which limit their choices. This industry explanation gives the lie to this commonplace belief.

Every state government requires realtors to be licensed. State agencies were complicit in the industry's discriminatory practices, in some cases even lifting licenses of agents who didn't enforce segregation. Into the 1960s, local real estate boards expelled members for selling homes in white neighborhoods to black families.

In 1962, the National Association of Realtors promoted President Kennedy's refusal to support a ban on private-sector racial discrimination in housing. The prohibition in his executive order applied only to government agencies. A year later, the association published a "Property Owners' Bill of Rights" that asserted a homeowner's freedom from any government requirement to be nondiscriminatory. This was a long held position. Claiming that the right to practice racial discrimination was protected by the Constitution, the association ran expensive but successful advertising campaigns to defeat state and local nondiscrimination proposals in the 1950s and '60s. The most prominent was a 1964 California campaign that repealed a state anti-discrimination law.

The industry's powerful lobbyists also tried to prevent passage of the national Fair Housing Act in 1968 and almost prevailed. They successfully won an exemption for homes "sold by owner." Many real estate agents then fictionalized sales as private transactions to mask refusals to black households. In response to the act becoming law, the association's president told members that "the first civil right" was freedom from crime, which would presumably rise if a neighborhood became racially diverse.

Were it not for realtors, their agents, and their associations, we would not today have the segregated neighborhoods that maintain so much of our racial inequality.

The real estate industry has much to make up for.

Speed It Up! Reform of the Real Estate Industry Proceeds Too Slowly

After a spring and summer of Black Lives Matter demonstrations in 2020, National Association of Realtors president Charles Oppler apologized: "What Realtors did was an outrage to our morals and our ideals. . . . It was a betrayal of our commitment to fairness and equality. . . . [O]n behalf of our industry, we can say that what Realtors did was shameful, and we are sorry."

The association then developed additional training materials on nondiscrimination and intensified efforts to diversify its ranks. National chains like Coldwell Banker and Keller-Williams, as well as many local associations, hired DEI officers to promote fair treatment of nonwhite realtors and sometimes to create programs that introduce more black households to homeownership.

Sincere though these steps may be, they do little to redress segregation for which the industry is responsible. The new efforts aim to prevent future discrimination but evade the industry's obligation to confront its past. Fairness in future sales will not open all-white neighborhoods that the industry closed. In his apology, Mr. Oppler added, "We can't go back to fix the mistakes of the past." This is untrue.

In response to the apology, the president of the black realtors' organization, formed when the national association barred black members, called on Mr. Oppler's group to go beyond internal diversity and pay "reparations." The African American leader didn't specify what he had in mind, but it might include funds to subsidize blacks to purchase homes in neighborhoods that realtors had previously closed to them. Real estate profits are substantial and can support such a program.

In 2021, the real estate industry handled about six million home sales, at an average price of about $325,000. That's roughly $2 trillion worth of houses. The usual realtor commission is 6 percent, with half usually going to the buyer's agent and half to the seller's. If the industry made a commitment to devote one-sixth of that commission to help "fix the mistakes of the past," it could create an annual fund of $20 billion to support black homeownership. Considering the industry's history, this seems like a small and reasonable step; it would make a difference. If the industry as a whole is unwilling to adopt such a program, local associations or firms can do so, and community groups should urge them to consider it.

Many law firms routinely assign attorneys to do pro bono legal work for nonprofit organizations or individuals in need. Shouldn't real estate agencies adopt a similar policy and handle home purchases by African Americans without a commission?

Modern-Day Redlining: Realtors' Racial Steering Remains Commonplace

Even prevention of future discrimination is still a work in progress for real estate professionals.

In 2019, reporters for *Newsday* on Long Island, New York, concluded that almost half the agents in their region engaged in racial steering—showing homes to white buyers only in white neighborhoods and to black buyers only in black ones. Or they engaged in more subtle steering, like telling a home buyer that he or she "wouldn't be happy" in an other-race neighborhood or that the home buyer would find only a same-race neighborhood to be a "very friendly place."

The newspaper hired blacks and whites to pose as home seekers. It recruited testers at churches and on social media, including a website where New York City's ready supply of unemployed actors and actresses looked for work. *Newsday* trained testers to ensure that they behaved similarly when they met with realtors; reporters gave documents to the recruits that described identical financial backgrounds, income, wealth, and employment histories. An editor even purchased identical purses for female testers. They wore buttonhole cameras and filmed interactions with realtors; when *Newsday* published its report, it included videos of agent behavior that illustrated the industry's unlawful practices.

One recorded agent refused to show homes to a black tester without mortgage preapproval but pressed a white tester to look at homes without it. *Newsday* identified by name the agent and the brokerage for which she worked. Another promoted a neighborhood to a black tester because residents were "the nicest people," while warning the white tester about gang activity in the same area. Another steered a white tester away from a neighborhood where African Americans lived, saying "Follow the school bus, see the moms that are hanging out on the corners." Agents told black testers there were no listings in their price range while giving listings to white testers with identical incomes. Realtors told white testers that homes in an area had poor resale values, while encouraging black testers to consider the same neighborhood. Overall, agents gave whites 50 percent more listings than blacks.

In fully half the tests, agents treated black buyers differently from whites; Hispanics experienced discrimination 40 percent of the time, and Asians, 20 percent. When the *Newsday* investigation ended, its director introduced the testers to one another. Only when the non-white testers learned how many more homes were shown to their counterparts did they realize they'd been victimized. This duplicates the experience of actual home buyers, who have no way to compare how others were treated.

Every ten years, the federal government sponsors similar matched-pair testing nationwide. Its reports garner little notice, because they only produce statistics that show ongoing discrimination without identifying realtors who offended, so enforcement, including discipline of violators, doesn't follow.

The last one, conducted in 2012, found that African Americans experienced discrimination about one-third of the time. It noted that this "probably understate[s]" violations, partly because government testers present themselves as fully qualified for homes they seek to purchase. In the actual transactions, agents motivated by the prospect of commissions go out of their way to help white home seekers improve their paper qualifications but do so less frequently for African Americans. The government surveys only tested initial contacts between purported house hunters and agents or landlords, but discrimination frequently occurs later in the process—for example, when a realtor drives a client around some neighborhoods but not others.

The best way to end such behavior is to discipline agents who discriminate. Sanctions can escalate from warnings to suspensions to state and municipal license revocation. States and cities should assess fines from brokers who hire and supervise agents that practice discrimination, as well as from agents themselves. A few dramatic and well-publicized cases would give real estate professionals incentives to behave lawfully. At present, state licensing agencies are mostly unconcerned with discrimination and tend to discipline brokers primarily if they mishandle clients' escrow funds. That is too narrow a definition of agencies' mission.

There is no reason to believe that Long Island realtors are dramatically worse than those elsewhere. The industry reacted with embarrassment to the *Newsday* report; its leaders acknowledged that to overcome its past, it faces enormous challenges. It needs help to do so.

Paired Testing Can Identify Real Estate Agents Who Discriminate

The federal Department of Justice should ensure compliance with the Fair Housing Act. Its Civil Rights Division has an enforcement program that can conduct paired testing. The department does almost nothing with this authority. Considering how commonplace discrimination remains, this failure is shameful.

The real estate industry once fought to prevent testing. In 1975, Wisconsin realtors successfully lobbied for a state law that prohibited it. A federal court ruled the ban unlawful and authorized civil rights groups to use the practice to identify discrimination. Other real estate associations sought similar prohibitions but backed off after Department of Justice warnings.

Fair housing centers like those in Louisiana and central Indiana exist in many cities. They are left with the primary responsibility for investigating housing discrimination. The government provides such minimal financial support that centers can rarely conduct random testing to expose discrimination; they usually limit themselves to investigating client suspicions. This leaves victims, who rarely know they were treated differently, with almost the entire responsibility for enforcing our fair housing law.

Random paired testing is expensive—paired tests of eighty-four agents cost *Newsday* nearly $200,000. Recruitment of testers is challenging—New York's large pool of unemployed actors and actresses is unusual—and once they've testified to support a complaint, they become known to the industry and lose their effectiveness.

Centers can file lawsuits or complaints with government agencies when they conclude that a client's claim of unlawful practices is valid. Sometimes, however, government attorneys consider that their ethical duty is only to the complaining home seeker, not the public interest. They may settle with an offending realtor or landlord to get the client into a home and forgo seeking substantial fines, other discipline, or admission of guilt by threatening a lawsuit or filing one.

Fair housing centers can avoid this narrow outcome by filing complaints or lawsuits that are separate from those of their clients. But litigation is more expensive than administrative complaints and requires greater sophistication, so with limited funds most fair housing centers shy away from it. When they do go to court, they can win judgments or settlements that take account of the public interest, such as banning the violator from further work in the industry, payments to help finance centers' repeated testing of the offender to ensure future compliance, or payments to subsidize centers' ongoing programs of testing for discrimination.

In practice, even fair housing centers that undertake testing use their limited resources mostly to investigate landlords for rental discrimination. The centers are more oriented to serving lower-income populations; rental testing is less expensive than for-sale testing and can often be done by phone: if a landlord tells a tester with an African American–sounding name that an advertised apartment has been rented but tells a subsequent white tester a different story, probable discrimination is easier to establish. Landlords may advertise vacancies as "no Section 8." Although lawful in many places, the practice may disguise racial discrimination. Centers may test these landlords with black and white applicants whose paperwork shows they can afford the apartment without Section 8 subsidies, to determine if the black applicants experience more frequent rejection.

With funds so limited, a large share of fair housing center complaints allege discrimination against persons with disabilities or sexual harassment by property managers, not racial discrimination. It's easier to prove that a building lacks an accessible entrance than that a landlord is biased against black tenants. If a property manager sexually harasses a tenant, it's not necessary to produce another tenant who wasn't harassed to prove the claim. Landlords may openly tell applicants that they won't rent to someone with a seeing-eye dog, a violation of the Fair Housing Act. But landlords who want to exclude African Americans are aware that it's illegal and find pretexts for discrimination.

Insurance Agents Also Violate Nondiscrimination Laws

African American home buyers don't just face racial discrimination in appraisals, property listings, credit scores, and mortgages. After overcoming these hurdles, they need to take out homeowner's insurance. Racial discrimination here is more difficult to uncover but probably just as pervasive.

In this market, black applicants are also unlikely to know whether they were treated worse than white applicants. They can find out only if a fair housing center can send white testers to seek similar insurance from the same agents. To learn whether insurance agencies systematically overcharge or deny coverage to African American and Hispanic applicants, a fair housing center has to conduct a paired testing program. Centers, though, rarely have the budget to investigate discrimination by local insurance agencies.

In 1992, the federal government gave funds to the National Fair Housing Alliance, the umbrella group for local fair housing centers, to conduct paired testing of three major insurance firms: Nationwide, Allstate, and State Farm. The inquiry, which covered nine cities, exposed racial discrimination as great as, if not greater than, in real estate. State Farm was the worst, discriminating against black and Hispanic applicants 85 percent of the time. Allstate and Nationwide discriminated about half the time.

In some cases, insurance agents quoted premium prices for African Americans that were higher—in some cases, twice as much—as quotes for whites who sought coverage for houses of similar value. Agents offered policies that included coverage not only for building structure but also for personal property to whites but not to blacks. Insurance agencies were more likely to return calls from potential customers with identifiably white ethnic names than from those with seemingly African American names. Agents offered discounts for protective devices (such as deadbolt locks or smoke alarms) more frequently to white testers than to black ones. The industry also had seemingly race-neutral policies whose effect was discriminatory—for example, requiring a minimum insured value that excluded more black than white applicants, because black-owned homes, on average, were lower-priced than white ones.

Following the paired testing investigation, local fair housing groups and their national association filed lawsuits and administrative complaints. The settlements promised some reforms, such as ending the minimum value requirement, better fair housing training for agents, and placement of more local offices in black and Hispanic neighborhoods. Fair housing center leaders believe that the insurance industry is far less discriminatory now than it was three decades ago. Ongoing testing, though, is still essential to make certain that the industry continues to live up to its commitment.

Fair Housing Centers Need Funds to Test Realtors and Landlords

Community groups should press their local real estate, banking, and insurance firms to fund fair housing centers at levels needed for extensive and regular testing. Centers themselves should enhance their credibility for this role by including establishment figures as well as civil rights activists on their boards. Many already do. Their programs should produce not merely statistics like federal reports or advice to companies about educating their agents, but discipline and penalties that will send a signal to others. As one director of a local real estate board put it, "I don't want statistics, I want to know which of my members are practicing discrimination so I can end it."

Fair housing centers could do more testing, even with limited funds, if more white and black supporters volunteered and agreed to be trained as testers. For supporters of racial justice who wish they could do more, contributing in this way would help to reduce the discriminatory practices of the real estate, banking, and insurance industries.

Although hidden buttonhole cameras are not permitted in a few states, testers can use them in most places to document their conversations. Even where visual or audio confirmation is not practical or affordable, other documentation is acceptable; for example, realtors may give testers copies of open house listings that differ for black and white home seekers. Even without documentary evidence, experts can review testers' written reports after interviews have been completed. This is good evidence in litigation.

Realtors' Self-Monitoring Falls Short, but Is Better than Nothing

Some large real estate firms and local associations now hope to hire fair housing centers for private testing that can identify discrimination in their ranks. The firms hope to use this information to improve Fair Housing Act compliance with training but with no obligation to take disciplinary action based on results. The act is now more than fifty years old. The time to rely only on more training sessions for agents has passed.

Private testing is a poor substitute for independent enforcement, but may be better than nothing, especially if centers make clear that if they uncover discrimination, they have a legal obligation to take action. This includes retesting the offender, perhaps multiple times, to see if discrimination is consistent and to do so before centers disclose likely violations to firms that commissioned their investigations; otherwise, realtors or landlords may get warning of a retest, which would undermine its validity. Firms that contract with fair housing centers for testing should provide sufficient funds to support not only initial tests but necessary follow-up.

A city east of the Missisippi was the site of an early collaboration between a realtors association and fair housing center. The president of the association reported in mid-2022:

> We are entering into the third set of testing. We are experiencing approximately 40 percent of those tested steer, give advice, and/or behave in a manner that is unprofessional and violates Fair Housing laws. For example, they detect an accent or ID a consumer's name as "different" and do not respond and pass them off to another agent. The training is

working only so-so, I have had some resistance from both brokers and agents initially denying the allegations.

In a few instances, racial discrimination was so severe that offenders were referred back to the fair housing center for further investigation, possibly leading to prosecution.

Self-testing by private firms is not unusual in other fields. Fast food corporations send testers to purchase meals at franchised restaurants to ensure maintenance of quality standards. Retailers send testers to stores to see if salespersons are courteous. Companies have strong financial incentives to ensure that meals are standardized or customers have good experiences. Real estate companies, in contrast, have an ethical and legal obligation, not only a financial one, to eliminate racial discrimination. Although we should take seriously the insurance industry's claims that it has reformed, its sorry history does not yet justify leaving nondiscrimination enforcement to the agencies themselves. The midwestern city's arrangement was apparently working well, but private testing in most metropolitan areas cannot be an adequate substitute for a fair housing center's fully independent and fully funded program of paired testing.

State Licensing Agencies Fall Down on the Job

To qualify for license renewal, agents must take refresher courses that include nondiscrimination. *Newsday* reporters recorded six courses and asked experts to evaluate them. Five, including one taught by the then-president of the Long Island Board of Realtors, failed to include legally required hours of nondiscrimination training. The minimal attention paid to it in that course was, in an expert's evaluation, "shockingly thin in content." Another instructor, a former association president, told agents that obeying fair housing laws is voluntary, like whether to obey a speed limit when you are in a hurry: "You get to choose whether you break the law."

Few, if any, state agencies sufficiently evaluate these courses, making the licensing agencies complicit in ongoing discrimination. Many sessions are now online and easy to observe. Local civil rights groups can monitor them and press state real estate groups to use their extensive lobbying powers (employed so often in the past to empower racial discrimination) to reform licensing agencies, making them partners in campaigns to clean up the industry. Activists should insist that state agencies withhold renewals of agents whose training lacks a comprehensive exploration of their obligations. If, in the twentieth century, state agencies had lifted a few licenses of realtors who engaged in racial discrimination, it would have sent a message throughout the industry, which would have resulted in a country much less segregated than it is today. A similar message now can't undo the past, but it can help put the real estate industry on the side of reform.

The national realtors association has now adopted Chief Justice John Roberts's simple-minded view that "the way to stop discriminating on the basis of race is to stop discriminating on the basis of race." The group insists that realtor descriptions of neighborhoods' racial composition violate the Fair Housing Act. The association has published a pamphlet that advises members they could lose their licenses if they promote integration. It continues to issue strong warnings that members must be race-blind and that the law requires it.

On the contrary, the Fair Housing Act encourages realtors to steer white clients away from segregated white suburbs and toward diverse communities. The act's requirement that government "affirmatively further" its purposes is a call for promoting integrated neighborhoods, as well as a warning against and taking action to prevent white flight from neighborhoods in transition.

Oak Park, Illinois, 1966. Citizens Committee for Human Rights members marched every Saturday during the spring and summer, protesting real estate agency listings that forbade showing homes to African Americans.

Chapter 12

Desegregate for the Long Term
Maintaining Integrated Communities and Schools

We can think of a neighborhood as desegregated when its racial makeup reflects that of the surrounding metropolitan area. Frequently, however, a suburban neighborhood can seem to be desegregated when it is in transition—for example, when a formerly exclusive community experiences white flight as its African American population grows. Temporarily, it may seem to be diverse as it converts from a white segregated neighborhood to a black one. Stable desegregation that persists for a sustained period is rare but possible to achieve with intentional effort.

Although most whites and blacks say that they would prefer to live in a diverse neighborhood, a small minority actually does. When a suburb starts to desegregate, lenders and realtors often promote white flight on the basis that property values will fall. But middle-class integrated neighborhoods can stabilize if they can field housing demand from more potential home buyers, both African Americans and whites who seek diversity. In some places, residents have organized and succeeded in maintaining their community as one where both blacks and whites feel at home.

Stabilizing desegregation will always be controversial. In a changing neighborhood, stemming white flight necessarily means limiting housing opportunities in that neighborhood for black families. Yet African Americans will also suffer if we allow segregation to persist, simply moving from one community to another. We don't confront the severe consequences of residential segregation if we permit segregated and mostly white neighborhoods to flip into mostly black ones.

West Mount Airy, Pennsylvania; Oak Park, Illinois; and Cleveland Heights, Ohio, are three mid-twentieth-century examples of communities that developed shared values and an identity of being integrated. In each, activists used person-to-person mobilization and community building to challenge whites' fears and replace them with positive personal interactions between residents of different races. To varying degrees, they pressed local governments, school districts, banks, and real estate agencies to support integration. Today's advocates of racial justice can learn from their experiences and adapt them to modern times.

West Mount Airy, Pennsylvania

The northwest Philadelphia neighborhood of West Mount Airy was an all-white community of 18,000 in the 1950s when middle-class African Americans started to move there from the central city. Its location not far from the urban core, its mix of housing types accessible to a wide range of households, and its easy access to open space appealed to everyone, attracting blacks and making whites hesitant to leave.

In 1953, when realtors began blockbusting and racial steering, leaders of Jewish, Episcopalian, Protestant, and Unitarian congregations created a joint council to respond. The group studied census and housing data, city charters, state, federal, and international constitutions, and religious, sociological, and human relations literature. A few months later, it began to coordinate efforts to use sermons and living room conversations to transform congregants' understanding of integration to something they should welcome, not resist. It distributed a pamphlet—"This We Believe About Our Neighborhood"—to discourage white flight and encourage hospitality to their new black neighbors: "[R]unning away is detrimental to the community. It forces too many sales in too short a time. . . . People who love good homes, gracious living, a cultural atmosphere, should be encouraged to stay. People who appreciate and can contribute to such an environment should be encouraged to buy or rent in the neighborhood."

The religious council then inspired the formation of the West Mount Airy Neighbors Association, a secular group that sought out white residents of blocks undergoing racial transition and persuaded them not to flee. While many initial association members were white residents driven more by a desire to preserve property values than a moral commitment to integration, the organization was dedicated to being biracial.

It helped to create a food co-op and an arts center, where blacks and whites could build relationships and share experiences. The group worked on school quality, youth services, and better communication among residents. It met with local bankers to ask that they offer equally favorable loan terms to qualified buyers regardless of race and persuaded a few to distribute brochures that marketed the neighborhood as stable and integrated. Members built relationships with realtors and asked them to sign a code of ethics that included an obligation to show all available homes to both white and black home buyers. The association challenged panic selling by pressing realtors to remove "for sale" or "sold" signs from lawns to avoid the image of a racially changing neighborhood. By 1962, nearly two dozen real estate offices had adopted the ethical pledge, and the West Mount Airy Neighbors promoted the favored realtors in newspaper ads and brochures.

That year, the organization also devised a creative way to advertise its goals, by hosting a United Nations Delegates Weekend, during which two hundred representatives from thirty-one U.N. member countries stayed with West Mount Airy families. Europeans stayed with black families and Africans with whites.

The association boosted housing demand (and, therefore, property values) by marketing West Mount Airy to whites through local and national press coverage that promoted the integrationist ideal. Blacks, motivated less by living the ideal of integration than by the amenities, services, and economic stability the neighborhood offered, didn't need as much convincing.

By the 1970s, West Mount Airy had established a shared culture and identity as an integrated community. But then, deindustrialization, divestment in central cities, increases in crime, and loss of jobs all led the neighborhood association to shift from promoting racial integration to issues of economic stability and neighborhood safety.

As part of Philadelphia, West Mount Airy does not have its own government or school district, which has complicated its integration efforts, especially those aimed at desegregating its elementary schools. Starting in the 1950s, the citywide district redrew attendance boundaries several times so the neighborhood's schools drew more black students from downtown areas and became overcrowded. Court-ordered busing in the 1970s continued these trends. Meanwhile, the state inadequately funded public education; whites and blacks who could afford to do so took their children out of local public schools, which now predominantly served poorer African American children from other areas. Racially imbalanced schools were a contrast to the careful residential desegregation that the association had worked so hard to achieve.

In the early 2000s, Yvonne Haskins, a longtime black resident of West Mount Airy and former president of the neighborhood association, observed, "I saw all these black kids in the school yard and only one little white girl, and I was shocked, and I started talking about it to everybody, what are we doing that our schools don't represent who we are, as a community."

Today, West Mount Airy activists are working to diminish the threat that segregated schools pose to residential integration. Together with school administrators, they are using the same one-on-one tactics employed decades earlier to persuade whites not to flee the neighborhood, now to convince white families not to flee the public schools. Enrollment is still majority-black and not reflective of the neighborhood's racial mix, but recent efforts, including revived parent organizations, monthly school tours, campus beautification, new music, science, technology, and math curricula, and a principal committed to integration, have begun to shift the demographic pattern.

West Mount Airy remains an attractive community for both black and white Philadelphians with means, but the neighborhood is now difficult to buy into. Rising home prices threaten neighborhood desegregation, as wealthier whites outbid African Americans for house purchases and more expensive rentals. Targeted marketing to prospective buyers is once again needed, only this time to middle-class African Americans. Inclusionary zoning, home buyer assistance, renter protections, and other strategies to make housing more affordable are now necessary to prevent resegregation.

Maintaining racial diversity, even in a community that has done so successfully for half a century, is a task that can never be considered complete. In West Mount Airy, residents have become aware that they cannot be complacent. The association again seeks to attract black residents to maintain the neighborhood's balance and sponsors speaker forums on racial issues. Ms. Haskins is optimistic: "The stability that we want to preserve is pretty much locked in now. It's a part of our culture, that we're not afraid of each other and that we relish differences."

Oak Park, Illinois

Residents of the predominantly white Village of Oak Park, a town of 63,000 on Chicago's western border, started talking about challenging their community's segregation in 1950 after Percy Julian, an African American research chemist, bought a house there. Before his family moved in, it was firebombed, followed the next year by a similar attack. Several white residents wrote letters to the local newspaper denouncing the violence. Some started to meet to discuss how to challenge the segregation that had characterized Oak Park since its founding fifty years earlier.

Yet little changed during the next decade. In 1963, Carole Anderson, an African American violinist, appeared for her first rehearsal with the Oak Park Symphony and was promptly fired. The symphony's board chair defended the dismissal, saying that "[n]othing is integrated in Oak Park as yet." Twenty-five of the symphony's eighty-three musicians, along with its conductor, resigned in protest. More than a thousand Oak Park residents then signed a newspaper ad defending the "right of all people to live where they choose." Protestant and Catholic churches created social action committees that evolved into a broadly based and secular committee for human rights. Members held protest marches and demonstrations in front of realty offices and sent prospective white and black home buyers and renters to test whether agents engaged in racial steering or other discriminatory practices. They distributed leaflets to African Americans who worked in Oak Park to encourage them to move to the village; and they sent letters to black newspapers in Chicago and held open houses, potluck dinners, and block parties in order to introduce prospective residents to Oak Park and to build community among those living there.

One of the first African American families to settle in the village was Harriette and Mac Robinet and their six children. She was a microbiologist, he a physicist. No realtor would sell them a home, so in 1965 a white family bought one and sold it to them. The police required that they move in during the middle of a day and in the middle of a week, when few people would be around to notice. Within a month of their arrival, a next-door neighbor fled the village. But others welcomed them, giving the Robinets a washing machine, refrigerator, and piano to inaugurate their new home.

Oak Park has long had an almost equal mix of rented and owned housing, making it attractive and accessible to people of various income levels. Unlike West Mount Airy, Oak Park has its own municipal government, which gave committee members an accessible target to advocate for a fair housing ordinance, which the village board adopted in 1968 and then assigned staff to enforce two years later. Elected officials were now on board, with a goal that the village's population should reflect the greater Chicago area's racial makeup and that, rather than segregating African Americans in mostly black neighborhoods, diversity should exist throughout the town. The village government supplemented its housing discrimination ordinance with two other measures designed to prevent realtors from creating panic among white homeowners: it prohibited "for sale" signs on lawns, which speculators were using to create the impression of an unstable neighborhood, and it created a registry so residents could join a no-solicitation list that prevented realtors from attempting to persuade them to sell. The school district supported integration by adjusting attendance boundaries to promote racial diversity in each of its elementary and middle schools.

The village adopted a diversity statement in 1973 to establish its commitment to a policy of integration: "Oak Park has committed itself to equality not only because it is legal, but because it is right; not only because equality is ethical, but because it is desirable for us and our children. . . . Our goal is for people of widely differing backgrounds to do more than live next to one another. Through interaction, we believe we can reconcile the apparent paradox of appreciating and even celebrating our differences while at the same time developing consensus on a shared vision for the future."

Five years later, in 1978, Oak Park adopted a home-equity insurance program to provide owners a guarantee against future property value declines. All homeowners paid a 1 percent property tax to fund it; those who enrolled paid a nominal fee. The policy promised to reimburse 80 percent of lost equity if a family sold its home after at least five years in the program. This undercut realtors' ability to stoke fear and incite white flight, encouraged residents to stay and invest in their homes, and bolstered confidence in the neighborhood's stability. It aimed to reduce racial tensions by taking the imagined economic threat out of desegregation.

The insurance program ended after thirty years because it proved unnecessary: no participant ever required reimbursement. Perhaps because worried homeowners knew they could protect their property values rather than move, home prices increased, and fewer than two hundred homeowners worried enough about equity loss to enroll in the program.

Until 1972, Oak Park activists had been solely concerned with integration of homeownership. But then, they turned their attention to rentals and obtained local government and philanthropic support to found the nonprofit Oak Park Housing Center to promote apartment integration. Tenant turnover is faster than that of homeowners—30 percent of Oak Park tenants move every year—so segregation can happen quickly in an apartment building and affect the surrounding neighborhood. But an intentional strategy can also integrate apartment buildings quickly. To promote building-level integration, the center uses census data to assess the racial composition of village neighborhoods. It uses this information, along with its knowledge of the apartment buildings in each neighborhood, to determine which buildings and areas are most segregated; it then provides counseling and referrals to apartment seekers to bolster integration. It refers whites to predominantly black areas and blacks to predominantly white ones.

The housing center also encourages landlords in neighborhoods most susceptible to resegregation to find tenants through its referral program. In exchange for marketing units through the center for three years, landlords can receive matching grants of up to $10,000 for rehabilitation from the village and can also get one year of rental reimbursement to cover vacancies while they await tenants who would further their buildings' integration.

The affirmative marketing program in Oak Park is unique in its focus on diversity of small areas, its attention to the rental market, the support and cooperation its supporters have won from local government, and the race-conscious nature of its efforts. In 2016, the housing center reported that 83 percent of assisted tenants made moves that promoted desegregation.

The village remains about evenly divided between owners and renters. Forty percent of black Oak Parkers now own their homes while 60 percent rent. For whites, the opposite holds true—60 percent homeowners and 40 percent renters. Oak Park's integration was moderately paced. It went from a population that was 1 percent African American in 1970 and 11 percent ten years later to 19 percent in 1990 and 22 percent in 2000 and 2010, but it's now down to 18 percent as the community becomes less affordable. Yet the village has met its goal of reflecting the racial mix of the Chicago metropolitan area, whose overall population is now 16 percent African American.

Cleveland Heights, Ohio

In 1963, Martin Luther King Jr. made a fund-raising visit to Cleveland that helped inspire a new civil rights coalition of the city's civic and religious groups, which organized marches and rallies and launched a campaign to desegregate public schools.

Cleveland's school board was committed to segregation. When schools in its black neighborhood of Glenville became overcrowded, the district bused children to white schools in other neighborhoods where space was available, but it kept those black students in separate classrooms.

In 1964, the district began to build new schools in Glenville to avoid continuing to send black children to nearby white schools. Many recognized this as a tactic to avoid integration. Protesters, including black civil rights activists, Glenville parents, and white supporters, sat in ditches at the site to stop the construction of yet another segregated school. Many were arrested.

Some who engaged in this civil disobedience were from the affluent suburb of Cleveland Heights, whose population of 62,000 was almost all white. Many had been inspired by a sermon Dr. King delivered in their town during his recent visit to the area. One participant in the Glenville demonstration, a Presbyterian minister from the suburb, was accidentally run over and killed by a bulldozer. This got the attention of his Cleveland Heights community, where many of the residents who supported the protests had not considered how their own town's exclusive, white character contributed to Cleveland's segregation of African Americans. This soon changed.

Three women lobbied the Cleveland Heights school board to open its summer schools to black students from Cleveland, raised money for scholarships, and recruited city students to enroll. Another woman had recently moved with her family to Cleveland Heights for the purpose of organizing for its desegregation. She gathered together a group, including the summer school program advocates, to establish the Heights Citizens for Human Rights to challenge the suburb's racial exclusivity.

Initially, its goal was to bring one black family to every street to avoid creating a black ghetto in a pocket of the suburb. But some members disagreed that they should direct where African Americans could live. The organization's goal evolved to balancing black families' choices of where to live with neighborhood integration. This meant challenging white realtors, convincing African Americans that they would be welcome, and ensuring that whites would, in fact, be welcoming.

In 1967, the group led forty living room discussions, attended by five hundred white residents. It created a speaker's bureau, produced an educational series on black heritage, organized a letter-to-the-editor campaign, and held community forums, all to build support for integration. The group surveyed local real estate brokers and found that almost none would sell to a black home buyer, so it created a competing nonprofit association of the few who would. In its seven years in business, its members sold 199 homes to African Americans in previously all-white neighborhoods.

The organization trained members to search newspaper ads, identify whites who'd put their homes up for sale, and then attempt to persuade them to work with the nondiscriminatory realtors. The volunteers used a "Home Sellers Project Worksheet" that outlined the best arguments to use to address each potential home seller's interests and concerns—patriotic, religious, or legal—and provide answers to those questions they were most likely to hear:

> What will the neighbors think?
> Will property values go down?
> I don't want to rock the boat.
> Isn't it true that whites won't buy after Negroes move in?
> Isn't it true that Negroes don't keep up their property?
> Isn't it better for people to live with their own kind?

The group recruited African Americans to move to the area by attending community events in Cleveland and contacting black organizations there. It conducted monthly suburban house tours for Clevelanders and matched potential black home buyers, identified through their church and community groups, with white volunteers tasked with neighborhood promotion. Escorts contacted brokers and accompanied black home buyers and renters to ensure fair treatment and to document any discrimination that occurred. When African Americans were told a house or apartment was no longer available, a white tester then visited the same residence to see whether the treatment and information were the same. A Catholic church social action committee sent paired black and white volunteers to inquire about apartments and homes for sale to document different treatment. The group used their findings—that ten prominent real estate firms discriminated against blacks—to campaign for the city government to adopt an ordinance to prohibit such practices.

After several years of this volunteer activity, Cleveland Heights religious leaders formed the Heights Community Congress, which absorbed members of the original human rights group and expanded to include religious, business, civic, and neighborhood associations. The new organization received funding from a local foundation to hire a director and six staff members. In 1974, its housing task force initiated litigation against a local realty company, one of the first lawsuits in the nation to test the Fair Housing Act. The plaintiffs included white Cleveland Heights residents who wanted to live in integrated neighborhoods but were denied that right by the realtors' practices. The suit was settled for $15,000 ($80,000), which the community congress used to support its desegregation activities.

Desegregation activists were also active politically and in the early 1970s elected supporters to the Cleveland Heights city council, which then banned steering, blockbusting, and unwanted solicitation, while implementing fair housing training for realtors (completion resulted in being named a preferred realtor). To refute expectations that integration leads to lower home values, the city stepped up code enforcement and a church formed a nonprofit corporation, with funds from several churches and other charitable organizations, to offer home-repair loans. To resist and offset white flight, the local Jewish federation started a down payment assistance program that offered interest-free loans to Jewish families buying homes in the town.

This was followed in 1985 by the Ohio state program that set aside low-interest mortgage assistance for home buyers whose purchases furthered integration. As the black population of Cleveland Heights grew, state support went to white buyers to help stabilize the community's racial composition. Black realtors objected, and in response the program added an additional set-aside for minorities buying homes in any neighborhood. Cleveland Heights partnered with a neighboring suburb to provide additional mortgage incentives to first-time home buyers in the state agency and Jewish federation programs. Most homeowners assisted by the city's program were also whites buying in Cleveland Heights.

From less than 1 percent of the population in 1970, African Americans are now 40 percent of the suburb's residents.

The Work Is Never Done

As in West Mount Airy and Oak Park, other issues have become more pressing in Cleveland Heights. Its poverty rate is growing, vacant and foreclosed homes are common, the population is declining and aging (as is the housing stock), and issues of integration and discrimination within the public schools have returned as concerns. The suburb no longer has an organization focused on residential desegregation. While the town has maintained its diversity, public schools have not. In the high school, most students are African American.

Rising home values threaten desegregation in all three places. Activists will now have to press for economic reforms and housing subsidies to preserve their communities as welcoming to moderate-income and racially diverse newcomers. The key to ongoing economic, not to mention racial, stability may be to attract young professionals, with an intentional focus on maintaining a racial balance of those who move in.

To assure black and white residents of the community's racial stability, its integration must go beyond who lives there to who holds decision-making power. City boards and commissions should reflect the community's population and provide for leadership sharing by people of different races. Local activists should ensure this balance is achieved and address barriers to participation.

While not the only places to intentionally integrate, West Mount Airy, Oak Park, and Cleveland Heights illustrate how local groups can pursue active racial stabilization. Despite what many in West Mount Airy and Oak Park saw as inevitable when black families first settled, resegregation has not occurred.

These accounts are not historic curiosities. Throughout the nation today, inner-ring suburbs become racially and ethnically diverse as African American and other nonwhite families leave cities for more affordable and higher-quality housing. As in the twentieth century, whites may leave, tipping towns from diverse to segregated. Meanwhile, the outer-ring suburbs to which whites flee remain segregated, with African Americans excluded.

Civil rights supporters in both kinds of places have work to do, stabilizing desegregation of inner-ring suburbs and opening the outer ring to racially diverse populations. The West Mount Airy, Oak Park, and Cleveland Heights activists have much to teach us about how to proceed.

Desegregation of Schools and Communities Go Hand in Hand

A racial justice group might begin by investigating its community's school segregation—and its effects. Although no reforms that we describe in this book are easy to accomplish, there are some advantages to starting here: many potential supporters have children in schools and an interest in their improvement; it may be easier (although not easy) to influence school boards than city councils or state governments.

Several activists described in this book did so. The Montgomery Travelers, for example, organized around racial incidents in Wilmette's mostly white public high school. The Presbyterian Inter-Racial Dialogue pressed the Winston-Salem district to add African American history to its curriculum and then defended the instruction when board members moved to end it. Shane Wiegand's research into companies that benefited from Rochester's racial deed restrictions began in his classroom and is now a curriculum taught throughout the region. Cleveland Heights residents who worked to diversify their white community began with protests of school segregation in neighboring black Glenville.

School segregation makes neighborhood integration difficult, if not impossible, and neighborhood segregation makes school segregation inevitable.

Many benefits of integrated neighborhoods are conveyed through their schools. As well as having better educational and employment outcomes than others, students educated with other-race peers are more likely to attend diverse colleges, choose to live in diverse communities, and have healthier cross-race relationships as adults. They are also more likely to send their own children to integrated schools.

Yet a powerful countervailing force now intensifies school and neighborhood segregation. In 2001, Congress passed and President George W. Bush signed the No Child Left Behind Act, which required annual student testing and the publication of average scores by race. The legislation was based on the ludicrous theory that lower average achievement of African Americans resulted from lazy teachers who didn't try to educate black students. The law's proponents dismissed the importance of social and economic challenges that students from low-income, segregated neighborhoods encounter and predicted that test scores' publication would shame teachers into greater effort and make the achievement gap disappear. Not surprisingly, this approach failed. The racial achievement gap isn't much different from its size twenty years ago; what the law accomplished was to give educators incentives to prioritize test-taking tricks and easily tested basic skills over a well-rounded curriculum with more complex material.

The law accomplished something even worse: by requiring publication of school test results, it gave parents and realtors a tool that falsely identified desirable neighborhoods as those with high average math and reading scores. But these are not necessarily the best schools. Test results mostly reflect the social and economic challenges that pupils may or may not confront. A school with many children of college-educated parents will post high averages even if it also has teachers who are lazy, or worse. One with pupils from economically disadvantaged families will have lower academic achievement even if its teachers are hardworking, dedicated, and devoted to every child's success. One with a diverse population is likely to have moderate average test scores, which disclose nothing about the quality of instruction. The only way for parents, or prospective homeowners, to learn if a neighborhood school is worthy of their children is to visit it and to meet the parents, teachers, and administrators who compose its adult community.

It is no longer controversial that No Child Left Behind was deeply flawed, considering its utter inability to significantly narrow the achievement gap. The National Association of Realtors warns its members not to promote neighborhood test results to indicate community desirability. It advises agents that using scores in this way intensifies segregation, because white clients are hesitant to buy homes in neighborhoods with mediocre test reports and instead seek homogeneously white areas with higher scores. But even if realtors take their association's advice (and few do), the tests are hard to avoid. Real estate websites promote them. These companies acknowledge that scores are more likely to signal white segregation than school quality, but the business of promoting test reports is too lucrative to ignore. They attempt to minimize the harm by reporting other data—high school graduation rates, for example. But without the time-consuming and expensive effort to hire experts with the experience needed to visit and evaluate a school, accurate published evaluations are out of reach.

Local realtor groups, in cooperation with other credible organizations, should undertake investigations of their community's school quality to uncover more useful information to provide to clients. In Pasadena, California, a local foundation that supports public education is challenging real estate agents' perceptions of the district, including their reliance on test score data and outdated or exaggerated stories about struggling, segregated schools. The group has developed a course to counter these views. It sends monthly newsletters with profiles of schools and students, offers campus tours, and provides ongoing information to realtors. It invites them to volunteer in schools, as "Principal of the Day," for example, so they can make personal connections and see the environments firsthand. The agents can also participate in adopt-a-school partnerships, where they pledge a portion of their commission to local schools.

The Pasadena Educational Foundation encourages school visits by realtors, who then develop an appreciation of public education and avoid steering clients away from integrated campuses. Here, realtor Robb Buzzini reads to a kindergarten class. He recalls, "It was commonplace for realtors to tell clients, 'You'd better get a bargain, because you'll have to save money for private school.' But when realtors become familiar with the public system, they can describe its excellent programs. If you are only looking at Redfin or Zillow, you're not getting an accurate picture."

Sixty realtors have completed the course, and several have become active members of the educational advocacy group. They have changed, for the better, how they talk to clients about the district's educational quality. The national real estate association has developed a tool kit for local associations based on these efforts.

Real estate agents can improve how they promote neighborhoods with integrated schools to white and black home buyers, emphasizing that children cannot be well educated if their classmates have identical racial backgrounds.

In most places, segregated schools are still the norm. Realtors' endorsements of diverse learning environments can help start to desegregate them.

The School-to-Prison Pipeline

A horrible consequence of school segregation is the harsher discipline of African American students, especially in more racially isolated schools. It begins as early as preschool. Reform here should be a high priority for community groups. The percentage of African American students predicts the severity of security measures more than any other school characteristic. Schools with similar levels of misconduct are more likely, if they have large numbers of black students, to have metal detectors, random contraband sweeps, security guards, police officers, and security cameras. African American students are then, not surprisingly, arrested at school more often than whites.

When police are posted in schools, their mission easily expands to criminalize conduct that was previously handled by educators. Officers may operate under zero tolerance policies that require severe consequences for any misbehavior. They respond to minor infractions, such as classroom disorder or disruption, by citing or arresting students.

In suburban schools where most students are white, counselors or school administrators address similar instances more humanely, with concern for the root of the problem. In these schools, suspensions are often reserved only for the most serious offenses. Diverse schools use harsh discipline less often overall but apply it unequally; discipline of black students is consistently more severe than for whites, especially for low-level misbehavior.

When youth have frequent contact with police, they exhibit higher stress levels. They feel more threatened and on guard around law enforcement officers, which may be perceived as defiance or disobedience, leading to tougher disciplinary action and even more police contact.

Black pupils who attend schools with harsher security measures and higher suspension rates are more likely to drop out, fail to attend college, and be arrested and incarcerated as adults than students in schools with less punitive disciplinary policies. Rather than preparing students for a career, these schools tend to funnel them to prison and a life of involvement with the criminal justice system. This too frequent pathway is commonly called the *school-to-prison pipeline*.

Schools overall now contain more police officers than social workers, based on the misguided belief that campuses are increasingly more dangerous. However, there is no evidence that this is the case. Students are no more violent or prone to criminality than previously. Juvenile crime rates and drug use are at a historic low. School shootings are less likely to be perpetrated by students than by adults or intruders, challenging the notion that stricter discipline of students will make them safer. Students are more protected in school than outside of it. Only 3 percent of children murdered each year are killed in schools. Despite highly publicized mass shootings, this rate hasn't changed in decades.

Giving police responsibility for managing behavior increases student alienation and impedes their ability to learn. Local activists can seek to change their schools' racially discriminatory disciplinary policies. They can pressure school boards to end zero tolerance policies and to use suspensions only for the most serious misconduct. They can also advocate removing police officers' responsibility for nonviolent misbehavior and returning it to teachers, counselors, social workers, and administrators, where it belongs. Schools with mental health providers see improved school safety, improved attendance, lower suspension and expulsion rates, lower rates of disciplinary action, and improved academic achievement, graduation rates, and career preparation.

When police are assigned to campuses, police departments should provide the officers with mandatory training on adolescent development, stereotype formation, and how to de-escalate tense interactions.

Local activists should also advocate alternative disciplinary policies, especially in predominantly African American schools that rely too heavily on policing. Some schools have adopted less punitive approaches to discipline. In Baltimore, Chicago, St. Paul, Los Angeles, and elsewhere, administrators have implemented restorative justice programs, which use professionally guided discussions with the offending students, the victims, and anyone else affected by the misbehavior, to repair the harm caused, rather than punish and suspend. In other places, schools use disciplinary review boards in which trained students hear from and question those who misbehave and come up with a sentence, such as community service or writing a paper about their behavior, after which the offender's record is wiped clean.

Local Action for School Desegregation

Comprehensive challenges to school segregation are mostly beyond the capacity of local racial justice groups, but in addition to the highest priority—ending the criminalization of black student behavior—other steps are possible.

- Activists can raise funds to commission local school evaluations by experts who understand that the opportunity to learn from racially and ethnically diverse teachers and classmates is a characteristic of a high-quality school.
- Alumni of competitive colleges and universities can organize campaigns to persuade their alma maters to give admission preferences to applicants who live in diverse neighborhoods and attend their local public schools.
- Many districts maintain attendance zones that unintentionally or purposefully assign students to schools in ways that ensure they are segregated. Opportunities sometimes exist to reconfigure them so children can attend more diverse schools that are still near their homes. In some cases, it may be necessary to press adjoining school districts to develop a collaboration that can make such reform possible.

In 1974, civil rights lawyers challenged Detroit's segregation of blacks in urban schools and whites in suburban ones. Evidence showed that the region's housing policies were responsible, and the plaintiffs sought to open suburban educational opportunities for city children. But the Supreme Court rejected the proposal, ruling that white suburbs had no responsibility for Detroit's segregation, so their districts could not be required to participate in a remedy. It was another decision in the *Dred Scott* tradition that ignored the reality of how segregation was imposed. As a result, federal court-ordered desegregation plans that require districts to accept students from outside their boundaries are now forbidden nationwide. But civil rights groups can still campaign to get their school districts to enact such plans voluntarily. This is a limited remedy that works best when predominantly black and white attendance zones are in close proximity, so that children do not face long bus rides. There are more opportunities to do this than most people realize.

Chief Justice John Roberts's call for the nation to be race-blind came in a 2007 Supreme Court opinion that prohibited school districts from considering students' race in voluntary desegregation programs. Some districts instead now use the racial composition of students' neighborhoods or their families' income for school assignments. Not surprisingly, these race-neutral programs are not as effective at achieving integration as race-based programs would be.

Some white suburbs have excess school capacity as birthrates fall and populations age. A voluntary busing program can offer those seats to urban African American families who seek integrated educations for their children. Boston has maintained such voluntary busing for many years, with enormous benefit to the children who participated.

Suburban and urban school districts can also allow students to voluntarily cross their boundaries. The receiving schools should invest in making their campuses welcoming environments to children from other districts by offering mentoring to those students and professional development to teachers and staff. Transportation authorities can offer free trips to students traveling to more distant schools.

But permitting students to transfer to more diverse environments can harm the neighborhood schools from which they depart by reducing enrollments and the per-pupil funding that results, and by removing the influence of the most educationally sophisticated parents (and their children). Additional state funds should flow to those schools to make up for the revenue they lose when children choose suburban districts.

In 1989, families in Hartford, Connecticut, sued in state court over the inferior education that black and Hispanic students received in their segregated and underfunded schools. As a result, the state now allows students in the area to attend schools outside of their district; Hartford students can enroll in more than twenty suburban districts, and suburban students can do so in Hartford schools. When students from Hartford travel, the state increases funding to the receiving schools and does not reduce the city school budgets. Connecticut has also created forty magnet schools, almost half in Hartford itself. They are open to any student and use affirmative marketing to ensure diverse populations. As a result, almost half of Hartford's nonwhite students now attend desegregated schools. Racial justice activists can organize to persuade their local school districts to implement voluntarily the strategies that were court ordered in Hartford.

Affluent communities frequently augment classroom resources with voluntary parent contributions. Donors can insist that their support is shared with schools in nearby lower-income areas. Community groups can also press local governments to equalize opportunities by making supplementary contributions to schools where families don't have such resources. Local philanthropic foundations should participate and offer unrestricted funding to help schools attract and maintain racially and economically diverse student populations.

In areas with a mix of middle- and low-income families, those who can afford to opt out of the public system often do so, leaving it with disproportionately poor students. Without middle-income parents and their greater resources and political power, the schools inevitably suffer. Parents in these communities should send their children to local public schools, get involved with parent associations, and advocate for improvements. This was part of Luke Davenport's advice to conscientious gentrifiers.

The Obama administration's Affirmatively Furthering Fair Housing rule required varied government agencies to work together to address their region's segregation and its impacts. School districts should participate in this collaboration. Communities conducting fair housing assessments should include in their analyses how school and neighborhood segregation are interconnected. The plans they produce should include appropriate school desegregation strategies. Local activists engaged in this planning process can ensure this is not overlooked.

Modesto, California. Sharon Froba (right) spent three years speaking to civic and religious groups about their neighborhoods' segregation. After a city-owned golf course was closed, she and Wendy Byrd (left), NAACP chapter president, campaigned to use the site for mixed-income housing, including market-rate, moderate-income, and deeply subsidized units. On September 30, 2022, they displayed an architectural model of their proposal to a local social services organization.

EPILOGUE

Throughout this book, we've described what activists or advocates can do to redress segregation, yet many readers may not see themselves in those roles. They may have never spoken at a city council meeting, written a letter to an elected official, or participated in the political process beyond voting. For significant progress, it's not necessary for every person who cares about an issue to engage in such activities, but some must. For the change this book imagines to be possible, many more will have to step into these roles and see themselves as activists, and many others will need to support them.

Opportunities for community action are enormous in variety. This book has only described a few. Which strategies your racial justice group embraces will vary from place to place, but there are enough options that no committee should find itself lacking in ideas. White supporters of racial equality have no excuse: you can't sit out the fight and expect change to result if too few of you step forward.

We are hopeful that this book will give readers tools to get involved and become activists, but we are also realistic. Most readers who've made it this far will not lead actions to challenge segregation and shouldn't be expected to do so. But those readers are now aware of the many paths they can take. Some will attend meetings or protests but not direct them. Others will add their donations and votes to help make activists successful. A movement to redress segregation requires participants in all of these roles.

Some whites today may hesitate to join active campaigns to narrow inequality because they've been told they have unconscious biases that render them inadequate partners in fights to confront segregation. Of course, they have such biases. We all do. But this should not stop or even delay taking steps to advance racial equality. Examining our internal prejudices and learning about the historical forces that shaped them is important. But taking action is what will lead to change.

Segregation does not only hurt African Americans. Whites also suffer its effects. Segregated black neighborhoods, denied the resources they need to thrive, reinforce whites' stereotypes of African Americans as lower-class people to be feared. Affluent whites with the means to do so then form communities that artificially inflate home prices to maintain exclusivity. Middle-class and lower-income whites and blacks alike are priced out of these highly resourced communities and pay a cost of maintaining segregation. The same stereotypes also lead many whites to act against their own self-interest. They oppose policies that would benefit them rather than support something that they see as helping only the most needy African Americans.

The change we need requires both place-based and mobility approaches. We should pursue activities that improve resources in segregated African American communities as well as those that increase access to segregated white neighborhoods for black families that choose to live in them. Focusing on one of these strategies and ignoring the other will not be sufficient to challenge the varied causes and effects of segregation. The redress of segregation also requires both past- and future-focused efforts: we should accept the obligation to change policies and practices that perpetuate segregation and adopt those that compensate for past injustices.

We all do better when we are not separated from one another. Now is the time to join together in our own communities to remedy the racial segregation that harms us all.

In 2022, Virginia governor Glenn Youngkin banned teaching "critical race theory" and "inherently divisive concepts" in public education. Antoinette Waters, an Arlington high school history teacher was not intimidated. She says: "I do not teach CRT or indoctrination. I educate students to learn our whole story, rooted in historical facts. I teach African American studies, not American nostalgia. Our children deserve to know the truth, so they can clean up the mess made in the past and not repeat it in the future."

FREQUENTLY ASKED QUESTIONS

You don't capitalize the "B" in black? Why not?

It has recently become more commonplace to capitalize the "B" in black but not the "w" in white. When the Associated Press adopted this style, it explained that "people who are Black have . . . the shared experience of discrimination due solely to the color of one's skin. . . . White people generally do not share the same history and culture, or the experience of being discriminated against because of skin color." We don't disagree with these statements. What's more, whites who seek to create a racial identity that is comparable to black identity may be asserting the false notion that they suffer from discrimination on account of their race. In actuality, this is an attempt to suppress the effort to reduce racial inequality, not advance it. So we don't capitalize white.

Some media companies, however, have decided to capitalize white as well. The *Washington Post* asserted that whites are "a distinct cultural identity in the United States" and that "[i]n American history, many White Europeans who entered the country during times of mass migration were the targets of racial and ethnic discrimination." A few black scholars supported the decision, saying that if white were capitalized, it would prevent white supremacists from doing it themselves as an act of defiance. We reject this rationalization. Implying that whites are a racial group with a shared experience of discrimination similar to that of black people undermines our obligation to understand the unique suffering, abuse, and exploitation of African Americans.

Our reason for not capitalizing black is this: one mission of *Just Action* is to persuade white Americans who are not sophisticated advocates of racial equality that there are ways they can take steps to advance the principles they express. Throughout, we avoid code words, always thinking that clear explanation is preferable. Many readers will not be familiar with how one letter in the word *Black* can be used to symbolize African Americans' history of exploitation and suffering and will be confused by what will seem to be an inconsistency between the uppercase "B" and the lowercase "w." Our default approach has always been to use terms and styles with which the broadest share of readers is familiar and to explain rather than use jargon, abbreviations, or symbols. Our goal has always been to persuade people to do the right thing and to avoid actions that will alienate potential allies. When the time comes that nonspecialists become familiar with reasoning like that of the Associated Press, and the symbolism becomes obvious, we will consider adopting its style.

I expected you to show how we can dismantle "racist" practices, and to denounce "racism" and "white privilege." But you don't use these terms at all. Why not?

The term *racist* has become a weapon, not a description. Charging someone or something as being racist ends a discussion; it does not explain inequality and does not recruit allies to redress it.

The term is now so widely used that it has lost all meaning. We call it racist if a white worker insensitively asks a black colleague about her hairstyle, if we maintain a regressive tax system, if an elite high school relies on test scores to decide whom to admit, if a state legislature attempts to make it more difficult for African Americans to vote, if a white senator charges a black nominee of being soft on crime, if a policeman murders a black man by keeping a knee on his victim's neck, and if our criminal justice system incarcerates many young black men on trivial pretexts that it overlooks when young white men are concerned. We should, to varying degrees, worry about all of these. But if we don't make distinctions, we can't find the proper strategies to counteract and address the problems. To lump them into a single category of "racism" makes it more difficult to do so. A term that means everything means nothing.

As more Americans have learned the history of residential segregation, some characterize our system as one of *white privilege*. That term is troublesome and can even be harmful.

Certainly, many whites (and fewer African Americans) have contemptible privileges in our society. Recently, the federal government prosecuted privileged white parents who bribed admissions officers, athletic coaches, and testing administrators to admit children to competitive colleges to which they may not otherwise have been eligible. In our increasingly unequal society, those at the top of the economic ladder have more ways of using their wealth to jump to the head of the line for opportunities that should be available to all.

In many other ways, public policy promotes privileges that are disproportionately enjoyed by whites. One is how we permit the transfer of wealth and assets to subsequent generations, defying our claim to be a society based on merit, in which everyone starts off equally and achieves success by discipline, hard work, and skill. A free society shouldn't eliminate gifts from parents to children (and grandchildren), but our tax system can restrict them much more than it does, so that success is less dependent on the family into which one is born. Individuals (yes, disproportionately white) should not feel guilty about a privilege given to them by public policy, although they should support politicians who attempt to narrow it and consider whether the balance between their charitable giving and their bequest plans are consistent with their views about the redress of segregation and the role of earned merit.

Another privilege, disproportionately of whites, is the practice of many competitive colleges to give admission preferences to alumni children. This is also an indefensible transfer of advantage to the next generation. Some institutions have abandoned this policy, and all should do so. The federal government could prohibit universities that receive federal funds from utilizing such preferences. Until it does, alumni concerned with enhancing racial equality should organize or join campaigns to withhold contributions to their alma maters as long as the institutions retain this policy.

Chapter 10 described how affluent suburbs adopt zoning rules that exclude moderate- and lower-income blacks. Residents of these areas convert homeownership into indefensible privilege.

But we should not reinterpret privileges of inheritances, legacy admissions, and exclusionary zoning as a claim that persons should feel privileged (and guilty about it) simply because they are white. Working-class whites, subsidized after World War II to move to racially exclusive suburbs, did not exercise a privilege; they claimed a right. A decent government would ensure that all citizens have a right to safe and affordable housing. Every veteran—and nonveteran—should have received a homeownership subsidy. The problem is not that whites were privileged but that blacks were denied an equal right.

We should think of many economic rights in this way. During the New Deal, Congress adopted federal minimum wage and social security programs that purposely excluded occupations in which African Americans were predominant, like domestic work and agriculture. White workers and retirees whose economic security then improved were not privileged; they claimed a right to which everyone should have been entitled. That African Americans were denied it was the shame, not that whites were privileged to claim it. We should rise to our responsibility to correct the effects of that denial.

The concept of white privilege also encourages guilt that is neither justifiable nor an effective basis on which to organize a new civil rights movement to remedy residential segregation. All Americans have an obligation to enforce constitutional rights, not from guilt about privilege but from an understanding that the denial of rights demands both their restoration and a remedy for the effects of that denial. Unless we step up to that obligation, our democracy cannot survive.

We're going backward on racial equality. How can you talk of a new civil rights movement when we have so little chance of success?

A recent survey found: "Seventy-one percent of Republicans say the U.S. has made a lot of progress over the past fifty years in ensuring equal rights for all Americans, regardless of race, while just 29 percent of Democrats say this. . . . Only 19 percent of black adults say the country has made a lot of progress, while 80 percent say it has made only a little or no progress at all."

The Republicans are right; Democrats are wrong.
The facts:

- Today we are arguing about how many ballot drop boxes there should be in black neighborhoods and whether voters should routinely get mail-in ballots or have to request them. Sixty years ago, African Americans were lynched for trying to register, and civil rights workers were killed for trying to help them do so.
- Today, the military is the most integrated institution in American society; we've had a black secretary of defense and a black chairman of the Joint Chiefs of Staff. Seventy-five years ago, African Americans were restricted to segregated infantry units commanded by white officers.
- Today, every significant American corporation has African Americans in supervisory positions. Fifty-five years ago, a survey of Chicago corporations found not a single one in a position as high as "shipping and receiving manager."
- Today, the black high school graduation rate is nearly identical to the white rate; fifty years ago, it was three-fourths of the white rate. Today, the share of young adult African Americans with a graduate degree is more than half of the white rate; twenty-five years ago, it was one-third. Indeed, the share of young blacks with a graduate degree today is the same as the white share as recently as 1995.
- Today, African American children are in poverty at three times the white rate. Fifty years ago, it was four times.
- Fifty years ago, there were almost no predominantly white neighborhoods in which African Americans were living. Today, although many white neighborhoods are mostly all-white, the number with no African Americans is small.

In each of these areas, progress has been too slow and much more should be achieved.

Some things have not improved. African American homeownership rates are no better today than they were fifty years ago. More low-income African Americans live in neighborhoods with highly concentrated poverty than fifty years ago, largely because middle-class

African Americans have had more opportunities to leave. Although African Americans are now found in almost all executive suites, there are almost none at the top—only five CEOs in the Fortune 500 are black.

And some things have gotten much worse, in particular the mass incarceration of African Americans—today, 1 in 81 are imprisoned, up from 1 in 271 in 1970. A black man in his twenties now has a 1-in-3 chance of being confined to prison at some time in his life. This has a devastating impact on African American families and communities.

Why is it so important that we get this right? If you believe that there's been little progress, you won't appreciate the hard, deliberate, patient work that past racial justice activists undertook, and you'll have little incentive to learn how to duplicate that work. Past progress wasn't easy, and it wasn't accomplished just by marches and sit-ins. Those were important, but they were built on years of local organizing work, of the kind that racial justice activists should duplicate today.

We millennials have not seen national movement on issues we care about—like climate change, racial justice, income inequality—and so we've grown numb to issues that affect our lives and disillusioned with our ability to do anything about it. Issues the 1960s civil rights movement fought were strongly evident: segregated environments, denial of the right to vote, lynchings, church bombings, and the dreadful list continues. Changes happened nationally around these issues. How can we build a new movement when change seems less attainable?

In the 1950s and '60s, many African Americans in the South felt helpless to change conditions that affected their lives. Some felt that it was pointless to try to overcome them while others accepted that segregation and hardship was somehow their own fault. It was tough for civil rights activists to organize in the face of this resignation and the real dangers that taking action presented. Someone who had the courage to register to vote faced being fired, evicted from a home, denied credit—and being killed. Whites and blacks faced beatings, even assassination, for participating in civil rights activities. Even reporters and federal government officials were beaten for observing civil rights demonstrations.

White liberals who supported the civil rights movement also had to overcome their helplessness, as well as their indoctrination that African Americans' disadvantages resulted from blacks being less motivated, ambitious, and disciplined. The same feelings of powerlessness exist today, but less so.

The first challenge of racial justice activists is to educate potential recruits. Taking the next step, from awareness to action, was difficult then, and is now. But knowledge about the legacies of slavery and Jim Crow is deeper now than at any previous time in American history. That gives a contemporary civil rights movement a head start that the previous one never enjoyed.

Some states now prohibit teaching "critical race theory" or that the United States suffers from a legacy of systemic racism. Do you think that a teacher who describes our obligation to redress segregation would run afoul of those laws? It strikes me that even the unassailable facts documented in your previous book, The Color of Law, *would be off limits in many American public schools.*

When I (Richard) was a student in an all-white New York City public school in the 1950s, virtually nothing useful was taught about slavery or Jim Crow. I read a lot at home, and my seventh-grade teacher chastised me when I referred to the Civil War; she insisted that I was always to refer to it as the "War Between the States," because it was only about states' rights. So our first reaction to your question is that if some states are now trying to prevent the teaching of how racial inequality arose and has been perpetuated, that can only be because teachers are doing more than they have before, and that's progress.

Your question assumes that teachers are easily intimidated and won't teach an accurate account if states pass laws that seem to prohibit it (or, in a few cases, do prohibit it). That's not correct. Hundreds of thousands of teachers continue to teach accurately, even in states that attempt to frighten them. Where textbooks lie about our history, accurate material is available on the web, and many teachers use it.

In the 1920s, Tennessee prohibited teaching the Darwinian theory of evolution and required instruction in the biblical account of creation. Famously, a teacher named John T. Scopes defied the law and was prosecuted. He was convicted and fined, but his trial was a national sensation and made a mockery of the law. Teachers today should watch a somewhat fictionalized version of the Scopes trial, *Inherit the Wind* (1960), and take inspiration from his courage. If states were to fire or prosecute contemporary teachers for explaining our racial history, they will likewise inspire millions. Racial justice groups in states that are threatening to do this might establish funds to protect teachers from lost income if they are fired for fulfilling their professional responsibility to teach truth.

However: the laws to which you refer, in almost every state where they have been adopted, say that teachers *should* teach the history of slavery and segregation. Certainly, demagogues have ignored the words of the laws and implied the opposite. But what most of the laws prohibit is teaching children that they are personally responsible for these crimes, because they are white or because their family's economic circumstances are better as a result. We agree with this guidance. What teachers should explain is that each of us, regardless of our ancestry or race, has an obligation as an American to remedy the actions that created the apartheid society in which we live today.

As for "critical race theory," "systemic racism," and "structural racism," teachers should avoid these terms and teach in ways that children can understand. As this book explains, when we have a racially hierarchical society, even race-neutral policies can deepen inequality (recall our discussions of how property tax and credit-scoring systems are frequently discriminatory in effect, though not in intent). Both the Fourteenth Amendment to our Constitution and the Fair Housing Act prohibit actions that have such a disparate impact, even if unintentional, provided that a legitimate purpose can be accomplished without such discrimination. If teachers explain this, students can understand it without sloganeering.

How can we encourage more whites to get involved?

We've emphasized that local civil rights groups should be led by African Americans, but white leadership and participation are also essential. In the last decade, more Americans have become aware of heroic actions not only of black leaders but also of ordinary African Americans in struggles for equality. Many children, including whites, now see more positive images of African Americans, Hispanics, and Asians in books they get from libraries and in schools than previous generations. What they encounter less are accounts of whites who, alongside and in support of blacks, also sacrificed in campaigns for desegregation. Without the inspiration of such examples, there is a danger that whites who are civil rights supporters may come to see themselves as passive bystanders in fights for racial justice. This can doom those efforts to weakness.

White children require role models who have participated in the fight for desegregation. We have mentioned a few in passing from the twentieth century: Viola Liuzzo, Andrew Goodman, and Michael Schwerner, assassinated because they tried to help black Mississippians register to vote; and others, described but unnamed in earlier pages, like Bobbi Raymond, whose life's work was to desegregate the rental market of Chicago's Oak Park, or the many whites in West Mount Airy and Cleveland Heights who fought to open up their neighborhoods and then preserve their biracial characters.

Chapter 11 described how the real estate industry spent huge sums to defeat referenda that would have prohibited discrimination in housing. One, for example, was the 1964 vote in California (then a politically conservative state) that, by a two-to-one margin, protected the "right" to discriminate. But voting against the realtors were 1.5 million white Californians, including members of labor unions, women's organizations, religious groups, and teacher associations. Today, as then, when white majorities support segregation there are also large numbers of dissenters who can band together to fight for racial equality. Along with biographies of heroes and heroines like Rosa Parks, Martin Luther King Jr., Sojourner Truth, John Lewis, Thurgood Marshall, Frederick Douglass and many, many others, children should also be taught the stories of white supporters.

We might begin with Eleanor Roosevelt, who shared many assumptions of white superiority that were characteristic of her upper-class upbringing and milieu. Her husband, President Franklin Roosevelt, was a polio survivor, paralyzed and unable easily to travel. In his place, Mrs. Roosevelt became his "eyes and ears," traveling the country on his behalf. As she did so and met more African Americans, her views started to evolve.

Omaha, Nebraska, 1962. Shocked to learn that an African American surgeon could not purchase a home in middle-class neighborhoods, Lois Stalvey organized a diverse "Panel of Americans" to educate churches and synagogues about racial prejudice. Presenters included (left to right) Alice Trustin (Jewish), Lois Stalvey (Protestant), Sister Mary Catherine (Catholic), Elizabeth Organ (African American), and Susan Buffett (Protestant). In retaliation, the firm employing Mrs. Stalvey's husband then transferred him out of the city; the family relocated to Philadelphia, where she organized a similar "Panel of Philadelphians."

In 1938 she was invited to address a social welfare conference in Birmingham, Alabama, attended by about fifteen hundred policy advocates from across the South. The conference began on a Sunday evening, and when the police chief, Bull Connor, learned that blacks and whites had sat together in the meeting, he came the next morning, announced that the meeting was illegal, and surrounded the auditorium with police. He ordered whites to sit on one side of the auditorium and blacks on the other. When the First Lady arrived, she surveyed the scene and then took her seat on what had been designated the black side of the room. When a policeman ordered her to move to the white side, she demanded a folding chair and a yardstick. She then measured the distance between the black and white sides of the auditorium, plunked down her chair precisely above the midpoint, and sat there in the aisle until she was later called upon to speak.

The White House press secretary, Steve Early, had a firm policy of prohibiting black journalists from attending presidential press conferences. When Mrs. Roosevelt refused to obey the rule for her own meetings with reporters, he protested to President Roosevelt, who was unsuccessful in persuading his wife to comply. He might have been afraid to try.

Because of these and many similar actions, Dr. King referred to Eleanor Roosevelt as "perhaps the greatest woman of our time."

When in the twentieth century African Americans first attempted to move to previously all-white suburbs, almost no realtor would sell to them. They could move out of a segregated neighborhood only if a white supporter bought a home and then resold it to the African American family. These were called *straw purchases*, and there were many. That's how the Robinets became one of the first black families to own a home in Oak Park. In Louisville, Kentucky, a straw buyer got a fifteen-year jail sentence for buying and then selling a home in his own neighborhood to a black family. In Omaha, Nebraska, Lois Stalvey and her family were driven out of the city in the early 1960s for attempting to help an African American surgeon find an adequate home. She wrote an autobiography describing her evolution from a conventional white Protestant housewife to a racial justice crusader. It should be rewritten in a version for young adults. Whites like Mrs. Stalvey who defied neighbors to welcome black families to their neighborhoods were heroic. Schoolchildren should learn about them.

You write about whites and blacks. But others who are Asian or Hispanic or from other backgrounds also want to fix the harms of residential segregation. Where do we fit in?

In most parts of the country, African Americans and whites are the largest groups. Policies of segregation that the nation employed to impose inequality were, almost everywhere, specifically aimed at suppressing the well-being of the black population. In the west and southwest, Chinese, Japanese, and Mexican immigrants and their descendants were also the targets of discriminatory programs and policy, mostly by state, not federal government. Genocidal policies were enacted against Native Americans.

One does not have to be a member of a targeted racial or ethnic group to participate fully and equally in a racial justice committee. *Just Action* emphasizes the role of blacks because the legacies of slavery and Jim Crow remain with us today in many more places and to a much greater extent than the consequences of discrimination against others. And we emphasize the role of whites because in most parts of the country, they remain the dominant group, without whose political power racial justice campaigns are unlikely to win important victories. But Americans of all backgrounds can, and should, actively participate in committees to redress segregation.

Many of the reforms that *Just Action* advocates would benefit all racial and ethnic groups, even where an important justification for a reform is the historic targeting of African Americans. This is particularly true in the case of Hispanics, many of whom also live in areas of concentrated disadvantage and would benefit, for example, from the place-based programs that Part III of this book describes.

You write that if we improve conditions in low-income African American neighborhoods, we cannot expect those neighborhoods to remain entirely black because as they improve, middle-class whites will start to move in. Aren't you ignoring high-quality middle-class African American communities, like Prince George's County in Maryland, or Ladera Heights in California, that are both middle class and black?

We describe two types of neighborhoods that undergo racial transition. Type 1: those that were once almost all-black and low-income but are now becoming more white as housing stock and retail improve; and Type 2: places that were once all-white and in which large numbers of middle-class African Americans have settled.

As Type 1 neighborhoods improve, whites begin to move in. The arrival of these new residents is frequently called gentrification. It can occur either because whites begin to arrive and then attract higher-quality retail and housing or because the introduction of better retail and housing attracts whites to follow. Part II of this book describes policies and programs that can limit the number of black households who are displaced, but we don't think there is a way to prevent all displacement, retain the entire black population, and admit no others. It is unlikely (and as yet unseen) for a low-income segregated black community to remain all-black as it becomes middle- or upper-income

Type 2 neighborhoods can develop in several ways. Chapter 12 tells how white residents of Cleveland Heights made deliberate efforts to attract black neighbors. Oak Park and West Mount Airy citizens took similar action and responded to the influx of African Americans with actions to stabilize their community as desegregated.

As exclusionary suburban policies have diminished, middle-class black families have relocated to other formerly white places, like Prince George's County and Ladera Heights. Whites in these communities did not try or were not able to restrict this movement. African Americans are now a majority of both places. But their black populations seem to have peaked. Prince George's County was 64 percent black in 2010 but down to 59 percent in 2020, mostly because its Hispanic population has grown. Ladera Heights was 72 percent black in 2010, but down to 64 percent in 2020, as both the white and Asian populations have grown. In all these Type 2 communities, there are clusters where the black population is higher, just as there are clusters of other groups—such as Jews, Italians, and others—in communities throughout the nation.

High-quality middle-class black communities do exist and are attractive places to live for those that can afford them. But as they become attractive to middle-income blacks, middle-income whites and other ethnic groups tend to follow.

A NOTE ON WORD USAGE

This book is aimed not at policy experts but at people who want to take the initial steps to redress segregation and narrow racial inequality in their own communities. In some cases, we use terms that are not always technically precise but that make our words easier, we hope, to understand.

- We use *bank* to refer to local financial institutions that invest in mortgages, so this applies both to federally chartered banks and to state chartered savings-and-loan associations. Both banks and S&Ls are supervised by federal agencies today.
- There are two federal government-sponsored enterprises that provide mortgage funds to banks. One, the Federal National Mortgage Association (FNMA, or Fannie Mae) was created to replenish bank funds. The other, the Federal Home Loan Mortgage Corporation (Freddie Mac), was created to replenish S&L funds. Today, Fannie Mae and Freddie Mac remain separate but perform nearly identical functions. We ignore the distinction between the two and use *Fannie Mae* to refer to activities of either or both.
- We use *family* and *household* interchangeably, although families include only related individuals and households can include unrelated members. The Department of Housing and Urban Development refers to "family income" in calculating eligibility for subsidies, but its definition of *family* includes single persons living alone or unrelated individuals living together, which is how the Census Bureau defines a nonfamily household.
- We use *neighborhood, community, area, jurisdiction, place,*

city, and *municipality* interchangeably. When we use *neighborhood*, we do not necessarily mean a census tract, its technical definition.

- We use *project*, *development*, and *complex* interchangeably. When we write *project*, we do not mean a public housing project.

- Chapter 2 says that racially explicit remedial policies are needed to remedy racially explicit discriminatory policies that created a segregated and unequal society. Lawyers and judges use various terms, sometimes inconsistently, to describe them: *race-targeted*, *race-specific*, *race-based*, even *race-conscious*, although policymakers can be race-conscious without affirmatively favoring African Americans. We use the terms interchangeably.

- Housing policy is frequently based on a family's *median income* for a community (or an area's *median rent*). This is income that is higher than half of the family incomes in the area and lower than the other half (and similarly for median rent). The federal government defines "extremely low income" as less than 30 percent of area median income (AMI); very low income as 30 to 50 percent of AMI; and low income as 50 to 80 percent of AMI. When we use *low* or *lower income*, we are not referring to these specific government cutoffs. Depending on context, we could be referring to any or all of them. Median income is different from average income, which can be higher than the median if the richest families have incomes that are further above the median income than the incomes of the poorest families are below the median. We sometimes use *typical income* (or rent), by which we mean the median.

- When experts refer to the unaffordability of housing not only for low-income families but for lower-middle or even middle-income families, like teachers or nurses, retail or construction workers, they frequently say that we need workforce housing for this group. *Workforce housing* is an unfortunate phrase because it implies that low-income families who need deep housing subsidies are not in the workforce, which is mostly untrue. These households usually have jobs, sometimes multiple jobs, to make ends meet. The problem is not that they are out of the workforce, but that their wages are too low to make housing affordable in the current market. Except when we mention a specific "Workforce Housing" program where the phrase is in its official title, we generally refer to housing for lower-middle and middle-income households as *moderate-income housing* or *missing-middle housing*. Because rental subsidies are rarely available to families with incomes above 60 percent of AMI, we include 60 to 120 percent as the missing-middle range. This is not consistent with the government's definition of low income as 50 to 80 percent.

In the development field, missing-middle housing can refer not to unaffordability but to architectural type. In a neighborhood of single-family detached homes, missing-middle housing may consist of town houses, duplexes, and garden apartments. This use overlaps but is not identical to our use. In an affluent community, missing-middle structures like town houses might still be unaffordable to missing-middle households.

- We use *law*, *ordinance*, *rule*, and *regulation* interchangeably to describe municipal policy, although only states pass laws; cities adopt ordinances.
- We also use *middle-class* and *middle-income* interchangeably, although sociologists count many characteristics as contributing to middle-class status, in addition or even instead of income. (Impoverished graduate students may have low incomes, and their children may be eligible for free lunch in school, but they are still middle-class because of education, status, and behavior.) Similarly, *lower-class* in sociology refers to a group that not only has less income but also other below-average characteristics, like poor educational attainment. However, the term has taken on a pejorative connotation, so we avoid it; when we use *lower-income*, we sometimes are referring to *lower-class*, as sociologists use the term.

ACKNOWLEDGMENTS

A father-daughter collaboration is risky, success not inevitable. In this case, though, it could not have been more rewarding. The father came to appreciate how much insight, skill, knowledge, and passion the daughter had acquired in previous careers; the daughter, that there might be something to be said for the wisdom of old age. We often worked from different time zones but spent many nearly full days on an open phone line, discussing content and presentation of every topic in this book. She initially drafted some chapters, he others, but we hope that few readers will be able to guess who tackled which first. In what follows, *we* can refer to either or both of us.

We dedicate this book to each other.

Our appreciation of Bob Weil's commitment and dedication to this project can't be overstated. He "retired" as editor in chief of Liveright just before we presented the proposal for *Just Action,* but this was one venture he would not relinquish, to our good fortune. When he read our first draft, he politely observed that perhaps twenty-eight chapters was too much and that, to guide the reader through, our chapter titles might be more enticing and our subtitles more descriptive. As he proposed for *The Color of Law,* here, too, it was Bob's notion that an illustration to introduce each chapter would make the book attractive—thankfully, he made this recommendation after we abandoned the twenty-eight-chapter idea.

On the few occasions when we resisted Bob's counsel, our ever attentive literary agent, Gloria Loomis, was able to intervene and explain why Bob was right and we were wrong. Without her role in presenting both *The Color of Law* and *Just Action* to Bob, and her patience as we developed this sequel over too many years, neither book would have emerged. Authors are used to agents pestering them about when we would be done; Gloria understood that stoic silence was the most effective prod.

Bob's unique talent also includes his assembly of a remarkable team at Liveright. His deputy, Haley Bracken, expertly managed the entire process from draft manuscript to printed book and was always available to assist. If you think, as we do, that this is an attractive book, thank Anna Oler, who designed the inside, and Steve Attardo, our cover artist. We're grateful to Trent Duffy, our copyeditor, who instructed us in twenty-first-century grammar styles. You are able to get this book only because of the efforts of Steven Pace, who oversees sales, and Peter Miller (ably assisted by Cordelia Calvert), who organized (and organizes) publicity while Nick Curley and Pete Wentz handle marketing. All are part of a smoothly functioning team that makes editor Bob Weil seem infallible. Perhaps *seem* is not the right word.

Speaking of editors: readers rarely appreciate how essential good editing is. We had the good fortune to be able to hire a superb private editor to supplement Bob's work. Kit Rachlis spent several months going over *Just Action* chapter by chapter, raising questions about the arguments we were making, asking that we let the words "breathe" when he thought we came to a conclusion too quickly, while urging us to "trust the readers" when we had provided sufficient information to allow them to arrive at a conclusion on their own. Then, after all that was done, he spent days with us, going over the final manuscript line by line and word by word to ensure that we explained ourselves effectively. We said in *The Color of Law* and say again here: Kit Rachlis is truly a co-author of this book.

Supplementing Liveright's publicity team has been our indefatigable personal publicist, Johanna Ramos-Boyer. As we developed this book, she arranged presentations to a variety of audiences with whom we could explore our thinking. She continues to do so. Thank you, Johanna.

We set out to write a book that would guide readers who cared about racial justice to take steps in their own communities to redress it. Although all metropolitan areas in this country are needlessly and tragically segregated, all have distinct histories and opportunities. Our challenge was to present as many alternative areas of action as possible, so that local groups could be inspired to seize those that were most appropriate to their circumstances.

There are experts in each of the many housing policy areas that we determined to summarize, but none expert in all of them. To prepare to write this book, we had to learn a little bit about a lot of issues, but not a lot about any one of them. This required imposing on a large number of professionals in the housing field who had the patience to educate us about the fields in which they specialized. We consulted with them by phone, email, and video conference, in some cases multiple times as we found ourselves needing further explanation of housing challenges we mistakenly thought we already understood. We identify these authorities in the bibliography, listed by the first chapter for which they provided tutoring, although several explained more than one topic to us.

Four, however, deserve special mention:

- If you are concerned about racial inequality in housing, particularly those strategies we've referred to as place-based, subscribing to *Shelterforce.org* is essential. Many of its articles introduced us to policy challenges of which we had not previously been aware; its editor, Miriam Axel-Lute, read the entire manuscript and identified problems that we thought we had solved but had not.
- To understand mobility policy, the website of the Poverty & Race Research Action Council is equally essential. Phil Tegeler, its executive director, not only has deep knowledge of every aspect of the field but is acquainted with advocates everywhere who attempt to challenge segregation. He also read the manuscript, caught errors, and gave us invaluable advice.
- Lisa Rice, president of the National Fair Housing Alliance, can fairly be called the nation's chief of antidiscrimination advocacy and litigation. When Fannie Mae settled a lawsuit alleging that its foreclosed homes in white neighborhoods were maintained in better condition than those in black and Hispanic ones, that was Lisa at work. We made many revisions to our manuscript after she pointed out our initial errors.
- Greg Squires, a recently retired professor at George Wash-

ington University, has produced (indeed, continues to do so) scholarship on fair housing policy and practice that others in the field have learned to consult first. His career demonstrates that perhaps we were wrong when we said nobody can know a lot about a lot of housing policy issues. His comments on a draft of our manuscript also influenced this final version.

We worked for years on this book before anyone else set eyes on it. We hoped it would make sense and be informative to those who hadn't thought about these issues much, as well as to those who devote much of their time to them. But we couldn't know whether what we created accomplished this without careful reviews by a diverse group, one that included activists, scholars, and practitioners as well as typical readers whom we had encountered in church and book groups. Reading a not yet polished manuscript is not easy, yet their advice was consistently valuable. While we made many changes they recommended, mistakes or flaws that remain in *Just Action* may result from our failure to adopt more of their suggestions. Thanks to Tim Ambrose, Michael Ansara, Michelle Boyd, John Comer, Barbara Clutter, Bob Kuttner, Tiffany Manuel, Rochelle Miles, Josie Mooney, Kori Peragine, Natosha Reid Rice, and Jill Van Zanten.

Richard has had the good fortune of an unpaid appointment as a senior fellow of the Othering and Belonging Institute of the University of California, Berkeley. Its director, john a. powell, and assistant director, Steve Menendian, continue to educate him about race and housing, and he expresses his gratitude. The institute has provided him with summer research assistants, without whom this book could not have been produced. We look forward to following their inevitable success in postcollege careers. For now, we express our gratitude to Sophie Bandarkar, Caroline Buhse, Nemesio Cabral, Brianna Guerrero, Aaron Kinard, Maya Smith, Emily Stratmeyer, and Eva Thomas.

And thanks also to our virtual assistant, Melissa DeLacey, whose transcriptions of interviews are a trove of fair housing documentation.

Leah: A great gift of embarking on this project with my dad has been to witness up close the remarkable influence and contribution he's made with *The Color of Law* and the broad range of people who have been deeply affected by his work. I'm grateful to him for giving me the opportunity to join him in carrying it on, as well as his persistence in convincing me to do so. Writing a book, even with a co-author, can be a solitary endeavor. I am so appreciative for all those, especially my partner, Skye, who served as sounding boards and cheerleaders and made this feel like a team effort. It truly was. Thank you all.

Richard: I promised my wife and companion, Judith Petersen, that I would retire after publication of *The Color of Law*. I broke that promise. Judi: I pledge not to do it again. Your tolerance of my absences for this work, not only because you supported its mission but from your generosity and compassion, can never be fully repaid, but I'll try. I was also sustained in this endeavor by my children (biological and acquired), their spouses, and my grandchildren, Jesse, Joanie, Amy, Steven, Sam, Andy, Dorothy, and Oliver . . . and, of course, Leah. Thanks to all of you.

NOTES

These notes provide some added detail and sources for the general reader seeking more information. Source citations are reported by page and full paragraph number. Sources citing evidence described in a particular paragraph are assembled in a single note identified by that paragraph. Citations applying to a description in a paragraph that continues from one page to the next are identified in a note referring to the page on which that paragraph begins. If an article or book is the source of multiple statements in a chapter, the citation appears only at its first use. When an interview or email is the source, the name of the interviewee appears in the bibliography under the first chapter for which she or he provided information.

We only include citations here that are easily accessible and do not require paid subscriptions. An exception, though: we do cite here articles in major national newspapers and magazines that are behind paywalls; many readers of this book are familiar with obtaining articles from these publications. When an available resource such as a newspaper article summarizes scholarly work in a subscription-only, peer-reviewed journal, we cite the newspaper article, which will guide readers to more information. However, where a scholar has posted his or her journal article on a publicly available website, that source is cited.

We do not include state or federal government websites because subsequent administrations often remove documents from their sites and so, where possible, we cite articles or reports that refer to this information.

Sources not available to the general public, such as those in subscription-only, peer-reviewed journals or on websites behind a paywall, as well as some extended discussion and expanded index, are available at *justactionbook.org*. We will update this online resource, as necessary, for two years following publication of *Just Action*.

Introduction

p. 2, ¶ 1   Kluger 1976.

p. 3, ¶ 2   Rothstein 2004; Morsy and Rothstein 2019.

p. 4, ¶ 3   The census reports a black-white income gap of 60 percent. Estimates of the black-white wealth gap vary, partly because of different definitions (e.g., should wealth include the present value of an automobile that depreciates or a house that may appreciate or depreciate?) and partly because no government agency requires households to report their wealth. Estimates of the wealth gap range from 1 percent to 15 percent. We use 5 percent as the approximate average of these estimates.

p. 4, ¶ 5   McGhee 2021 emphasizes the explicit desire of conservative politicians to deny benefits to African Americans, while we highlight the cynical manipulation of white racial hostility to gather support for low taxes and impoverished government services. Both play a role.

p. 8, ¶ 2   Logan and Stults 2021: "There has been almost no change in the share of white neighbors for the average African American in this whole period."

In the southwest and California, immigrants and their descendants from Mexico, China, and Japan have suffered from discrimination and segregation. In California some school districts created Mexican attendance zones and offered whites who lived in them the opportunity to transfer out. This continued until 1946 when a federal court prohibited it. Fedbarblog 2021. In Texas, after Congress established the United States Housing Authority in 1937, the first public housing consisted of three projects in Austin—one for whites, one for blacks, and one for Mexicans. The black population of Austin was effectively forced to move to the area where the black project was located. But Hispanics who did not live in the public housing project continued to live anywhere in the city. Rothstein 2017. The impact of segregation on Mexican Americans in the southwest should be investigated further, and remedies enacted, but it does not explain contemporary inequality between whites and Hispanics in the rest of the country.

p. 8, ¶ 4   Alba and Islam 2009.

p. 9, ¶ 4   Cashin 2004.

p. 10, ¶ 2   In 2020, middle-class African American families with incomes greater than about $90,000, or about 134 percent of national median income, lived in neighborhoods with low-income rates of 12 percent (incomes of less than $45,000, or about 67 percent of national median income); for middle-class whites, it was only 8 percent. Logan, Stults, and McKane 2022.

p. 11, ¶ 1   As of the 2020 census, in the largest metropolitan areas of the country, 54 percent of African Americans live in suburbs. Frey 2022.

p. 11, ¶ 2   In 1950, average school completion for white males was 12.4 years; for nonwhites, 8.4 years. Average school completion for white females was 12.2 years; for nonwhites, 8.9 years. In 1952, 2 percent of whites and 10 percent of nonwhites were illiterate. Census 1961.

p. 12, ¶ 1   Lowery et al. 2018. For a repository of studies on black-white discrepancies in all aspects of policing, sentencing, and charging, see Balko 2020.

Chapter 1: You Should Just Do It

p. 15, ¶ 1   It is more probable that blacks would have white friends than whites would have black friends, because there are fewer African Americans than whites in the population. That two-thirds of whites in 2022 had an all-white social network was an improvement from a decade earlier, when three-quarters of whites had no nonwhite friends. Jones et al. 2022.

p. 16, ¶ 1   Steele 1997.

p. 20, ¶ 2   Johnson online-a and online-b; ABC7 2018.

p. 20, ¶ 3   Chicago Bungalow Association 2021a and 2021b.

p. 24, ¶ 1   McCutchan 2012.

p. 29, ¶ 2   Green and Hagiwara 2020.

p. 30, ¶ 4   Blackmon 2008.

p. 33, ¶ 2   Froba and Froba 2020.

p. 33, ¶ 4   Adjua Kwarteng is a pseudonym.

p. 35, ¶ 4   Ms. Byrd and Ms. Froba recruited other local organizations to join in their affordable housing advocacy, including Faith in the Valley and the LGBTQ+ Collaborative.

p. 37, ¶ 1   Neiman 2019. Contrary to Neiman's argument, we consider Germany's reckoning with its Nazi past to have little relevance for challenges Americans face. Although some Jews have now returned to Germany, and although antisemitic incidents are increasing (as they are in the United States), almost all Jews who were targets of Nazis were exterminated or fled the country. Germany has made reparation payments to many victims' descendants (most of whom live abroad), but Jews living in Germany today are not economically subjugated and segregated. Confronting its past does not require Germany to undertake major domestic economic and social reforms. In contrast, confronting the legacies of slavery and Jim Crow require Americans to undertake a substantial restructuring of economic and social arrangements. The ongoing subjugation of the black African population in South Africa, even after that country undertook a "truth and reconciliation" process that surpasses ours in honesty, has more relevant and troubling lessons for the United States than how Germany confronts its past.

p. 37, ¶ 3   States that have passed laws making it easier for owners to strike through or redact racial covenants in their deeds include Maryland, Virginia, Florida, Washington, California, and Minnesota. Biron 2021; Moyer 2020; Rios 2022.

p. 38, ¶ 2   Marin County 2021.

p. 38, ¶ 3   Nikole Hannah-Jones, creator of the "1619 Project" at *The New York*

Times Magazine, urges that the racial language should be removed everywhere. "We don't need to maintain that language in a document to understand the history of where we've come from," she wrote. Watt and Hannah 2020. We disagree. So much education is required to persuade Americans of the need for redress, we can ill afford to abandon an opportunity for education where it presents itself.

Chapter 2: Dare to Defy

p. 41, ¶ 3   In a 1972 opinion for a unanimous Supreme Court, Justice William O. Douglas quoted with approval the Fair Housing Act's Senate sponsor, Walter Mondale of Minnesota, who said: "the reach of the proposed law was to replace the ghettos 'by truly integrated and balanced living patterns.' " *Trafficante* 1972. See also *Starrett City* 1988.

p. 42, ¶ 1   The law is the Equal Credit Opportunity Act; it authorizes the Special Purpose Credit Program. Hayes 2020.

p. 43, ¶ 1   The Civil Rights Act of 1866 states: "All persons within the jurisdiction of the United States shall have the same right in every State and Territory to make and enforce contracts, to sue, be parties, give evidence, and to the full and equal benefit of all laws and proceedings for the security of persons and property as is enjoyed by white citizens." In 1883, the Court ruled that Congress lacked the Constitutional authority to extend such protection. *Civil Rights Cases* 1883; *Plessy* 1896; *Brown* 1954; *Corrigan* 1926; *Shelley* 1948; *Jones* 1968; *Steelworkers* 1979; *Wygant* 1986; *Adarand* 1995.

p. 43, ¶ 3   *Parents Involved* 2007. From Chief Justice Roberts's decision: "The way to stop discrimination on the basis of race is to stop discriminating on the basis of race."

p. 43, ¶ 4   *Grutter* 2003. From Justice Sandra Day O'Connor's majority opinion: "We expect that 25 years from now, the use of racial preferences will no longer be necessary."

p. 44, ¶ 3   *Cruikshank* 1876. It took the assassination of two white civil rights workers, Andrew Goodman and Mickey Schwerner (along with their African American co-worker, James Chaney) in 1964 for the Supreme Court to conclude that the federal government could prosecute Klansmen and sheriffs who participated in the crimes and not defer to state governments that either didn't prosecute or did so halfheartedly. *Price* 1966. For a description of the Ohio law, see Keating 1994.

p. 45, ¶ 2   *Dred Scott* 1857. The Court declared that the Missouri Compromise was unconstitutional. The Missouri Compromise was an 1820 act of Congress that admitted Missouri to the union as a state where slavery was permitted but prohibited slavery in any future territories which were located north of a line extended westward from Missouri's southern border. Blumenthal 2019 is a recent compelling and comprehensive history of the *Dred Scott* decision and the controversy that followed it.

p. 46, ¶ 2   Lincoln 1861: "[I]f the policy of the Government upon vital questions affecting the whole people is to be irrevocably fixed by decisions of the Supreme Court, the instant they are made in ordinary litigation between parties in personal actions the people will have ceased to be their own rulers, having to that extent practically resigned their Government into the hands of that eminent tribunal." Lincoln's view was that the Supreme Court could decide specific cases, but decisions in those cases should have no applicability to policy in general; opponents of slavery could take action after action to protect runaway slaves. Lincoln's expectation was that this process would eventually lead to the Court's deferral to congressional policy to protect former slaves in free states and to prohibit the extension of slavery to the territories.

p. 48, ¶ 3   Abandoning Supreme Court supremacy may not make it easier to narrow racial inequality in neighborhoods. Activists will have to persuade citizens to support racially explicit programs that diminish the legacies of slavery and Jim Crow. Americans don't presently favor this approach. A recent poll (Graf 2019) found that 73 percent of Americans oppose affirmative action in college admissions. A majority of African Americans, 62 percent, were also opposed, as were 65 percent of Hispanics and 63 percent of Democrats. We take a risk if we become a democracy, but it pales compared to the price we've paid by allowing an unelected court to rule.

p. 48, ¶ 4   Chemerinsky 2021 demonstrates that the Court, except for the Warren years, has consistently denied criminal defendants their constitutional rights. He urges police reformers to direct efforts to state constitutional and legislative improvement and abandon hopes that the Supreme Court will change. His recommendation also applies to residential racial segregation. Rare exceptions to the Court's endorsement of residential segregation were *Buchanan* 1917, which banned explicit racial zoning (its primary rationale was protection of property rights of homeowners who chose to sell or rent to opposite-race buyers or tenants), and *Shelley* 1948, which prohibited judicial enforcement of racially restrictive covenants, though it did not block covenants themselves as private agreements.

p. 49, ¶ 2   "In interpreting the Fourteenth Amendment, the Court reduced the 'privileges or immunities' guaranteed to citizens to virtual insignificance. . . . Increasingly, the Court construed the Fourteenth Amendment as a vehicle for protecting corporate rights rather than those of the former slaves." Foner 2019.

p. 53, ¶ 2   Bowie 2021a and 2021b.

p. 53, ¶ 4   Article III, Section 2 of the Constitution states: "[T]he supreme Court shall have appellate Jurisdiction, both as to Law and Fact, with such Exceptions, and under such Regulations as the Congress shall make." Hartmann 2022; Bouie 2022.

Chapter 3: Make a Plan

p. 56   The housing development was a partnership between the historically black Bethlehem Lutheran Church, which owned the land, and Tulane University's URBANbuild program, which provided the labor. The URBANbuild program began in 2005; it uses undergraduate and graduate students in the School of Architecture to design and construct affordable housing throughout New Orleans. The students complete all of the construction work that does not require a licensed professional.

p. 57, ¶ 1   The rule covers cities, counties, and states that receive housing and community development funds from the federal Department of Housing and Urban Development (HUD). Practically speaking, all communities are entitled to such funds, although they can escape coverage by refusing the grants. Hannah-Jones 2015.

p. 57, ¶ 2   HUD 2015. Although the rule did not explicitly apply to housing authorities, many jurisdictions that completed a plan before 2018 did so as collaborations between local governments and housing authorities.

p. 59, ¶ 1   New Orleans 2016, especially appendices B and C.

p. 60, ¶ 1   In 2021, the Louisiana Fair Housing Action Center analyzed the demographics of the city's neighborhood associations and tracked their activity in land-use debates. Over fifteen years, these associations helped block 422 affordable units from being built and delayed 184 more. The associations' board members were disproportionately white and homeowners compared with the neighborhoods they represented. LFHAC 2021.

Chapter 4: Is Homeownership the Answer? It's Complicated

p. 63, ¶ 2   Rothstein 2017; see especially chapter 4.

p. 63, ¶ 3   Chaskin and Joseph 2013.

p. 63, ¶ 4   "[A] decline in Black ownership of 10 points, quite common in many states, is associated with a 3.3-point drop in Black voter turnout net of other trends like the presence or absence of Obama on the ballot and the proliferation of strict voter ID laws." Rugh 2020.

p. 64, ¶ 3   A comparison between present rent and the monthly costs of a prospective home purchase should include, in addition to principal and interest, taxes, insurance, utilities, and maintenance costs. Home buyers should also anticipate possible future increases in tax or insurance costs.

p. 64, ¶ 5   The example is oversimplified because it assumes no inflation over these thirty years.

p. 65, ¶ 1   Census 2021; Reid 2021.

p. 65, ¶ 2   Badger and Bui 2022.

p. 65, ¶ 3   Choi, McCargo, and Goodman 2019.

p. 67, ¶ 1   Goodman and Zhu 2021.

p. 67, ¶ 4   Young adults are more likely to buy a home if parental wealth is more than $200,000, a threshold that half of white parents but only 10 percent of African American parents meet. The difference in homeownership and wealth between black and white parents explains 12 percent of the gap in homeownership between black and white young adults. Choi, Zhu, and Goodman 2018; Yun et al. 2021.

p. 67, ¶ 6   Freeman and Harden 2014.

p. 68, ¶ 2   The program was authorized in the Assets for Independence Act of 1998. Households are eligible if they receive benefits from the Temporary Assistance to Needy Families program or earn less than 200 percent of the poverty line and have less than $10,000 in assets.

p. 68, ¶ 3   The savings program is called the Family Self-Sufficiency Program; public housing residents and Section 8 recipients are eligible. Households enrolled in the program establish financial goals and receive additional services to help meet them. The funds are available when participants reach their objectives (usually within five years); there are no restrictions on how they use the savings. Brown 2017.

p. 68, ¶ 4   Housing finance agencies (HFAs) receive federal and state funding and usually contract with banks to administer their mortgage products, which may have different eligibility criteria and terms. Stegman and Loftin 2021.

p. 69, ¶ 1   In limiting (Iowa) or encouraging (Georgia) recipients to purchase homes in low-income neighborhoods, these programs reinforce segregation. Assistance should be designed to allow home purchases in any neighborhood.

p. 69, ¶ 4   Bailey et al. 2021.

p. 70, ¶ 3   The settlement includes a nonadmission clause, in which Wells Fargo denies it acted unlawfully. Mui 2012. Eligible home buyers in Minneapolis–St. Paul can receive $15,000, and those in the San Francisco Bay Area can receive $25,000 through this program.

p. 70, ¶ 4   Katzanek 2019. The Bank of America program is open to households with incomes up to 150 percent of the area median. Gross 2022.

p. 71, ¶ 1   See the reference to the Special Purpose Credit Program in the notes for chapter 2. Financial institutions are required to justify using this authority; requirements are less onerous for nonprofits. The ESL Credit Union in Rochester, New York, has adopted such a program targeted to black and Hispanic home buyers purchasing homes anywhere in the greater Rochester area (see chapter 11). The Bank of America program, described just above, and a down payment assistance program of JP Morgan Chase are justified as Special Purpose Credit Programs. Instead of targeting black and Hispanic home buyers who wish to purchase homes in any neighborhood, these bank programs assist home buyers of any race who wish to purchase in census tracts that are majority-black or majority-Hispanic. They thus attempt to improve black and Hispanic homeownership rates but in doing so, reinforce these groups' segregation.

p. 71, ¶ 2   The California Association of Realtors offers a Special Purpose Credit Program to first-time home buyers that grants up to $10,000 in closing cost assistance to low- or moderate-income African Americans and other members of an "underserved community." CAR online.

p. 71, ¶ 5   BirdSEED online.

p. 73, ¶ 2   Sackett 2016.

p. 74, ¶ 2   Malloy 2017.

p. 74, ¶ 3   Lenders can only sell loans to Fannie Mae in which borrowers meet minimum credit score standards. Banks rely on credit-scoring companies to provide this information. One company, the Fair Isaac Corporation, provides almost all credit-scoring information. Credit scores, therefore, are frequently called *FICO scores*. In most cases, banks don't get this information directly from FICO but through three credit-reporting companies—Equifax, Experian, and Transamerica. Mercator 2018.

p. 75, ¶ 1   FICO scores are weighted averages of the following: history of paying bills on time (35 percent); using a low percentage of available credit limits (30 percent); length of time making debt payments (15 percent); using different kinds of debt (10 percent); and not having new debt (10 percent). However, FICO's methods are not transparent for allocating points within these categories, and it retains considerable judgment in the calculation of individual scores. FICO online.

p. 75, ¶ 2   One-third of African Americans have no credit score, compared with 17 percent of whites. Of those with scores, 21 percent of African Americans have scores over 700, the level typically required for a mortgage, compared with 51 percent of whites. Choi, J., et al. 2019.

p. 75, ¶ 3   Pew 2012.

p. 76, ¶ 1   Reddy 2010.

p. 76, ¶ 2   Experian and FICO now permit borrowers to boost their scores by providing payment histories for utility and cell phone accounts. Consumers must sign up for this service with each company. Carr, Zonta, and Spriggs 2021; Kaul 2021.

p. 77, ¶ 3   A 2014 pilot program of the nonprofit Credit Builders Alliance investigated the effect of reporting rental history on credit scores. It studied 1,255 low-income tenants; 79 percent had an increase in their credit scores. Chenven and Schulte 2015; Goodman and Zhu 2018.

p. 77, ¶ 4   Hutson and Axel-Lute 2022.

p. 78, ¶ 2   Martinez and Kirchner 2021; Fannie Mae 2021; Lieber 2021.

Chapter 5: Mix 'Em Up!

p. 81, ¶ 2   For discussion of the federal program that gives tax breaks to developers, see chapter 10.

p. 82, ¶ 1   The 1931 Davis-Bacon Act requires contractors on federally funded projects to pay workers prevailing wages. In practice this means paying no less than rates negotiated by unions in the local area. The act removes the incentive for developers to replace existing union workers (more likely to be white) with lower-paid black and Hispanic workers willing to work for less to get the jobs. Many affordable-housing developers who oppose the law claim to be representing the interests of historically excluded groups. They are correct, but their arguments are no different from those used to oppose labor legislation generally, like minimum wage laws, the protection of the right to organize, and international labor standards.

p. 83, ¶ 1   Children from families in the lower half of the income distribution who have the opportunity to make friends in the upper half and who take advantage of that opportunity have better lifetime outcomes than similar children who don't make higher-income friends. Chetty et al. 2022; Miller et al. 2022.

p. 83, ¶ 5   Badger and Bui 2022. National median household income in 2020 was $67,521. Twenty-eight percent of African Americans have incomes between 60 and 120 percent of national median income. We consider these moderate- or middle-income. Another 28 percent are above 120 percent.

p. 84, ¶ 1   Kasakove and Gebeloff 2022. Economists refer to the tendency to marry partners with similar educational attainment as *assortative mating*. It has increased over the last half century.

African Americans may be an exception to this trend. Black marriage rates have been falling overall. College graduation rates for black women have been growing but remain low for black men. This makes assortative mating among African Americans less likely because college-educated black women have greater difficulty finding a college-educated black man as a spouse. Interracial marriages don't offset this trend, because most black-white marriages are between a black man and a white woman. Reeves and Rodrigue 2015.

p. 84, ¶ 3   Cytron 2011; Wilson 1987.

p. 85, ¶ 5   Eaton 2001; Wells et al. 2009.

p. 86, ¶ 3   Chaskin and Joseph 2015. When the projects were demolished, nearby whites voted for more liberal candidates. This held true even after accounting for changes in the overall political situation that might otherwise have explained whites voting for candidates with more racially liberal views. Enos 2016.

In other instances, projects termed "mixed-income" don't include nonpoor families. Many that are subsidized with tax credits (see chapter 10) are located in low-income, predominantly African American neighborhoods where property values are so low that market-rate rents are affordable to families whose incomes are only slightly above the subsidy level of 60 percent of the area median. Bostic et al. 2019; Chaskin et al. 2015. We do not consider projects to be mixed-income if they don't include middle-class households.

p. 86, ¶ 4   The relative alacrity with which young poorly educated black men respond to improved employment opportunities was demonstrated more than thirty years ago by Freeman (1991) and recently by Aaronson et al. (2019). Nonetheless, the white stereotype that African Americans lack a strong work ethic persists. The racial gap in labor force participation of these young men narrows in an improving economy, although the black rate remains below the white one. The persisting difference is perhaps attributable in part to a lesser work ethic or to discrimination—either on account of race alone or because of prior criminal records.

p. 87, ¶ 4   The first quoted interview is of a low-income resident of Oakwood Shores, where most residents, including new homeowners, were black. The second is of a low-income resident of Westhaven Park, where new homeowners included not only whites but Asians and Hispanics as well.

p. 88, ¶ 1   Cuozzo 2013; Greene 2015; Moyer 2015; Jacobus 2016.

p. 88, ¶ 3   Davis, Carter, and Hepner 2020.

p. 89, ¶ 5   Theodos, Stacy, and Teles 2021.

p. 89, ¶ 7   Kimura 2016.

p. 92, ¶ 1   Park 2020.

Chapter 6: Invest in Place

p. 97, ¶ 1   Kerubo 2021; Badger, Bui, and Gebeloff 2019.

p. 100, ¶ 3   In many areas, an increase in investment in a poor neighborhood does not lead to rapid housing appreciation and rent increases. Axel-Lute 2019. Nonetheless, rising rents remain a serious problem in low-income neighborhoods throughout the country, forcing renters to move even in the absence of gentrification. Mallach 2019. Whatever the cause, renter protection measures can mitigate the displacement of low-income renters and their cultural institutions.

p. 100, ¶ 5   Price 2014; Rose 2001; Greene, Ramakrishnan, and Morales-Burnett 2020; PWF 2019.

p. 101, ¶ 3   Wang and Balachandran 2021. On how inclusionary zoning policy can promote racial equity, see Reyes and Khare 2021.

p. 103, ¶ 2   DeSilver 2018; Gartland 2020; Sammon 2022.

p. 103, ¶ 4   Chew and Treuhaft 2019.

p. 104   The coalition of tenant organizations was coordinated by the Association for Neighborhood and Housing Development (ANHD), which created a set of anti-displacement principles to which Signature Bank agreed, following the groups' campaign. Ms. Rosero was president of the Brooklyn-based United Neighbors Organization, a coalition member.

p. 104, ¶ 1   A system that limits increases for new tenants is called *vacancy control*. Regulation that places no limit on rent increases when apartments turn over is called *vacancy decontrol*.

p. 104, ¶ 2   Barton 2019.

p. 105, ¶ 2   Rajasekaran, Treskon, and Greene 2019.

p. 107, ¶ 6   New Jersey and New Hampshire have statewide just-cause eviction rules. Cities with such rules include Seattle, Portland, San Francisco, Oakland, East Palo Alto, Los Angeles, San Diego, Boston, Chicago, New Orleans, Philadelphia, and Washington, D.C. The regulations are typically not strong enough to have a big impact on the eviction rate but make a small difference. LHS online; Howard 2020.

p. 108, ¶ 2   NCCRC online 2022a.

p. 109, ¶ 1   NCCRC online 2022b. In Cleveland, one cooperating philanthropy, Catholic Charities, does not have a requirement of public school attendance for provision of rental aid.

p. 109, ¶ 2   Park 2016

p. 109, ¶ 3   CPD 1976.

p. 110, ¶ 1   Park 2020.

p. 110, ¶ 2   Broadwater 2015.

p. 110, ¶ 3   Porch online.

p. 111, ¶ 1   Eberlin 2020.

p. 111, ¶ 3   Duong 2021.

p. 112, ¶ 2   Williamson 2020.

p. 112, ¶ 5   Washington, D.C.'s law, and others modeled after it, are known as Tenant Opportunity to Purchase Acts (TOPA). Gilgoff 2020.

p. 113, ¶ 4   Sentencing Project 2018; ACLU 2020.

p. 114, ¶ 1   Friedman 2015; NAACP online.

p. 114, ¶ 2   Because of its disparate impact on African Americans, such a blanket refusal probably violates the Fair Housing Act, but like most violations, enforcement requires victims to be more proactive in bringing complaints than we can reasonably expect. De La Garza 2020.

p. 114, ¶ 5   Couloute 2018.

p. 115, ¶ 2   Christman and Rodriguez 2016.

p. 115, ¶ 3   For more on the efficacy of ban-the-box ordinances in employment and hiring, see Emsellem and Avery 2016.

p. 115, ¶ 4   The state of Colorado as well as the cities of Seattle, Newark, Chicago, Detroit, Oakland, Berkeley, Washington, D.C., and others have also adopted ban-the-box rules for housing.

p. 116, ¶ 2   Subramanian, Moreno, and Gebreselassie 2014.

p. 117, ¶ 1   Smith 2020; Archer 2019.

p. 117, ¶ 3   Prieto 2011.

p. 118, ¶ 1   Michaels 2019.

p. 119, ¶ 3   For more information on existing community land trusts and resources for starting and managing them, see: Grounded Solutions online-a.

p. 120, ¶ 6   Yeoman 2018.

p. 123, ¶ 1   The trade-off between creating wealth and preserving affordable housing is also a challenge for other attempts to improve housing opportunities for African Americans, such as down payment assistance, which we describe in chapter 4. This aid can make homeownership affordable to black households that lack inherited wealth, but it does not add to the stock of affordable housing to help future home buyers. When families later sell, they can charge market rates, and a new buyer without inherited wealth will again require down payment aid to purchase the home.

Chapter 7: Stop the Fraud

p. 125, ¶ 1   Beryl Satter, a historian and the daughter of a lawyer who represented victims of contract sales, described the scheme as it operated in Chicago. Consider her book, *Family Properties* (2009), a companion to this one. See also McPherson 1972 and Finley 2016.

p. 126, ¶ 4   It is impossible to know precisely how many contracts were renegotiated because not all were reported. The estimated number is probably fewer than five hundred, out of three thousand victims in the Lawndale neighborhood alone.

p. 128, ¶ 1   Hirsch 1983.

p. 128, ¶ 2   Sugrue 1996.

p. 128, ¶ 3   Rothstein 2017 (see especially chapter 6); Downie and Hoagland 1969.

p. 130, ¶ 1   CTLTC online.

p. 130, ¶ 2   George et al. 2019; *Chicago Tribune* 1973.

p. 131, ¶ 5   Reed 2021.

p. 132, ¶ 2   Maryland 1955; Pietila 2010.

p. 132, ¶ 3   Other Baltimore banks that financed this speculation included Patapsco Federal Savings and Loan, Uptown Federal Savings and Loan, Maryland National Bank, Equitable Trust Company, First National Bank of Maryland, and National City Bank of Baltimore.

p. 132, ¶ 4   Goldseker Foundation online.

p. 133, ¶ 4   Contract sales take many forms and can be called *contract for deed, rent to own, land contracts,* and *rent for deed*. In our discussion, we do not attempt to distinguish the differences, if any, among these forms and instead discuss the characteristics they share.

p. 133, ¶ 5   Rothstein 2012. For more on the foreclosure crisis, see Lewis 2011.

p. 133, ¶ 6   Duca 2013.

p. 134, ¶ 2   In 2016, the National Fair Housing Alliance and twenty fair housing organizations sued Fannie Mae, alleging that after the 2008 foreclosure crisis, it maintained and marketed its foreclosed homes in white neighborhoods while allowing foreclosed homes in black and Hispanic neighborhoods to deteriorate, destabilizing those communities. In February 2022, Fannie settled the lawsuit with a payment of $53 million. Fair housing organizations plan to use $35 million of the funds for subsidizing home repair, home purchases, and neighborhood improvements for residents of the victimized black and Hispanic neighborhoods as well as ongoing investigation of discrimination that violates the Fair Housing Act. Goldstein 2022.

p. 134, ¶ 3   Goldstein and Stevenson 2016; Battle et al. 2016.

p. 134, ¶ 5   Stevenson and Goldstein 2016; NCLC 2020.

p. 135, ¶ 1   Kurth 2016; Burns 2017.

p. 135, ¶ 2   Two firms, Apollo Global Management and Home Servicing, have been active in southeastern cities. Another large buyer was Shelter Growth Capital Partners, founded by former Goldman Sachs executives. Yet another was Battery Point Financial, the project of another Goldman Sachs trader, who was responsible for buying collections of subprime mortgages during the run-up to the financial collapse and later bought the same (or similar) properties at bargain prices to sell on contract to the same (or similar) black and Hispanic victims.

p. 136, ¶ 2   Schaul and O'Connell 2022.

p. 136, ¶ 4   Burns 2015.

p. 137, ¶ 3   Allegheny County 2021.

p. 137, ¶ 4   Finney 2018; Leggate 2018.

p. 138, ¶ 4   NCLC and Pew 2021.

Chapter 8: What's a House Worth?

p. 144, ¶ 3   Alvernaz 2021.

p. 145, ¶ 1   Berry 2021; Avenancio-León and Howard 2020; *NYT* 2021.

p. 145, ¶ 2   Grotto 2021.

p. 146, ¶ 2   Knauss and Breidenbach 2019. This account of Syracuse's assessment inequity was previously published by Richard Rothstein in *The New York Times* (Rothstein 2020a). Many cities and counties specify that assessed values should be a certain percent of a home's real market price. There is nothing unfair about this, provided the same percentage is used for all property throughout the jurisdiction. For example, if all assessed values are 50 percent of market values, when the tax assessor divides the total of public budgets (school districts, fire departments, public libraries, etc.) by the total of assessed values, a rate results that is twice as high as the rate resulting if budgets were divided by assessed values at the full market price. With this twice-as-high-rate, homeowners pay taxes on only half the value of their homes, so the tax paid is no different than it would be if the assessed value was the actual value but the tax rate was only half as high. The problem lies with underlying assessments that have different relationships to market values in different neighborhoods, not with the uniform percentage applied to the underlying assessments for purposes of reporting taxable assessed value.

p. 146, ¶ 4   Wilson and Kuang 2020; Ferretti 2017.

p. 147, ¶ 2   Kaegi 2021a.

p. 149, ¶ 3   Schmidt 2021; Wilson 2021.

p. 150, ¶ 2   Kaegi 2021b.

p. 150, ¶ 3   Neavling 2020, 2021, and 2022.

p. 152, ¶ 5   For some specific stories, see Malagón 2020; Lisa Rice presentation in HUD 2021; Kamin 2020; Glover 2021; Burris 2021; Kamin 2022b.

p. 153, ¶ 1   Narragon et al. 2021.

p. 153, ¶ 2   In almost all comparisons of racial inequality, Hispanics suffer less discrimination than blacks. But in home appraisals it's reversed. Appraisals of homes being purchased by Hispanics and appraisals of homes in majority-Hispanic neighborhoods average further below actual sale prices than appraisals for African Americans. Yap et al. 2022.

p. 154, ¶ 1   Parker et al. 2021. Until the 1970s, national appraiser training materials instructed to take into account: "The neighborhood is entirely Caucasian. It appears that there is no adverse effect by minority groups." Squires and Goldstein 2021; Louis 1997.

p. 154, ¶ 4   Harney 2007.

p. 155, ¶ 2   Kamin 2022a.

p. 157, ¶ 2   N'namdi and Yoes 2022; Rao 2012.

p. 157, ¶ 3   In some states, homeowners can collect their home's auction price less the tax lien amount, interest, and fees, but they must know about this provision and how to apply for it. Even when they do, the amount they collect is typically far less than the equity in the home. Montag 2020.

p. 159, ¶ 1   Badger and Bui 2022.

p. 159, ¶ 2   Cenziper, Sallah, and Rich 2013. A 2017 class action lawsuit against the District of Columbia won a $1 million settlement for twenty-one homeowners who lost all equity in their properties through the tax lien foreclosure process. Some of these liens may have been due to billing errors. Hsu 2017.

p. 159, ¶ 3   HAI 2021.

p. 160, ¶ 1   Montag 2019.

p. 161, ¶ 3   Way 2022.

p. 161, ¶ 4   Abrams 2019.

Chapter 9: Where the Money Flows

p. 162   In 2018, the California Reinvestment Coalition and the Anti-Eviction Mapping Project analyzed banks' financing of the displacement of low-income renters and identified First Republic as the worst offender in its lending to Oakland landlords. The coalition called for reforms on the city, state, and federal level, including more effective use of the Community Reinvestment Act to prevent this practice.

p. 163, ¶ 3   The Home Mortgage Disclosure Act makes this information public, and there are several online services where users can access and analyze data for a nominal fee.

p. 163, ¶ 4   FHCCI 2021.

p. 164, ¶ 4   The Community Reinvestment Act is intended to combat the history and legacy of redlining, but it is race-neutral, concerned with banks' performance in low- and moderate-income communities.

p. 165, ¶ 3   Odendahl 2021.

p. 166, ¶ 1   NCRC 2022.

Chapter 10: Make the Exclusive Inclusive

p. 171, ¶ 2   *Mhany* 2016 and *Avenue 6E* 2016 established that the racially charged code words used by city officials or their constituents to defend exclusionary zoning can be evidence of intentional racial discrimination and that their zoning ordinances therefore violate the Fair Housing Act.

p. 171, ¶ 3   Ikeda and Washington 2015.

p. 172, ¶ 2   Viala-Gaudefroy 2020.

p. 173, ¶ 1   Prevost 2021.

p. 173, ¶ 2   Frank and OCA 2020; Bronin 2021; Putterman 2021.

p. 173, ¶ 3   Whitten 1922.

p. 174, ¶ 1   The Census "Quick Facts" tool reports city population and homeownership data by race. The Partnership for Strong Communities' Housing Data Profiles report the median home values in Connecticut's cities and counties. Thomas 2020c.

p. 174, ¶ 2   Ellickson 2020.

p. 175, ¶ 1   Thomas 2020d.

p. 175, ¶ 3   Thomas 2020b.

p. 175, ¶ 4   Breen 2020; Glassman 2021; Prevost 2022.

p. 176, ¶ 2   Massey et al. 2013.

p. 176, ¶ 3   An analysis of more than three thousand federally subsidized low-income, affordable-housing developments in the country's twenty least affordable markets found they usually had no significant impact on surrounding property values. Young 2016.

p. 177, ¶ 4   Chapple et al. 2020.

p. 178, ¶ 1   One California town claimed that permitting duplexes within its boundaries would violate endangered species laws because the entire town was a "mountain lion habitat." Another town prohibited residents of new duplexes from either parking on the street or off it. Dougherty and Karlamangla 2022.

p. 178, ¶ 2   Massachusetts's Chapter 40B law requires jurisdictions to approve affordable-housing developments regardless of local zoning ordinances, unless the jurisdiction has achieved low- and moderate-income housing production goals. New Jersey's 1985 Fair Share Act mandates every jurisdiction provide its fair share of its region's housing need for low- and moderate-income households, regardless of zoning. Although both states define "moderate income" as those earning up to 80 percent of area median income, we consider those earning up to 120 percent AMI as moderate income.

p. 178, ¶ 3   Twin Cities PBS 2018.

p. 179, ¶ 2   The plan, "Minneapolis 2040," also allowed more dense housing near transit, eliminated parking requirements, increased funding for affordable housing, and implemented inclusionary zoning. Kahlenberg 2019. Large single-family lots are those of 5,000 square feet or more. Badger and Bui 2019.

p. 179, ¶ 4   Freemark and Lo 2022.

p. 180, ¶ 1   Mallach 2020.

p. 182, ¶ 1   Grounded Solutions online-b.

p. 182, ¶ 3   WCNC 2013.

p. 182, ¶ 4   Reyes and Khare 2021.

p. 183, ¶ 2   Scally, Gold, and DuBois 2018. Almost half (47 percent) of tenants in Low-Income Housing Tax Credit developments earn 30 percent of area median income or less. Lawrence 2021.

p. 183, ¶ 3   Forty-one percent of tax-credit tenants use federal, state, or local rental assistance to pay for the already subsidized units. Of these, more than half use Section 8 rental subsidies.

p. 183, ¶ 4   Fischer 2018.

p. 184, ¶ 3   At year fourteen, the owner of a tax-credit property may request that the state's tax-credit allocating agency seek a qualified buyer who will purchase the property and maintain it as affordable for the second fifteen-year period. Federal regulations set a formula for determining the required price for such a purchase, which in most cases significantly exceeds the project's market price as affordable housing. When the allocating agency fails to find a buyer within one year, the property is released from its affordability requirements and the owner is free to sell it at market value or continue to own the property and charge market-rate rents. However, the federal government could revise the program regulations to lower the required purchase price for such transactions, so that these projects are more likely to remain affordable for the second fifteen-year period.

p. 185, ¶ 3   Section 8 is now called the Housing Choice Voucher program. Since it is most commonly known as Section 8, that is how we refer to it. The maximum rent a voucher can support (the area's fair market rent) is usually set at the 40th percentile of market rents, or just below the area's median rent. Voucher holders can lease a unit that exceeds the area's fair market rent, but their contribution cannot be more than 40 percent of their income.

p. 185, ¶ 4   King 2021.

p. 185, ¶ 5   Sard et al 2018.

p. 186, ¶ 1   If not for these obstacles, many more voucher holders could live in high-opportunity communities. In the country's fifty largest metropolitan areas, 18 percent of voucher-affordable units are located in high-opportunity areas, but only 5 percent of voucher holders live in these neighborhoods. Mazzara and Knudson 2019; Thomas 2020a.

p. 186, ¶ 2   PRRAC 2020; PRRAC 2022

p. 186, ¶ 3   In many jurisdictions with a source of income discrimination law, landlords require tenants' income be three times the rent and do not consider vouchers as income, making all Section 8 recipients ineligible. Some source-of-income discrimination laws, such as Washington State's, explicitly prohibit this practice, but it continues. Advocates have filed several lawsuits against landlords in Washington who discriminate against Section 8 tenants.

p. 186, ¶ 4   Bell, Sard, and Koepnick 2018.

p. 188, ¶ 3   The neighborhood-based payment standards are called *small area fair market rents* (SAFMRs). Before HUD required housing authorities in twenty-three metropolitan areas to implement SAFMRs in 2018 (including Dallas, twenty-four are now required to do so), the agency studied the effects of seven housing authorities using the new payment standard. Results showed that the number of voucher holders living in high-opportunity areas rose in agencies using SAFMRs, while those in comparison agencies where payment standards remained unchanged did not. Patterson and Silverman 2019; CBPP and PRRAC 2018.

p. 188, ¶ 4   Housing authorities that voluntarily adopt SAFMRs have two options: they can use small area rent standards in individual zip codes without federal approval, or they can request authorization to apply SAFMRs metropolitan-wide. The former allows for increasing rent caps only in higher-cost neighborhoods, without reducing rent subsidies in lower-cost areas. The latter option provides more opportunity for voucher holders to move to high-cost areas and more potential for housing authorities to realize cost savings.

p. 189, ¶ 4   *Hills* 1976; Polikoff 2006; Sanbonmatsu et al. 2011; Rubinowitz and Rosenbaum 2000.

p. 192, ¶ 1   HONP online; Dimmick 2022; Fechter 2022.

p. 192, ¶ 2   Administrative changes can also ease landlords' participation in the voucher program. Housing authorities must inspect and approve voucher-eligible units, and they must be vacant at the time. Landlords often must wait for inspections, losing rental income during that period, which deters many from participating. Advocates can press their local housing authorities to ensure prompt inspections and approvals.

Chapter 11: Hold Them Accountable!

p. 195, ¶ 1   Fisher 1999.

p. 195, ¶ 2   Flanagan and Bender 2021.

p. 196, ¶ 1   Newlands 1909; *NYT* 1912; *NYT* 1916.

p. 196, ¶ 2   CCLC online; MHP online. The Census "Quick Facts" tool reports city population by race and median income data.

p. 196, ¶ 4   CCLC 2020.

p. 197, ¶ 4   The account here and in the following paragraphs of Hillsdale's segregation and the firms responsible for it was previously published by Richard Rothstein in *The New York Times* (Rothstein 2020b).

p. 198, ¶ 1   Coldwell Banker online.

p. 198, ¶ 2   The company has replaced this statement on its website with one that does not refer to helping organizations or serving causes. The original statement can still be found in web archives. Bohannon Companies online.

p. 198, ¶ 3   Wells Fargo 2019.

p. 199, ¶ 1   Jarovsky 1989.

p. 199, ¶ 6   City Roots 2020.

p. 200, ¶ 2   ESL online; ESL 2021.

p. 201, ¶ 3   Yager 2016.

p. 203, ¶ 1   Paschall 2021; Kaufman 1978.

p. 204, ¶ 1   Carreon 2021.

p. 204, ¶ 2   Howard Hanna online.

p. 204, ¶ 3   Virginia National Bank online.

p. 204, ¶ 4   Lee Building Company online.

p. 205, ¶ 1   *Baltimore Sun* Editorial Board 2022.

p. 207, ¶ 4   Moncrieff 2007.

p. 208, ¶ 2   Slater 2021; Moncrieff 2007; *NYT* 1964b.

p. 209, ¶ 1   Gittelsohn 2020.

p. 209, ¶ 2   CB online; Business Wire 2021; KW online.

p. 209, ¶ 6   NAR 2022.

p. 210, ¶ 3   Choi, A., et al. 2019.

p. 211, ¶ 3   HUD 2013; Freiberg 2013.

p. 212, ¶ 3   Freiberg 2019.

p. 214, ¶ 3   The cities were Akron, Atlanta, Chicago, Cincinnati, Los Angeles, Louisville, Memphis, Milwaukee, and Toledo. Smith and Cloud 1997.

p. 217, ¶ 2   McDermott 2019.

p. 218, ¶ 2   Turner and Rawlings 2009.

Chapter 12: Desegregate for the Long Term

p. 221, ¶ 2   Cashin 2004; Saltman 1990.

p. 222, ¶ 2   Perkiss 2014.

p. 224, ¶ 3   Notebook 2019.

p. 225, ¶ 2   McKenzie and Ruby 2002; Sheppard 1977.

p. 225, ¶ 3   OPRFM 2018.

p. 226, ¶ 1   Trainor 2022.

p. 226, ¶ 2   In 1977, a federal appeals court ruled bans on "for sale" signs unconstitutional. The village's ban remains in its code but is not enforced; residents encourage new realtors to comply with it, and most do. While blockbusting is no longer
a threat, compliance with the ban is a sign of respect for fair housing work done
decades ago. Jackson 2016; *Linmark* 1977; Breymaier 2018.

p. 228, ¶ 1   The center's affirmative marketing fulfills the Fair Housing Act's purpose of promoting integration. Wary of legal challenges, landlords do not accept
or deny tenants based on their race but agree only to market units through the
housing center; the center makes nonbinding referrals to the apartment owners.
OPRHC 2016.

p. 228, ¶ 2   The Census "Quick Facts" tool reports city population and homeownership data by race.

p. 228, ¶ 3   Kaeser 2020.

p. 230, ¶ 1   Keating 1994.

p. 230, ¶ 2   The defendant, the Rosenblatt Realty Company, continues to practice in
the Cleveland area.

p. 233, ¶ 3   Mickelson 2011; Wells et al. 2009.

p. 234, ¶ 1   Rothstein, Jacobsen, and Wilder 2008.

p. 234, ¶ 3   Miyake-Trapp 2018.

p. 236, ¶ 1   GAO 2018; Nance 2017; Whitaker et al. 2019.

p. 236, ¶ 5   Bacher-Hicks, Billings, and Deming 2019.

p. 236, ¶ 6   GAO 2020.

p. 237, ¶ 3   Cohen 2016.

p. 238, ¶ 2   *Milliken* 1974.

p. 239, ¶ 1   *Parents Involved* 2007; Cobb 2022.

p. 239, ¶ 5   *Sheff* 1992; Sheff Movement online.

Epilogue

p. 244, ¶ 2   Cashin 2021; McGhee 2021.

Frequently Asked Questions

p. 250, ¶ 4   Pew 2021.
p. 255, ¶ 2   *NYT* 1964a.
p. 256, ¶ 1   Gray 2019; Mancini 2018.
p. 257, ¶ 1   King 1962.

BIBLIOGRAPHY

INTERVIEWS

Interviews with the following experts took place in person or via email, phone, or videoconference. Although some of the experts gave advice regarding multiple chapters, they are listed here only by the first chapter for which they were consulted, although their contributions may have been even greater for later ones.

Chapter 1: You Should Just Do It

Marisol Aguilar, Cynthia Barnes-Slater, Bruce Bondy, Lauren Bondy, Kevin Bruce, Fran Buntman, Wendy Byrd, Pastor Harvey Carey, Chanda Causer, Jennifer Chan, Laurie Elkin, Dave Froba, Sharon Froba, Alfredo Garcia, Van Gilmer, Laurie Goldstein, Joan Grangenois-Thomas, Alan Hatchett, Kimberly Holley, Marcella Holmes, Ilene Jacobs, Tonika Johnson, Kelly Kent, Sue Kent, Jonathan Klein, Maria Krysan, Adjua Kwarteng, Amanda Lankerd, Rev. Debbie Layman, Rosemary Linares, Michelle Logan, (the late, and sorely missed) James Loewen, Rev. Steve McCutchan, Brighid O'Shaughnessy, Angela Pauldine, Jobanna Peralta, Chris Peterson, Edie Rasell, Heather Ross, Ankit Shah, Clara Silva, Rev. Sam Stevenson, Carmen Stratton, Nancy Taylor, Nanette Tucker, Vineeta Vijayaraghavan, Darshan Vijaykumar, Marianne Villalobos, Rev. Kent Walley, Glenda Wilks, Wade Wilson, Geri Wright.

Chapter 2: Dare to Defy

Anne Bloom, Courtney Hodapp and colleagues, Howard Husock, Rebecca Labov, David Oppenheimer, Samuel Rothstein.

Chapter 3: Make a Plan

Liz Darby, Cashauna Hill, Betsy Julian, Lisa Rice, Michael Strecker, Phil Tegeler.

Chapter 4: Is Home Ownership the Answer? It's Complicated

Taylor Andre, Brook Baird, Simone Boyd, Markita Bryant, Stephanie Christmas, Gregory Hettrick, Tony Keith, Charles Lewis, Peg Malloy, Linda Mann, Carolina Reid, Linette Rhodes, Jasmin Shupper, Dirk Swift, Chrissy Washburn, Farrah Wilder, John Williams, Lisa Wise.

Chapter 5: Mix 'Em Up!

Several tenants of Avondale, Zack Barowitz, Beverly Bates, Josh Bivens, Mara Blitzer, Daryl Carter, Patty Cooper, Kim Cranston, Alea Gage, Carol Galante, Devika Goetschius, Lauren Green-Hull, Chazzie Henderson and other Watson tenants, Rosie Hepner, Miles Hewstone, Mark Joseph, Stacy Kaplowitz, David Kemper, Dana Kenison, Keith Kintrea, Frederick Klein, Cynthia Lacasse, John Logan, Susan Longstreet, Jane Mansbridge, Stephen Menendian, Lawrence Mishel, Bart Mitchell, Carol Naughton, Cynthia Parker, Dan Parolek, Karen Parolek, Christopher Ptomey, Robert Putnam, Richard V. Reeves, Smitha Seshadri, Hugh Spitzer, Michael Spotts, Caroline Swinehart, Beverly Tatum, Mark Teden, Linda R. Tropp, Gilbert Winn.

Chapter 6: Invest in Place

Rachel Bratt, L. D. Burris, Adam Cederbaum, Robert Cherry, Reed Colfax, Sharon Cornelissen, Kristen Cox, Miniard Culpepper, Madeleine Daepp, Kenny Dalsheimer, Colleen Dawicki, Luke Davenport, Marybeth Dugan, Tom Fiddler, Joan Fitzgerald, Rebecca Fontaine, Reann Gibson, Mary Gies, Peter Gilbert, Laurie Goodman, Lisa Govoni, Erin Graves, Lauren Hamilton, Rachel Heydemann, Linda Hunt, Rick Jacobus, Alisa Johnson, John Koskinen, James Kushner, Rebecca Lane, Susan Levy, Nora Linares-Moeller, Joyce Linehan, Mark Lopez, Selina Mack, Sally Martin, Alicia Mazzara, Jen McCormick, Juanita McNeil, Bob Mendes, Louis Mirante, Eli Moore, Mary Pattillo, Sandy Perry, Natosha Reid Rice, Hazel Remesch, Carl Richie, Angie Rodgers, Sally Santangelo, Lorisa Seibel, Melanie Shakarian, Mitchell Silver, Beth Sorce, Phil Star, Abigail Staudt, Erik Tang, John Washington, Tes Welborn, Spencer Wells, Jim Yamin.

Chapter 7: Stop the Fraud

Sara Benson, Brian Brown, Mike Gallagher, Tanya Golash-Boza, Amber Hendley, Saul Kerpelman, Linlin Liang, Sarah Mancini, Linda Mullenbach, Carol Ott, Kimberly Rubens, Beryl Satter, Terry Staudenmaier, Kevin Stein.

Chapter 8: What's a House Worth?

Bernadette Atuahene, Carlos Avenancio-Leon, Christopher Berry, Michelle Boyd, Ira Goldstein, Jacquelyn Griffin, Staci Horwitz, Troup Howard, Junia Howell, Jacob Inwald, Reggie Jackson, Fritz Kaegi, Andrew Kahrl, Dennis Kaufman, Steve Miner, Coty Montag, Steve Neavling, Jerry Paffendorf, John Rao, Joanne Savage, Scott Smith, Greg Squires.

Chapter 9: Where the Money Flows

Michael Ansara, Barry Berman, Adam Briones, Lew Finfer, John Gamboa, Josh Gnaizda, Debi Gore-Mann, Rolando Guzman, Bob Kuttner, Brian Maxey, Amy Nelson, Robert Ross, Jerry Rubin, Claudia Viek, Jamie Weisberg.

Chapter 10: Make the Exclusive Inclusive

Grace Baranowski, Renata Beamon, Matthew Berke, Paul Berman, Laura Beshara, Erin Boggs, Camille Brown, Sarah Brundage, Mike Daniel, Peter Dreier, Antonia Fasanelli, Barbara Fields, Janne Flisrand, Sheila Foster, Kelli Furtado, Vonda Goodman, Tyler Graber, Alyson Griffin, Wendy Hamilton, Brian Hanlon, Tracewell Hanrahan, Jennifer Hernandez, Judy Hughes, Parisa Ijadi-Maghsoodi, Alice Ingerson, Dewanna Johnson, Monique Johnson, Cydney Jones, Peter Kye, Thomas Lindsey, Ann Lott, Tiffany Manuel, Matt McDermott, Lisa McDonald, Molly Metzger, Fernanda Nicola, Chrishelle Palay, Kori Peragine, Tom Poupard, Lois Quinn, Alana Rosenberg, Robert Rozen, Frank Schneiger, Evora Sykes, Heather Thomas, Nancy Torphy, Marshall Wildmann, Alice Woods.

Chapter 11: Hold Them Accountable!

Caris Adel, Harriet Avery, Mark Barker, Laurie Benner, Max Besbris, David Bohannon, Jan Brito, Tom Brown, Garin Burbank, Eliza Cava, Lee Davenport, Jon Deane, Bill Dedman, Jack Dougherty, DeAnna Eason, Len Elder, Karyl Eldridge, Franco Faraudo, Robert Fitzpatrick, Marie Flannery, Steve Francks, Fred Freiberg, Sena Friedman, Ryan Gorman, Bryan Greene, Karen Grove, Ulani Prater Gulstone, Ellen Haberle, Robert Haden, Chris Hammond, Sophia Heath, Jeffrey Hicks, Daniel Holland, Heather Hopkins, Beth Huffer, Orville Jackson, Rebecca Jacobsen, Devala Janardan, Gary Keller, John Kent, Ajamu Kitwana, Jamie Langowski, John Leonardi, Maura McDermott, Stuart Mitchell, Scott Morrell, Jeremy Newman, Maureen O'Connell, Alice O'Connor, Rich Pulvino, Brooke Raymond, Mahogany Rhodes, Carol Rose, Gail Sansbury, Gail Schechter, Daniel Schudson, Gene Slater, Alexia Smokler, Heather St.-Aime, Amanda Szakats, Brennon Thompson, Jenny Thompson, Fred Underwood, Eric Van Dusen, D. J. Waldie, Jen Ward, Kimberley Wiedefeld, Shane Wiegand, Thomas Wills, Jordy Yager.

Chapter 12: Desegregate for the Long Term

Patrick Conyers, Alan Greenberger, Tammie Grossman, Yvonne Haskins, Dennis Keating, Steve Kendall, Andrea Krieg, Daniel Lauber, Diane Lauber, Frank Lipo, Monica Lopez, Sara Mosle, Myron Orfield, Abigail Perkiss, Don Register, Nureed Saeed, Peter Shapiro and his students, Eleanor Sharpe, Josh Spodek, Jennifer Waddell.

Frequently Asked Questions

Kalyn Belsha, Bill Bigelow, Scott Browne, Rachel Cohen, Heidi Erstad, Sam Heath, Jessica Lee, Anne McCracken, Deborah Menkart, Maureen O'Connell, Stephen Rosenthal, Chris Shepard, Ranjani Sheshadri, Ursula Wolfe-Rocca.

COURT CASES (LISTED IN CHRONOLOGICAL ORDER)

Dred Scott v. Sandford. 1857. U.S. Supreme Court, 60 U.S. 393.
United States v. Cruikshank. 1876. U.S. Supreme Court, 92 U.S. 542.

Civil Rights Cases. 1883. U.S. Supreme Court, 109 U.S. 3.

Plessy v. Ferguson. 1896. U.S. Supreme Court, 163 US 537.

Buchanan v. Warley. 1917. U.S. Supreme Court, 245 US 60.

Corrigan v. Buckley. 1926. U.S. Supreme Court, 271 U.S. 323.

Shelley v. Kraemer. 1948. U.S. Supreme Court, 334 U.S. 1.

Brown v. Board of Education of Topeka. 1954. U.S. Supreme Court, 347 U.S. 483.

United States v. Price. 1966. U.S. Supreme Court, 383 U.S. 787.

Jones v. Mayer. 1968. U.S. Supreme Court, 392 U.S. 409.

Trafficante v. Metropolitan Life Ins. Co. 1972. U.S. Supreme Court, 409 U.S. 205.

Milliken v. Bradley. 1974. U.S. Supreme Court, 418 U.S. 717.

Hills v. Gautreaux. 1976. U.S. Supreme Court, 425 U.S. 284.

Linmark Associates, Inc. vs. Township of Willingboro. 1977. U.S. Court of Appeals, Third Circuit. 535 F.2d 786.

Steelworkers v. Weber. 1979. U.S. Supreme Court, 443 U.S. 193.

Wygant v. Jackson Board of Education. 1986. U.S. Supreme Court, 476 U.S. 267.

United States v. Starrett City Associates. 1988. U.S. Court of Appeals, Second Circuit, 840 F.2d 1096.

Sheff v. O'Neill. 1992. Conn. Superior Court, 609 A.2d 1072.

Adarand Constructors v. Pena. 1995. U.S. Supreme Court, 515 U.S. 200.

Grutter v. Bollinger. 2003. U.S. Supreme Court, 539 U.S. 306.

Parents Involved in Community Schools v. Seattle School Dist. No. 1, et al. 2007. U.S. Supreme Court, 551 U.S. 701.

Mhany Management, Inc. v. County of Nassau. 2016. U.S. Court of Appeals, Second Circuit. 819 F.3d 581.

Avenue 6E Investments v. City of Yuma. 2016. U.S. Court of Appeals, Ninth Circuit, No. 13–16159.

ARTICLES, BOOKS, WEBSITES

Aaronson, Stephanie R., et al. 2019. "Okun Revisited: Who Benefits Most from a Strong Economy?" *Brookings Papers on Economic Activity*, Spring: 333–403.

ABC7. 2018. "Folded Map Project: Capturing the Division of the City." *ABC7 Eyewitness News*, September 5.

Abrams, Amanda. 2019. "Helping At-Risk Homeowners Stay Put with a Land Trust." *Shelterforce.org*, April 25.

ACLU. 2020. *A Tale of Two Countries: Racially Targeted Arrests in the Era of Marijuana Reform.* American Civil Liberties Union.

Alba, Richard, and Tariqul Islam. 2009. "The Case of the Disappearing Mexican Americans: An Ethnic-Identity Mystery." *Population Research Policy Review* 28: 109–21.

Allegheny County, Pennsylvania. 2021. "Consent Petition for Final Decree." Court of Common Pleas. No. 18–9176, July 27.

Alvernaz, Christina. 2021. "Memorandum on Dept. of Housing and Urban Development Disparate Impact Rule." Equal Justice Society. March 29.

Archer, Deborah N. 2019. "The New Housing Segregation: The Jim Crow Effects of Crime-Free Housing Ordinances." *Michigan Law Review* 118 (2): 173–232.

Avenancio-León, Carlos, and Troup Howard. 2020. *The Assessment Gap: Racial Inequalities in Property Taxation.* June. Washington Center for Equitable Growth.

Axel-Lute, Miriam. 2019. "It Doesn't Matter if Your Neighborhood Is Going to Eventually Gentrify." *Shelterforce.org*, July 31.

Bacher-Hicks, Andrew, Stephen B. Billings, and David J. Deming. 2019. "The School to Prison Pipeline: Long-Run Impacts of School Suspensions on Adult Crime." National Bureau of Economic Research. September.

Badger, Emily, and Quoctrung Bui. 2019. "Cities Start to Question an American Ideal: A House with a Yard on Every Lot." *New York Times,* June 18.

———. 2022. "The Extraordinary Wealth Created by the Pandemic Housing Market." *New York Times*, May 1.

Badger, Emily, Quoctrung Bui, and Robert Gebeloff. 2019. "The Neighborhood Is Mostly Black. The Home Buyers Are Mostly White." *New York Times,* April 27.

Bailey, Nikitra, et al. 2021. "First Generation: Criteria for Targeted Down Payment Assistance Program." Center for Responsible Lending and the National Fair Housing Alliance. May 21.

Balko, Radley. 2020. "There's Overwhelming Evidence That the Criminal Justice System Is Racist. Here's the Proof." *Washington Post*, June 10.

Baltimore Sun Editorial Board. 2022. "We Are Deeply and Profoundly Sorry: For Decades, the Baltimore Sun Promoted Policies That Oppressed Black Marylanders; We Are Working to Make Amends." *Baltimore Sun*, February 18.

Barton, Stephen. 2019. "The Economics of Residential Rent Control: A Not-So-Simple Matter of Supply and Demand." *Dollars & Sense*, January–February: 14–20.

Battle, Jeremiah Jr., et al. 2016. "Toxic Transactions: How Land Installment Contracts Once Again Threaten Communities of Color." National Consumer Law Center. July.

Bell, Alison, Barbara Sard, and Becky Koepnick. 2018. "Prohibiting Discrimination Against Renters Using Housing Vouchers Improves Results." Center on Budget and Policy Priorities. December 20.

Berry, Christopher. 2021. "Reassessing the Property Tax." University of Chicago, Harris School of Public Policy. March 1.

BirdSEED. Online. "Our Programs: Housing Justice."

Biron, Carey. 2021. "U.S. Homeowners Fight Deeds that Exclude Buyers Based on Race." *Thomson Reuters Foundation*, January 5.

Blackmon, Douglas. 2008. *Slavery by Another Name*. New York: Anchor Books.

Blumenthal, Sidney. 2019. *All the Powers of Earth: The Political Life of Abraham Lincoln, 1856–1860*. New York: Simon and Schuster.

Bohannon Companies. Online. "About Us."

Bostic, Raphael, et al. 2019. "Mixed-Income LIHTC Developments in Chicago: A First Look at Their Income Characteristics and Spillover Impacts." In *What Works Vol-*

ume: *The Book*. Edited by Marc Joseph and Amy T. Khare. Cleveland: National Initiative on Mixed-Income Communities, Case Western Reserve University.

Bouie, Jamelle. 2022. "The Supreme Court Is the Final Word on Nothing." *New York Times*, July 1.

Bowie, Nikolas. 2021a. "The Contemporary Debate over Supreme Court Reform: Origins and Perspectives." Written Statement of Nikolas Bowie, Presidential Commission on the Supreme Court of the United States. June 30.

———. 2021b. "How the Supreme Court Dominates Our Democracy: Judicial Review Gives Any Five Justices Power over the Whole Government: Why?" *Washington Post*, July 16.

Breen, Thomas. 2020. "City, 'Burb Clash on Open-Housing Quest." *New Haven Independent*, December 1.

Breymaier, J. Robert. 2018. "The Social and Economic Value of Intentional Integration Programs in Oak Park, IL." In *A Shared Future: Fostering Communities of Inclusion in an Era of Inequality*. Edited by Christopher Herbert et al. Boston: Joint Center for Housing Studies at Harvard University. 422–35.

Broadwater, Luke. 2015. "Baltimore Eviction Rate Among Highest in Country, Study Says." *Baltimore Sun*, December 7.

Bronin, Sara C. 2021 (rev., 2022). "Zoning by a Thousand Cuts." *Social Science Research Network*. February 25.

Brown, Steven. 2017. "Does the Family Self-Sufficiency Program Work? National Evidence May Not Tell the Whole Story." Housing Matters: An Urban Institute Initiative. November 16.

Burns, Rebecca. 2015. "Public Pensions Invest Big in Blackstone's Controversial Rental Properties." *America AlJazeera*, October 16.

———. 2017. "The Infamous Practice of Contract Selling Is Back in Chicago." *Chicago Reader*, March 1.

Burris, Alexandria. 2021. "Black Homeowner Had a White Friend Stand In for Third Appraisal: Her Home Value Doubled." *Indianapolis Star*, May 13.

Business Wire. 2021. "Kwx Taps DEI Expert Julia Lashay Israel." May 25.

CAR. Online. "C.A.R.'s Housing Affordability Fund Closing Cost Assistance Grant Program." California Association of Realtors.

Carr, James H., Michela Zonta, and William Spriggs. 2021. "2021 State of Housing in Black America: Emerging from the Covid Pandemic Recession." National Association of Real Estate Brokers. November.

Carreon, Jennifer. 2021. "Reflecting on the 1968 Fair Housing Act and Homeownership Today." Howard Hanna Real Estate Services. February 25.

Cashin, Sheryll. 2004. *The Failures of Integration*. New York: Public Affairs.

———. 2021. *White Space, Black Hood: Opportunity Hoarding and Segregation in the Age of Inequality*. Boston: Beacon Press.

CB. Online. "Coldwell Banker Diversity."

CBPP and PRRAC. 2018. "A Guide to Small Area Fair Market Rents (SAFMRs): How State and Local Housing Agencies Can Expand Opportunity for Families in All

Metro Areas." Center on Budget and Policy Priorities/Poverty and Race Research Action Council. May 4.

CCLC. Online. "Giving Value Back to Our Neighborhoods."

———. 2020. "Coming Together to Build a More Inclusive Community: CCLC Company Statement." Chevy Chase Land Company. June 19.

Census. 1961. *Historical Statistics of the United States, Colonial Times to 1957*. Bureau of the Census, U.S. Department of Commerce.

———. 2021. "Quarterly Residential Vacancies and Homeownership, Fourth Quarter 2020." Release CB21–15, February 2. Bureau of the Census, U.S. Department of Commerce.

Cenziper, Deborah, Michael Sallah, and Steven Rich. 2013. "Mistakes Put Homes in Peril." *Washington Post*, September 10.

Chapple, Karen, et al. 2020. "Reaching California's ADU Potential: Progress to Date and the Need for ADU Finance." Terner Center for Housing Innovation, University of California–Berkeley. August 28.

Chaskin, Robert J., and Mark L. Joseph. 2013. "'Positive' Gentrification, Social Control and the 'Right to the City' in Mixed-Income Communities: Uses and Expectations of Space and Place." *International Journal of Urban and Regional Research* 37 (2; March): 480–502.

———. 2015. *Integrating the Inner City: The Promise and Perils of Mixed-Income Public Housing Transformation*. Chicago: University of Chicago Press.

Chaskin, Robert, et al. 2015. "The Enduring Significance of Race in Mixed-Income Developments." Research Brief 10: Mixed-Income Development Study. University of Chicago School of Social Service Administration/Case Western Reserve University Mandel School of Applied Social Sciences. February.

Chemerinsky, Erwin. 2021. *Presumed Guilty: How the Supreme Court Empowered the Police and Subverted Civil Rights*. New York: Liveright.

Chenven, Sarah, and Carolyn Schulte. 2015. *The Power of Rent Reporting Pilot: A Credit Building Strategy*. Credit Builders Alliance.

Chetty, Raj, et al. 2022. "Social Capital I: Measurement and Associations with Economic Mobility." *Nature* 608 (August): 108–21.

Chew, Amee, and Sarah Treuhaft. 2019. "Our Homes, Our Future: How Rent Control Can Build Healthy, Stable Communities." PolicyLink/Center for Popular Democracy/The Right to the City Alliance. February.

Chicago Bungalow Association. 2021a. "Seeking Chicago Bungalow Folded Map Twins." *Chicago Bungalow Association Blog*, February 24 (updated March 19).

———. 2021b. "Meet the Folded Map Bungalow Twins." Webinar, November 17.

Chicago Tribune. 1973. "Slumlord Guide—8 Steps to Profit: A Manual for Slumlords—8 Steps to Profit from Squalor." *Chicago Tribune*, May 9 (part of a series).

Choi, Ann, et al. 2019. "Long Island Divided." *Newsday*, November 17.

Choi, Jung Hyun, Allana McCargo, and Laurie Goodman. 2019. "Three Differences Between Black and White Homeownership That Add to the Housing Wealth Gap." Urban Institute. February 28 (updated March 13).

Choi, Jung Hyun, et al. 2019. "Explaining the Black-White Homeownership Gap: A Closer Look at Disparities Across Local Markets." Urban Institute. October.

Choi, Jung Hyun, Jun Zhu, and Laurie Goodman. 2018. "Intergenerational Home-ownership: The Impact of Parental Homeownership and Wealth on Young Adults' Tenure Choices." Urban Institute. October 25.

Christman, Anastasia, and Michelle Natividad Rodriguez. 2016. "Research Supports Fair Chance Policies." National Employment Law Project. August 1.

City Roots. 2020. "Confronting Racial Covenants: How They Segregated Monroe County and What to Do About Them." City Roots Community Land Trust/Yale Environmental Protection Clinic. July 29.

Cobb, Casey. 2022. "Do School Choice Programs Contribute to the Resegregation of American Schools?" Research Brief 15, National Coalition on School Diversity. March.

Cohen, Rachel M. 2016. "Rethinking School Discipline." *American Prospect,* November 2.

Coldwell Banker. Online. "Celebrating More Than 100 Years of Excellence."

Couloute, Lucius. 2018. "Nowhere to Go: Homelessness Among Formerly Incarcerated People." Prison Policy Initiative. August.

CPD. 1976. "Forestdale Rent Strike, Largest in City, Is Ended." *Cleveland Plain Dealer,* February 23.

CTLTC. Online. "Three Key Benefits of Land Trusts." Chicago Title Land Trust Company.

Cuozzo, Steve. 2013. "The Truth About the 'Poor Door.'" *New York Post,* August 27.

Cytron, Naomi. 2011. "Ties that Bind: Income Inequality and Income Segregation." *Community Investments* 23 (2; Fall): 8–40. Federal Reserve Bank of San Francisco.

Davis, Vicki, Daryl J. Carter, and Rosemarie Hepner. 2020. "What Works for Building and Sustaining Mixed-Income Communities: A Perspective from the Development Community." National Initiative on Mixed-Income Communities, Case Western Reserve University. April 24.

De La Garza, Ashley. 2020. "The Never-Ending Grasp of the Prison Walls: Banning the Box on Housing Applications." *Scholar* 22 (3; October): 422–28.

DeSilver, Drew. 2018. "For Most U.S. Workers, Real Wages Have Barely Budged in Decades." Pew Research Center. August 7.

Dimmick, Iris. 2022. "Here's Why a For-Profit Company Is Buying Homes to Rent to Section 8 Tenants." *San Antonio Report.com,* March 13.

Dougherty, Conor, and Soumya Karlamangla. 2022. "California Fights Its NIMBYs." *New York Times,* September 1.

Downie, Leonard Jr., and Jim Hoagland. 1969. "Mortgaging the Ghetto I: Slum Homes Exploited by Speculation System." *Washington Post,* January 5 (first of a series).

Duca, John V. 2013. "Subprime Mortgage Crisis: 2007–2010." Federal Reserve History. Federal Reserve Bank of St. Louis. November 22.

Duong, Brandon. 2021. "Landlords Don't Have to Control Security Deposits." *Shelterforce.org,* October 7.

Eaton, Susan E. 2001. *The Other Boston Busing Story*. New Haven: Yale University Press.

Eberlin, Erin. 2020. "5 Basics of Rental Property Security Deposits: Learn Why, When, and How to Collect." Balance Small Business. January 31.

Ellickson, Robert C. 2020. "Zoning and the Cost of Housing: Evidence from Silicon Valley, Greater New Haven, and Greater Austin." *Social Science Research Network*. January 13.

Emsellem, Maurice, and Beth Avery. 2016. "Racial Profiling in Hiring: A Critique of New 'Ban the Box' Studies." National Employment Law Project. August 11.

Enos, Ryan D. 2016. "What the Demolition of Public Housing Teaches Us About the Impact of Racial Threat on Political Behavior." *American Journal of Political Science* 60 (1; January): 123–42.

ESL. Online. "ESL First-Time Homebuyer Grant." ESL Federal Credit Union.

———. 2021. "ESL In the Community: 2021 Report." ESL Federal Credit Union.

Fannie Mae. 2021. "Press Release: Fannie Mae Introduces New Underwriting Innovation to Help More Renters Become Homeowners." August 11.

Fechter, Joshua. 2022. "A Neighborhood's New Anti-Section 8 Rules Will Push Many Black Residents Out of a North Texas Suburb." *Texas Tribune*, July 21.

Fedbarblog. 2021. "Mendez v. Westminster: The Mexican-American Fight for School Integration and Social Equality Pre–Brown v. Board of Education." Federal Bar Association. June 16.

Ferretti, Christine. 2017. "Property Taxes Going Down for over Half of Detroiters." *Detroit News*, January 23.

FHCCI. 2021. "*Fair Housing Center of Central Indiana v. Old National Bank. Amended Complaint.*" Fair Housing Center of Central Indiana. October 16.

FICO Online. "What's in My FICO Scores?" MyFico.com, Fair Isaac Corporation.

Finley, Mary Lou. 2016. "The Chicago Freedom Movement and the Fight for Fair Lending." In *The Chicago Freedom Movement: Martin Luther King Jr. and Civil Rights Activism in the North*. Edited by Mary Lou Finley et al. Lexington: University Press of Kentucky. 207–27.

Finney, Christopher P. 2018. "Finney Law Firm Successfully Challenges Harbor Portfolio Advisors in Land Installment Contract Litigation." Finney Law Firm. August 3.

Fischer, Will. 2018. "Low-Income Housing Tax Credit Could Do More to Expand Opportunity for Poor Families." Center on Budget and Policy Priorities. August 28.

Fisher, Marc. 1999. "Chevy Chase 1916: For Everyman, a New Lot in Life." *Washington Post*, February 15.

Flanagan, Neil, and Kimberly Bender. 2021. "Four Black Men Developed a Montgomery County Suburb to Provide a Better Life for Some in Their Community. They Received Something Very Different in Return." Greater Greater Washington. May 24.

Foner, Eric. 2019. *The Second Founding: How the Civil War and Reconstruction Remade the Constitution*. New York: W. W. Norton.

Frank and OCA. 2020. "Application to Amend Woodbridge Zoning Regulations and Plan of Conservation and Development." Jerome N. Frank Legal Services Organization/Open Communities Alliance, September 29.

Freeman, Allison, and Jeffrey J. Harden. 2014. "Affordable Homeownership: The Incidence and Effect of Down Payment Assistance," *Housing Policy Debate* 25 (2; July 22): 308–19.

Freeman, Richard B. 1991. "Employment and Earnings of Disadvantaged Young Men in a Labor Shortage Economy." In *The Urban Underclass*. Edited by Christopher Jencks and Paul E. Peterson. Washington, D.C.: Brookings Institution.

Freemark, Yonah, and Lydia Lo. 2022. "Effective Zoning Reform Isn't as Simple as It Seems." *Bloomberg*, May 24.

Freiberg, Fred. 2013. "Racial Discrimination in Housing: Underestimated and Overlooked." Fair Housing Justice Center.

———. 2019. "Prove It!" *Poverty and Race* 28 (3; September–December).

Frey, William H. 2022. "Today's Suburbs Are Symbolic of America's Rising Diversity: A 2020 Census Portrait." Brookings Institution, June 15.

Friedman, Matthew. 2015. "Just Facts: As Many Americans Have Criminal Records as College Diplomas." Brennan Center for Justice. November 17.

Froba, Dave, and Sharon Froba. 2020. "Modesto's Racial Housing History." *Modesto History Center Newsletter*. Issue 3, September.

GAO. 2018. *Discipline Disparities for Black Students, Boys, and Students with Disabilities.* Government Accountability Office. March.

———. 2020. "K-12 Education: Characteristics of School Shootings." Government Accountability Office. June.

Gartland, Erik. 2020. "2019 Income-Rent Gap Underscores Need for Rental Assistance, Census Data Show." Center on Budget and Policy Priorities. September 18.

George, Samuel, et al. 2019. "The Plunder of Black Wealth in Chicago: New Findings on the Lasting Toll of Predatory Housing Contracts." Samuel DuBois Cook Center on Social Equity at Duke University, May.

Gilgoff, Julie. 2020. "Giving Tenants the First Opportunity to Purchase Their Homes." *Shelterforce.org*, July 24.

Gittelsohn, John. 2020. "Realtors Apologize for Role in Housing Racial Discrimination." *Bloomberg News*, November 19.

Glassman, Ian H. 2021. "Opinion: Affordable Housing a Symptom of a Larger Issue." *New Haven Register*, May 21.

Glover, Julian. 2021. "Black California Couple Lowballed by $500K in Home Appraisal, Believe Race Was a Factor." *ABC News*, February 12.

Goldseker Foundation. Online. "2021 Annual Report."

Goldstein, Matthew. 2022. "Fannie Mae Agrees to Foreclosure Changes." *New York Times*, February 8.

Goldstein, Matthew, and Alexandra Stevenson. 2016. "Market for Fixer-Uppers Traps Low-Income Buyers." *New York Times*, February 20.

Goodman, Laurie, and Jun Zhu. 2018. "Rental Pay History Should Be Used to Assess the Creditworthiness of Mortgage Borrowers." Urban Institute. April 17.

———. 2021. "By 2040, the US Will Experience Modest Homeownership Declines. But for Black Households, the Impact Will Be Dramatic." Urban Institute, January 21.

Graf, Nikki. 2019. "Most Americans Say Colleges Should Not Consider Race or Ethnicity in Admissions." Pew Research Center, February 25.

Gray, Jeremy. 2019. "In 1938 Birmingham, Eleanor Roosevelt Faced Bull Connor's Wrath." Alabama Media Group, April 24.

Green, Tiffany L., and Nao Hagiwara. 2020. "The Problem with Implicit Bias Training: It's Well Motivated, but There's Little Evidence That It Leads to Meaningful Changes in Behavior." *Scientific American*, August 28.

Greene, Leonard. 2015. "Developer Bypasses 'Poor Doors' with Separate Low-Income Units." *New York Post*, June 29.

Greene, Solomon, Kriti Ramakrishnan, and Jorge Morales-Burnett. 2020. "State Preemption of Local Housing Protections Lessons from a Pandemic." Urban Institute, September.

Gross, Jenny. 2022. "Bank of America Tests No-Down-Payment Mortgages in Black and Hispanic Neighborhoods." *New York Times*, September 1.

Grotto, Jason 2021. "How Unfair Property Taxes Keep Black Families from Gaining Wealth." *Bloomberg*, March 9.

Grounded Solutions. Online-a. "Community Land Trusts." Grounded Solutions Network.

———. Online-b. "Inclusionary Housing Map and Program Database." Inclusionary Housing, Grounded Solutions Network.

HAI. 2021. "Racial Disparities and Cook County Sales Tax Evictions." Housing Action Illinois. November.

Hannah-Jones, Nikole. 2015. "Living Apart: How the Government Betrayed a Landmark Civil Rights Law." *ProPublica*, June 25.

Harney, Kenneth R. 2007. "Appraisers Under Pressure to Inflate Values." *Washington Post*, February 3.

Hartmann, Thom. 2022. "Is the Supreme Court Seriously Above the Law?" *Trial Lawyer*, Summer: 40–44.

Hayes, Stephen. 2020. "Special Purpose Credit Programs: How a Powerful Tool for Addressing Lending Disparities Fits Within the Antidiscrimination Law Ecosystem." Relman Colfax PLLC/National Fair Housing Alliance. November.

Hirsch, Arnold R. 1983. *Making the Second Ghetto: Race and Housing in Chicago, 1940–1960*. Chicago: University of Chicago Press.

Holder, Sarah, and Kriston Capps. 2022. "A Legal Showdown over Section 8 Discrimination Is Brewing in Dallas Suburb." *Bloomberg*, July 29.

HONP. Online. "Welcome to the Neighborhood. High Opportunity Neighborhood Partners Is a Full-Service Real Estate Company that Acquires Quality

Homes in High Opportunity Neighborhoods." High Opportunity Neighborhood Partners.

Howard, Annie. 2020. "Fighting No-Fault Evictions with a Just Cause Ordinance." *Shelterforce.org*, December 11.

Howard Hanna. Online. "About Howard Hanna Real Estate Services: Philanthropy."

Hsu, Spencer. 2017. "D.C. to Pay $1 Million to Settle Families' Claims for Homes Taken by Tax-Lien Program." *Washington Post*, January 10.

HUD. 2013. "Housing Discrimination Against Racial and Ethnic Minorities 2012." Office of Policy Development and Research (PD&R), U.S. Department of Housing and Urban Development. June.

———. 2015. "Affirmatively Furthering Fair Housing." Federal Register 80 (136), July 16 at 42272, U.S. Department of Housing and Urban Development.

———. 2021. "NFHTA Forum. Collateral Damage: Consequences of Racial Bias in the Residential Appraisal Process." National Fair Housing Training Academy, U.S. Department of Housing and Urban Development. May 19.

Hutson, Brittany, and Miriam Axel-Lute. 2022. "Making Homeownership Work Better." *Shelterforce.org*, March 15.

Ikeda, Sanford, and Emily Washington. 2015. "How Land Use Regulation Undermines Affordable Housing." Mercatus Center, George Mason University. November 4.

Jackson, Steven. 2016. "Not in Your Front Yard: Why 'For Sale' Signs Are Banned in Oak Park." *WBEZ Chicago*, March 21.

Jacobus, Rick. 2016. "The Challenges of Economic Integration: Is It More Important to Have Mixed-Income Buildings, or to Give More People Access to Mixed-Income Neighborhoods?" *Shelterforce.org*, May 4.

Jarovsky, Ben. 1989. "Housing Sting: Evanston Realtors Are Accused of Racial Steering." *Chicago Reader*, March 2.

Johnson, Tonika Lewis. Online-a. "Folded Map Project."

———. Online-b. "Folded Map Artist Talk with 'Map Twins.'" Tonika Lewis Johnson, Social Justice Artist.

Jones, Robert P., et al. 2022. "American Bubbles. Politics, Race, and Religion in Americans' Core Friendship Networks." Public Religion Research Institute. May 24.

Kaegi, Fritz. 2021a. "Cook County Assessor's Office Racial Equity and Real Estate Conversation." Cook County Assessor. YouTube, April 22.

———. 2021b. "In a Digital Economy, How Can Cities Create a More Equitable Property Tax System?" *Medium.com*, September 17.

Kaeser, Susan. 2020. *Resisting Segregation: Cleveland Heights Activists Shape Their Community, 1964—1976*. Cleveland: Cleveland Landmarks Press.

Kahlenberg, Richard D. 2019. "How Minneapolis Ended Single-Family Zoning." Century Foundation. October 24.

Kamin, Debra. 2020. "Black Homeowners Face Discrimination in Appraisals." *New York Times*, August 25.

———. 2022a. "Remote Appraisals of Homes Could Reduce Racial Bias." *New York Times*, March 21.

———. 2022b. "Educators' Housing Discrimination Suit Is Personal." *New York Times*, August 21.

Kasakove, Sophie, and Robert Gebeloff. 2022. "The Shrinking of the Middle-Class Neighborhood." *New York Times*, July 6.

Katzanek, Jack. 2019. "Bank of America Offers $17,500 Grants for Would-Be Home-buyers." *Orange County Register*, June 21.

Kaufman, Steven. 1978. "The Dynamic Merger King of Va. Banks." *Washington Post*, June 25.

Kaul, Karan. 2021. "Adopting Alternative Data in Credit Scoring Would Allow Millions of Consumers to Access Credit." Urban Institute. March 15.

Keating, W. Dennis. 1994. *The Suburban Racial Dilemma*. Philadelphia: Temple University Press.

Kerubo. Jacquelynn. 2021. "What Gentrification Means for Black Homeowners." *New York Times*, August 17.

Kimura, Donna. 2016. "MassHousing Launches Workforce Housing Fund." Affordable Housing Finance. May 17.

King Jr., Rev. Dr. Martin Luther. 1962. "Epitaph for a First Lady: Eleanor Roosevelt." November.

King, Shelby. 2021. "How to Make Universal Vouchers Actually Work." *Shelterforce.org*, October 15.

Kluger, Richard. 1976. *Simple Justice: The History of Brown v. Board of Education and Black America's Struggle for Equality*. New York: Alfred A. Knopf.

Knauss, Tim, and Michelle Breidenbach. 2019. "Syracuse's Unfair Property Tax System Hurts Poor the Most." *Syracuse.com*, September 19.

Kurth, Joel. 2016. "Land Contracts Trip Up Would-Be Homeowners." *Detroit News*, February 29.

KW. Online. "Gary Keller: We Stand in Support of Equality and Change." Keller Williams.

Lawrence, Peter. 2021. "HUD LIHTC Tenant Report Highlights 47% of LIHTC Residents Earn at or Below 30% AMI." Novogradac Affordable Housing Resource Center, April 20.

Lee Building Company. Online. "Our Story."

Leggate, James. 2018. " 'Predatory' Property Investors Agree to Pay Cincinnati, Change Practices to Settle Lawsuit." *WCPO (9-ABC)*, March 28 (updated December 12).

Lewis, Michael. 2011. *The Big Short*. New York: W. W. Norton.

LFHAC 2021. "Delayed Until Downsized or Denied: Neighborhood Associations Lead the Charge Against Affordable Housing and Perpetuate Segregation in New Orleans." Louisiana Fair Housing Action Center. October 7.

LHS. Online. "Just Cause Eviction Policies." Local Housing Solutions.

Lieber, Ron. 2021. "Always Pay the Rent? It May Help Your Mortgage Application." *New York Times*, September 11.

Lincoln, Abraham. 1861. "First Inaugural Address." Avalon Project, Yale Law School. March 4.

Logan, John R., Brian Stults, and Rachel McKane. 2022. "Less Separate, No Less Unequal." Diversity and Disparities Project of the American Communities Project, Brown University.

Logan, John R., and Brian Stults. 2021. "Metropolitan Segregation: No Breakthrough in Sight." Brown University Working Paper, September 27.

Louis, Errol T. 1997. "The Price Is Wrong." *Shelterforce.org*, May 1.

Lowery, Wesley, et al. 2018. "Where Killings Go Unsolved." *Washington Post*, June 6.

Malagón, Elvia. 2020. "Black Homeowner, 2 Appraisals, $62,000 Difference." *Chicago Sun Times*, October 7.

Mallach, Alan. 2019. "Whose Affordable Housing Crisis? Being Priced Out of Appreciating Neighborhoods Is Not the Housing Affordability Problem Most Americans Face. But They Are Facing One." *Shelterforce.org*, February 19.

———. 2020. "More Housing Could Increase Affordability—But Only if You Build It in the Right Places." *Shelterforce.org*, June 19.

Malloy, Peg. 2017. "Getting Your House in Order: Financial Literacy by Community Design." NeighborWorks America. February 3.

Mancini, Mark. 2018. "11 Inspiring Facts About Eleanor Roosevelt." *Mental Floss*, October 11.

Marin County. 2021. Meeting Highlights, Restrictive Covenant Program, County of Marin Board of Supervisors. May 25.

Martinez, Emmanuel, and Lauren Kirchner. 2021. "The Secret Bias Hidden in Mortgage-Approval Algorithms." Associated Press, August 25.

Maryland. 1955. "An American City in Transition." Maryland Commission on Interracial Problems and Relations and the Baltimore Commission on Human Relations.

Massey, Douglas, et al. 2013. *Climbing Mt. Laurel: The Struggle for Affordable Housing and Social Mobility in an American Suburb*. Princeton, N.J.: Princeton University Press.

Mazzara, Alicia, and Brian Knudson. 2019. "Where Families with Children Use Housing Vouchers: A Comparative Look at the 50 Largest Metropolitan Areas." Center on Budget and Policy Priorities/Poverty and Race Research Action Council. January 3.

McCutchan, Stephen P. 2012. *Let's Have Lunch: Conversation, Race, and Community; Celebrating 20 Years of the Presbyterian Interracial Dialogue*. Scotts Valley, Calif.: CreateSpace.

McDermott, Maura. 2019. "Inside LI Agents' Training." *Newsday*, November 17.

McGhee, Heather. 2021. *The Sum of Us: What Racism Costs Everyone*. New York: One World.

McKenzie, Evan, and Jay Ruby. 2002. "Reconsidering the Oak Park Strategy: The Conundrums of Integration." Midwest Political Science Association. April 25.

McPherson, James Alan. 1972. " 'In My Father's House There Are Many Mansions— and I'm Going to Get Me Some of Them Too': The Story of the Contract Buyers League." *Atlantic Monthly*, April. 52–82.

Mercator Research. 2018. "Press Release. FICO Scores Used in over 90% of Lending Decisions According to New Study." Mercator Advisory Group. February 27.

MHP. Online. "MHP Properties" and "Projects in Development." Montgomery Housing Partnership.

Michaels, Samantha. 2019. "Hundreds of Cities Have Adopted a New Strategy for Reducing Crime in Housing. Is It Making Neighborhoods Safer—or Whiter?" *Mother Jones,* November–December.

Mickelson, Roslyn Arlin. 2011. "The Reciprocal Relationship Between Housing and School Integration." Research Brief No. 7. National Coalition on School Diversity. October.

Miller, Clair Cain, et al. 2022. "Vast New Study Shows a Key to Reducing Poverty: More Friendships Between Rich and Poor." *New York Times,* August 1.

Miyake-Trapp, Jennifer. 2018. "Changing the Perception of Pasadena Unified School District Through an Innovative Realtor Outreach Program." Poverty and Race Research Action Council/National Coalition on School Diversity. April 1.

Moncrieff, Stacey, ed. 2007. *The National Association of Realtors: 100 Years in Celebration of the American Dream.* Chicago: Wiley Publishing.

Montag, Coty. 2019. "Water/Color: A Study of Race and the Water Affordability Crisis in America's Cities." NAACP Legal Defense and Educational Fund. June 10.

———. 2020. "Lien In: Challenging Municipalities' Discriminatory Water Practices Under the Fair Housing Act." *Harvard Civil Rights—Civil Liberties Law Review* 55 (1; July): 199–265.

Morsy, Leila, and Richard Rothstein. 2019. "Toxic Stress and Children's Outcomes." Economic Policy Institute and Opportunity Institute. May 1.

Moyer, Justin Wm. 2015. "NYC Bans 'Poor Doors'—Separate Entrances for Low-Income Tenants." *Washington Post,* June 30.

———. 2020. "Racist Housing Covenants Haunt Property Records Across the Country: New Laws Make Them Easier to Remove." *Washington Post,* October 22.

Mui, Ylan Q. 2012. "Wells Fargo, Justice Department Settle Discrimination Case for $175 Million." *Washington Post,* July 12.

NAACP. Online. "Criminal Justice Fact Sheet." National Association for the Advancement of Colored People.

Nance, Jason. 2017. "Student Surveillance, Racial Inequalities, and Implicit Racial Bias." *Emory Law Journal* 66 (4): 765–837.

NAR. 2022. "Annual Existing Home Sales Hit Highest Mark Since 2006." National Association of Realtors. January 20.

Narragon, Melissa, et al. 2021. "Racial and Ethnic Valuation Gaps in Home Purchase Appraisals." Economic and Housing Research Note. Freddie Mac. September.

NCCRC. Online, 2022a. "All About Cleveland's Eviction Right to Counsel." National Coalition for a Civil Right to Counsel, February 1.

———. Online, 2022b. "The Right to Counsel for Tenants Facing Eviction: Enacted Legislation." National Coalition for a Civil Right to Counsel. March.

NCLC. 2020. "LDF, ACLU of Michigan, National Consumer Law Center, and Michigan Poverty Law Program File Class Action Fair Housing Lawsuit Against Vision Property Management for Targeting Black Homebuyers in Home Purchase Scheme" (press release). National Consumer Law Center. September 29.

NCLC and Pew. 2021. "Less Than Half of States Have Laws Governing 'Land Contracts.'" National Consumer Law Center/Pew Charitable Trusts. April 30.

NCRC. 2022. "NCRC and Old National Announce $8.3 Billion Community Benefits Agreement to Strengthen Small Businesses, and Minority and Underserved Communities." National Community Reinvestment Coalition. February 3.

Neavling, Steve. 2020. "Duggan Unveils Plan to Help Homeowners Over-Billed by Inflated Tax Assessments." *Detroit Metro Times*, October 27.

———. 2021. "#BlackHomesMatter Advocates to Call on Whitmer to Compensate Over-Taxed Detroit Homeowners." *Detroit Metro Times*, January 6.

———. 2022. "Detroit Illegally Overtaxed Homeowners $600M. They're Still Waiting to Be Compensated." *Detroit Metro Times*, April 14.

Neiman, Susan. 2019. *Learning from the Germans. Race and the Memory of Evil.* New York: Picador/Farrar, Straus and Giroux.

Newlands, Francis G. 1909. "A Western View of the Race Question." *Annals of the American Academy of Political and Social Science* 34 (2; September): 269–71.

New Orleans. 2016. "Assessment of Fair Housing Tool." City of New Orleans and Housing Authority of New Orleans. October 4.

N'namdi, Nneka, and Sean Yoes. 2022. "Vacant Homes Wither Under Flawed Tax Sale System." *Shelterforce.org*, May 19.

Notebook. 2019. "Can a Diverse Neighborhood Now Integrate its Schools? In Mount Airy, It's Happening." *Chalkbeat Philadelphia*, December 6.

NYT. 1912. "Race Issue Plank for the Democrats." *New York Times*, June 17.

———. 1916. "Confirm Brandeis by Vote of 47–22." *New York Times*, June 2.

———. 1964a. "Fair Housing Law Loses in Seattle." *New York Times*, March 12.

———. 1964b. "Coast Vote Slap at Fair Housing; Trend at Polls Thus Far Is Against Antibias Laws." *New York Times*, November 9.

———. 2021. "How Lower-Income Americans Get Cheated on Property Taxes." *New York Times*, April 3.

Odendahl, Marilyn. 2021. "Settlement Reached in Redlining Lawsuit Against Old National Bank." Indiana Lawyer. December 17.

OPRFM. 2018. "Opening the Door: Oak Park's Fair Housing Ordinance." Oak Park River Forest Museum. May 31.

OPRHC. 2016. "2016 Annual Report." Oak Park Regional Housing Center.

Park, Julian Francis. 2020. "Tenant Organizing When Rising Rent Isn't the (Main) Issue." *Shelterforce.org*, January 22.

Park, Madison. 2016. "High-Rent School Districts Build Homes for Teachers." *USA Today*, March 21.

Parker, Cherelle L., et al. 2021. "Home Appraisals Drive America's Racial Wealth Gap—95% of Philly's Appraisers Are White." WHYY.org (PBS), February 25.

Paschall, CJ. 2021. "Roy Wheeler Realty Company Announces Merger with Howard Hanna Real Estate." *NBC29*, March 4.

Patterson, Kelly, and Robert Silverman. 2019. "Small Area Fair Market Rents (SAFMRs): An Analysis of First Year Implementation in Mandatory Metropolitan Areas and Barriers to Voluntary Implementation in Other Areas." Poverty and Race Research Action Council/Buffalo Center for Social Research at the University of Buffalo, September 18.

Perkiss, Abigail. 2014. *Making Good Neighbors: Civil Rights, Liberalism, and Integration in Postwar Philadelphia.* Ithaca, N.Y.: Cornell University Press.

Pew. 2012. "Payday Lending in America: Who Borrows, Where They Borrow, and Why." Pew Research Center, Pew Charitable Trusts. July 19.

———. 2021. "Deep Divisions in Americans' Views of the Nation's Racial History—and How to Address It." Pew Research Center, Pew Charitable Trusts. August 12.

Pietila, Antero. 2010. *Not in My Neighborhood: How Bigotry Shaped a Great American City.* Chicago: Ivan R. Dee.

Polikoff, Alexander. 2006. *Waiting for Gautreaux.* Evanston: Northwestern University Press.

Porch. Online. "Renters and Landlords." Porch.com.

Prevost, Lisa. 2021. "A Push for Zoning Reform in Connecticut." *New York Times*, February 26.

———. 2022. "Town After Town, Residents Are Fighting Affordable Housing in Connecticut." *New York Times*, September 4.

Price, David. 2014. "7 Policies That Could Prevent Gentrification." *Shelterforce.org*, May 23.

Prieto, Bianca. 2011. "Crime-Free Apartment Program Starting in Orlando." *Orlando Sentinel*, January 30.

PRRAC. 2020. "Crafting a Strong and Effective Source of Income Discrimination Law." Poverty and Race Research Action Council. March.

———. 2022. "State and Local Source-of-Income Nondiscrimination Laws: Protections that Expand Housing Choice and Access." Poverty and Race Research Action Council, January 31 (updated June).

Putterman, Alex. 2021. "West Hartford Is Mostly White, While Bloomfield Is Largely Black; How That Came to Be Tells the Story of Racism and Segregation in American Suburbs." *Hartford Courant*, February 21.

PWF. 2019. "Equitable Housing Being Preempted by Legislatures Throughout the Country: Searchable Map Highlights Prominent Examples of Local Affordable Housing Efforts Blunted by Preemption." Partnership for Working Families. January 29.

Rajasekaran, Prasanna, Mark Treskon, and Solomon Greene. 2019. "Rent Control: What Does the Research Tell Us About the Effectiveness of Local Action?" Urban Institute. January.

Rao, John. 2012. "The Other Foreclosure Crisis: Property Tax Lien Sales." National Consumer Law Center. July 10.

Reddy, Sudeep. 2010. "States to Protect Borrowers Who Turn to Cars for Cash." *Wall Street Journal*, July 18.

Reed, Atavia. 2021. "Black Chicagoans Were Cheated Out of Owning Homes for Decades. This Englewood Art Project Shows Racism's Lasting Impact." *Block Club Chicago*, November 17.

Reeves, Richard V., and Edward Rodrigue. 2015. "Single Black Female BA Seeks Educated Husband: Race, Assortative Mating and Inequality." Social Mobility Papers. Brookings Institution. April 9.

Reid, Carolina K. 2021. "Crisis, Response, and Recovery: The Federal Government and the Black/White Homeownership Gap." Terner Center for Housing Innovation, University of California–Berkeley. March.

Reyes, Stephanie, and Amy Khare. 2021. "Advancing Racial Equity in Inclusionary Housing Programs: A Guide for Policy and Practice." Grounded Solutions. February.

Rios, Simón. 2022. "Racist Covenants Still Stain Property Records: Mass. May Try to Have Them Removed." WBUR, January 22.

Rose, Kalima. 2001. "Beyond Gentrification." *Shelterforce.org*, May 1.

Rothstein, Richard. 2004. *Class and Schools: Using Social, Economic, and Educational Reform to Close the Black-White Achievement Gap*. New York: Teachers College Press.

———. 2012. "A Comment on Bank of America/Countrywide's Discriminatory Mortgage Lending and Its Implications for Racial Segregation." Economic Policy Institute. January 23.

———. 2017. *The Color of Law: A Forgotten History of How Our Government Segregated America*. New York: Liveright.

———. 2020a. "The Neighborhoods We Will Not Share." *New York Times*, January 20.

———. 2020b. "The Black Lives Next Door." *New York Times*, August 14.

Rothstein, Richard, Rebecca Jacobsen, and Tamara Wilder. 2008. *Grading Education: Getting Accountability Right*. Washington, D.C.: Economic Policy Institute/Teachers College Press.

Rubinowitz, Leonard S., and James E. Rosenbaum. 2000. *Crossing the Class and Color Lines: From Public Housing to White Suburbia*. Chicago: University of Chicago Press.

Rugh, Jacob. 2020. "Why Black and Latino Home Ownership Matter to the Color Line and Multiracial Democracy." *Race and Social Problems* 12: 57–76.

Sackett, Chase. 2016. "The Evidence on Homeownership Education and Counseling." *Evidence Matters*. Office of Policy Development and Research, U.S. Department of Housing and Urban Development. Spring: 13–20.

Saltman, Juliet. 1990. *A Fragile Movement: The Struggle for Neighborhood Stabilization*. Westport, Conn.: Greenwood Press.

Sammon, Alexander. 2022. "Skyrocketing Rent Is Driving Inflation." *American Prospect*, June 21.

Sanbonmatsu, Lisa, et al. 2011. *Moving to Opportunity for Fair Housing Demonstration*

Program: Final Impacts Evaluation. Office of Policy Development and Research, U.S. Department of Housing and Urban Development.

Sard, Barbara, et al. 2018. "Federal Policy Changes Can Help More Families with Housing Vouchers Live in Higher-Opportunity Areas." Center on Budget and Policy Priorities. September 4.

Satter, Beryl. 2009. *Family Properties: Race, Real Estate, and the Exploitation of Black Urban America.* New York: Metropolitan Books.

Scally, Corianne Payton, Amanda Gold, and Nicole DuBois. 2018. "The Low-Income Housing Tax Credit: How It Works and Who It Serves." Urban Institute. July.

Schaul, Kevin, and Jonathan O'Connell. 2022. "Investors Bought a Record Share of Homes in 2021. See Where." *Washington Post*, February 16.

Schmidt, Sophia. 2021. "New Castle County to Reassess Property by 2023 Under Latest Settlement in Education Funding Lawsuit." *Delaware Public Media*, February 1.

Sentencing Project. 2018. "Report to the United Nations on Disparities in the U.S. Criminal Justice System." April 19.

Sheff Movement. Online. "Remedies."

Sheppard Jr., Nathaniel. 1977. "Chicago Suburb Offers Novel Equity Program in Hope of Preserving Property Values." *New York Times*, December 26.

Slater, Gene. 2021. *Freedom to Discriminate: How Realtors Conspired to Segregate Housing and Divide America.* Berkeley, Calif.: Heyday Books.

Smith, Leora. 2020. "When the Police Call Your Landlord." *Atlantic*, March 13.

Smith, Shanna, and Cathy Cloud. 1997. "Documenting Discrimination by Homeowners Insurance Companies Through Testing." In *Insurance Redlining: Disinvestment, Reinvestment, and the Evolving Role of Financial Institutions.* Edited by Gregory D. Squires. Washington, D.C.: Urban Institute Press. 97–117.

Squires, Gregory D., and Ira Goldstein. 2021. "Property Valuation, Appraisals, and Racial Wealth Disparities." *Poverty and Race* 30 (2; May–August).

Steele, Claude M. 1997. "A Threat in the Air. How Stereotypes Shape Intellectual Identity and Performance." *American Psychologist* 52 (6): 613–29.

Stegman, Michael, and Mike Loftin. 2021. "An Essential Role for Down Payment Assistance in Closing America's Racial Homeownership and Wealth Gap." Urban Institute, April.

Stevenson, Alexandra, and Matthew Goldstein. 2016. "Law Center Calls Seller-Financed Home Sales 'Toxic Transactions.'" *New York Times*, July 14.

Subramanian, Ram, Rebecka Moreno, and Sophia Gebreselassie. 2014. "Relief in Sight? States Rethink the Collateral Consequences of Criminal Conviction, 2009–2014." Vera Institute of Justice. December.

Sugrue, Thomas J. 1996 [2005]. *The Origins of the Urban Crisis: Race and Inequality in Postwar Detroit.* Princeton, N.J.: Princeton University Press.

Theodos, Brett, Christina Plerhoples Stacy, and Daniel Teles. 2021. "Can Place-Based Investments Like New Markets and Opportunity Zones Help Low-Income Neighborhoods and Residents?" Urban Institute, April 28.

Thomas, Jacqueline Rabe. 2020a. "How Wealthy Towns Keep People with Housing Vouchers Out." *Connecticut Mirror* and *ProPublica*, January 9.

———. 2020b. "Hartford Mayor to State: Stop with the Segregation." *Connecticut Mirror*, January 17.

———. 2020c. "One of America's Wealthiest States Might Pass Up an Opportunity to Tackle Housing Segregation." *Connecticut Mirror* and *ProPublica*, June 29.

———. 2020d. "Civil Rights Attorneys Take Aim at Single-Family Zoning Using Woodbridge as Test Case." *Connecticut Mirror*, September 29.

Trainor, Ken. 2022. "The Power of Showing Up." *Wednesday Journal of Oak Park and River Forest*, March 29.

Turner, Margery Austin, and Lynette Rawlings. 2009. "Promoting Neighborhood Diversity: Benefits, Barriers, and Strategies." Urban Institute. August.

Twin Cities PBS. 2018. "Minnesota Experience." *Jim Crow of the North*. Season 1, episode 20. November 28.

Viala-Gaudefroy, Jérôme. 2020. "Fact Check US: Would the Democrats 'Ruin the Suburbs' as Donald Trump Claims?" *The Conversation*, October 19 (updated November 14).

Virginia National Bank. Online. "Our Story."

Wang, Ruoniu, and Sowmya Balachandran. 2021. *Inclusionary Housing in the United States: Prevalence, Practices, and Production in Local Jurisdictions as of 2019*. Grounded Solutions.

Watt, Nick, and Jack Hannah. 2020. "Racist Language Is Still Woven into Home Deeds Across America: Erasing It Isn't Easy, and Some Don't Want To." *CNN.com*, February 15.

Way, Heather. 2022. "Property Tax Relief Programs Don't Reach Many Homeowners of Color." *Shelterforce.org*, March 7.

WCNC. 2013. "Incentives for Developers Get Approval." *WCNC Charlotte*, February 19.

Wells, Amy Stuart, et al. 2009. *Both Sides Now: The Story of School Desegregation's Graduates*. Berkeley: University of California Press.

Wells Fargo. 2019. "Eileen Fitzgerald to Lead Wells Fargo's Housing Affordability Philanthropy" (press release). August 7.

Whitaker, Amir, et. al. 2019. "Cops and No Counselors: How the Lack of School Mental Health Staff Is Harming Students." American Civil Liberties Union. March.

Whitten, Robert Harvey. 1922. "The Atlanta Zone Plan: Report Outlining a Tentative Zone Plan for Atlanta." Atlanta City Planning Commission.

Williamson, Alex. 2020. "Misleading Marketing of 'Renters' Choice.'" *Shelterforce.org*, December 10.

Wilson, William Julius. 1987. *The Truly Disadvantaged: The Inner City, the Underclass, and Public Policy*. Chicago: University of Chicago Press.

Wilson, Xerxes. 2021. "Kent County Agrees to Reassess Property Taxes, Settle Lawsuit." *Delaware News Journal*, February 25.

Wilson, Xerxes, and Jeanne Kuang. 2020. "Judge Rules Delaware Property Tax System Unconstitutional; Major Changes to Residents' Bills Could Follow." *Delaware News Journal*, May 8.

Yager, Jordy. 2016. "Searching for Solutions: Why Are Black Kids Arrested More Often Than White Kids?" *C-ville.com*, June 15.

Yap, Maureen, et al. 2022. "Identifying Bias and Barriers, Promoting Equity: An Analysis of the USPAP Standards and Appraiser Qualifications Criteria." National Fair Housing Alliance. January.

Yeoman, Barry. 2018. "The Soul of Community." *Craftmanship Quarterly*, Fall.

Young, Cheryl. 2016. "There Doesn't Go the Neighborhood: Low-Income Housing Has No Impact on Nearby Home Values." Trulia. November 16 (updated November 29).

Yun, Lawrence, et al. 2021. "Snapshot of Race and Home Buying in America." National Association of Realtors. February.

ILLUSTRATION CREDITS

INDEX

Source notes have index references if they substantially expand on information in the text. Source notes that document information in the text, perhaps with minimal elaboration of that information, are not included in the index. Index entries to court cases are to the page(s) where the case(s) are discussed, although the text may not use the case name. In most cases, index references to persons, institutions, and firms are to the discussions, not the specific page, in which they appear.

ABOUT THE AUTHORS

Richard Rothstein, father of co-author Leah Rothstein, is now mostly retired. He was introduced to civil rights activity when, as a college student in 1960, a friend pulled him onto a picket line of the Northern Student Movement at a Woolworth's store in support of the Greensboro lunch counter sit-ins. As a young man, he was a research assistant at the Chicago Urban League, where he aided the plaintiff team in the *Gautreaux* litigation; it proved that racially explicit government policy had segregated public housing. The lesson stuck with him and helped to inspire his authorship, more than half a century later, of *The Color of Law*. He then worked as a union organizer in the Southern textile industry, where he mobilized both white and black workers, but where the black mill hands had the dirtiest and lowest-paid jobs. This experience, too, stayed with him and influenced his subsequent research and writing. He was later a research associate of the Economic Policy Institute, senior fellow at the Thurgood Marshall Institute of the NAACP Legal Defense Fund, and a weekly education columnist for the *New York Times*. His previous books include *Grading Education: Getting Accountability Right*, *Class and Schools: Using Social, Economic and Educational Reform to Close the Black-White Achievement Gap*, and *The Way We Were? The Myths and Realities of America's Student Achievement*. He and his wife, Judith, moved from retirement on Cape Cod to the San Francisco Bay Area to be near their three children and respective spouses, and their four grandchildren.

Leah Rothstein was raised going with her parents to protests and picket lines and doing homework in the back of community, union, and city council meetings. During college, she ventured into political organizing on her own, getting involved in student activism and eventually taking a leave from her studies to work fulltime on an election campaign to defend affirmative action in California. This led her to work as a community and labor organizer in the San Francisco Bay Area and throughout California, focusing on housing, police accountability, education, environmental justice, and worker health and safety issues. Driven by a desire to be a more effective advocate, she earned a master's degree in public policy and became even more interested in how housing and community development policy impacts the ways we relate to our communities and each other. She then worked as a financial and policy consultant to affordable-housing developers, cities, counties, and redevelopment agencies. She helped assemble financing and development teams for affordable-housing construction and assisted writing local housing policy and analyzing its impacts. Leah also directed research for two Bay Area counties on their community corrections policies, practices, and populations, to help promote a rehabilitative approach. Leah lives in Oakland, California, with her partner, Skye. To counter the isolation inherent in single-family housing, they have created an unofficial co-housing compound with friends, where they share yards, meals, and a dog, Chula.

JUST ACTIONS FOR REDRESSING RACIAL SEGREGATION

A summary and reference guide for the strategies described in *Just Action*, with the page numbers on which the discussion can be found.

In preparation: Understand that segregation created on purpose can be reversed on purpose

- Develop bi-racial and multi-ethnic relationships (pp. 15–29)
- Research and educate your neighbors about how your community was segregated (32–36)

Improve resources in low-income, predominantly black and Hispanic neighborhoods and prevent displacement from rising housing costs ("place-based" strategies)

- Adopt renter protections
  - o Rent regulation (105–107)
  - o Just cause eviction ordinance (107–108)
  - o Eviction right-to-counsel program (108–110)
  - o Bridge renters' security deposit needs (110–112)
  - o Freeze property assessments (113)
  - o Ban the box (113–118)

- Create new affordable housing without concentrating low-income households
  - Support mixed-income developments (82–92)
  - Inclusionary zoning (101–103)
  - Community land trust (118–123)

- Protect homebuyers and homeowners
  - Challenge discriminatory property tax assessments (144–151)
  - Reform tax lien system (156–161)
  - Demand fair home appraisals and monitor appraisers' performance (152–156)
  - Challenge unfair contract sales (125–140)

- Use the Community Reinvestment Act to press banks to increase investments in these communities (163–167)
- Practice conscientious gentrification (97–101)

Open racially exclusive white suburban neighborhoods to diverse residents ("mobility" strategies)

- Allow for a diversity of housing in suburban communities
  - Challenge single-family-only zoning (172–180)
  - Implement zoning changes that lower cost of housing production (178–180)
  - Inclusionary zoning (180–182)
  - Community land trust (118–123)
  - Prioritize mixed-income Low Income Housing Tax Credit projects in high opportunity areas (183–185)
  - Challenge NIMBY opposition to housing development (176–177)

- Enable Section 8 recipients to rent in higher opportunity areas
  - Adopt and enforce Source of Income discrimination ordinance (186–188)
  - Implement Small Area Fair Market Rent standard (188–189)
  - Encourage landlords to participate in Section 8 program (191–192)

- o   Adopt comprehensive mobility program (189–191)
- o   Allow Section 8 vouchers to be used for homeownership (191)

Increase housing opportunities everywhere

- Participate in Affirmatively Furthering Fair Housing planning process (57–60)
- Provide down payment assistance for African Americans (67–73)
- Reform the credit scoring system (74–79)
- Press financial institutions to enact Special Purpose Credit Programs (71)
- Create housing for middle-income families (81–85)
- Build truly mixed-income housing (85–92)
- Challenge the real estate industry's steering of homebuyers to same-race neighborhoods (209–214)
- Volunteer as fair housing testers (215–216)

Challenge school segregation

- Redraw attendance zones (238)
- Create partnerships between realtors and school districts (234–235)
- Reduce police presence in schools and increase use of alternative discipline (236–237)
- Adopt voluntary school desegregation efforts (238–240)
- Share resources from affluent districts with nearby lower-income area schools (240)

JUST ACTION

Richard Rothstein
and
Leah Rothstein

JUST ACTION

Richard Rothstein and Leah Rothstein

DISCUSSION QUESTIONS

1. The civil rights movement of the 1950s and '60s successfully challenged many forms of racial segregation, but residential segregation remains unchanged. Do you think that challenging residential segregation is also important for advancing civil rights?

2. *Just Action* says that it doesn't matter where you start to redress segregation, so long as you start somewhere. Which strategies that you read about could benefit your own community? What might the obstacles be to implementing them? Who would you involve to make each strategy successful?

3. The country has experienced a backlash against programs to advance racial justice, as well as a Supreme Court decision ending affirmative action. How can we continue to redress segregation in the face of such opposition?

4. Is gentrification a positive, negative, or mixed outcome for a lower-income community? Are *Just Action*'s proposals practical for mitigating its harms and preserving its benefits?

5. The authors warn that removing artifacts of segregation—such as racially restrictive covenants—risks erasing opportunities to be reminded of our history and motivated to remedy its harms. How should the balance be struck between avoiding the offense of segregation's symbols and learning from them?

6. We have limited funds for affordable housing. Should we spend them only on the lowest-income households most in need, even at the risk of concentrating these families in separate projects, or

should we spend limited funds on mixed-income buildings, using some of our scarce resources on modest subsidies for moderate-income households?

7. Why does *Just Action* say that there is not only an opportunity to redress segregation, but an obligation to do so?

8. Must we understand the history of segregation's creation in order to remedy it? Is there an example from the book where understanding history helped to craft and build support for a remedy?

9. Imagine your neighborhood in ten years. Realistically, what changes might you hope to see?

For a complete list of Norton's works with reading group guides, please go to wwnorton.com/reading-guides.

Diana Abu-Jaber	*Life Without a Recipe*
Diane Ackerman	*The Zookeeper's Wife*
Michelle Adelman	*Piece of Mind*
Molly Antopol	*The UnAmericans*
Andrea Barrett	*Archangel*
Rowan Hisayo Buchanan	*Harmless Like You*
Ada Calhoun	*Wedding Toasts I'll Never Give*
Bonnie Jo Campbell	*Mothers, Tell Your Daughters*
	Once Upon a River
Lan Samantha Chang	*Inheritance*
Ann Cherian	*A Good Indian Wife*
Evgenia Citkowitz	*The Shades*
Amanda Coe	*The Love She Left Behind*
Michael Cox	*The Meaning of Night*
Jeremy Dauber	*Jewish Comedy*
Jared Diamond	*Guns, Germs, and Steel*
Caitlin Doughty	*From Here to Eternity*
Andre Dubus III	*House of Sand and Fog*
	Townie: A Memoir
Anne Enright	*The Forgotten Waltz*
	The Green Road
Amanda Filipacchi	*The Unfortunate Importance of Beauty*
Beth Ann Fennelly	*Heating & Cooling*
Betty Friedan	*The Feminine Mystique*
Maureen Gibbon	*Paris Red*
Stephen Greenblatt	*The Swerve*
Lawrence Hill	*The Illegal*
	Someone Knows My Name
Ann Hood	*The Book That Matters Most*
	The Obituary Writer
Dara Horn	*A Guide for the Perplexed*
Blair Hurley	*The Devoted*

Meghan Kenny	*The Driest Season*
Nicole Krauss	*The History of Love*
Don Lee	*The Collective*
Amy Liptrot	*The Outrun: A Memoir*
Donna M. Lucey	*Sargent's Women*
Bernard MacLaverty	*Midwinter Break*
Maaza Mengiste	*Beneath the Lion's Gaze*
Claire Messud	*The Burning Girl*
	When the World Was Steady
Liz Moore	*Heft*
	The Unseen World
Neel Mukherjee	*The Lives of Others*
	A State of Freedom
Janice P. Nimura	*Daughters of the Samurai*
Rachel Pearson	*No Apparent Distress*
Richard Powers	*Orfeo*
Kirstin Valdez Quade	*Night at the Fiestas*
Jean Rhys	*Wide Sargasso Sea*
Mary Roach	*Packing for Mars*
Somini Sengupta	*The End of Karma*
Akhil Sharma	*Family Life*
	A Life of Adventure and Delight
Joan Silber	*Fools*
Johanna Skibsrud	*Quartet for the End of Time*
Mark Slouka	*Brewster*
Kate Southwood	*Evensong*
Manil Suri	*The City of Devi*
	The Age of Shiva
Madeleine Thien	*Do Not Say We Have Nothing*
	Dogs at the Perimeter
Vu Tran	*Dragonfish*
Rose Tremain	*The American Lover*
	The Gustav Sonata
Brady Udall	*The Lonely Polygamist*
Brad Watson	*Miss Jane*
Constance Fenimore Woolson	*Miss Grief and Other Stories*

MORE FROM
RICHARD ROTHSTEIN

A *New York Times* Bestseller and Notable Book of the Year
One of Bill Gates's "Amazing Books" of the Year
One of *Publishers Weekly*'s 10 Best Books of the Year
Longlisted for the National Book Award (Nonfiction)
An NPR Best Book of the Year

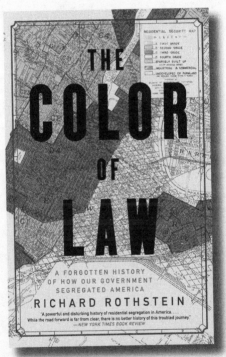

This "powerful and disturbing history" (*New York Times*)
exposes how American governments deliberately imposed racial
segregation on metropolitan areas nationwide.

Liveright Publishing Corporation

A Division of W. W. Norton & Company
Independent Publishers Since 1923